DO YOU KNOW·

– Why chopsticks are used to eat

– What the final Supreme Court d̶e̶ ̶ ̶ ̶ ̶ ̶ ̶ ̶ the internment of Japanese Americans d̶ ̶ ̶ ̶g World War II was?

– How Korean-American self-help credit organizations operate?

– What the special relationship between the United States and the Philippines was?

– How to tell Sikhs from other immigrants from India?

– Why cultural attitudes toward different ethnic groups are very different in Hawaii from the rest of the United States?

– How many Americans of Asian descent there are in our country today?

EVERYTHING YOU NEED TO KNOW ABOUT ASIAN-AMERICAN HISTORY

Lan Cao is professor of International Business Law at Brooklyn Law School. Born in Vietnam, she now lives in New York City.

Himilce Novas is a journalist, author, and talk-radio host who makes her home in Santa Barbara, CA. She is the author of numerous books, including *Everything You Need to Know About Latino History* (Plume).

EVERYTHING
YOU NEED TO
KNOW ABOUT
ASIAN
AMERICAN
HISTORY

Lan Cao and Himilce Novas

A PLUME BOOK

For Tao Thi Tran, V.V. Cao, and Joan Schmidt

PLUME
Published by the Penguin Group
Penguin Books USA Inc., 375 Hudson Street, New York, New York 10014, U.S.A.
Penguin Books Ltd, 27 Wrights Lane, London W8 5TZ, England
Penguin Books Australia Ltd, Ringwood, Victoria, Australia
Penguin Books Canada Ltd, 10 Alcorn Avenue, Toronto, Ontario, Canada M4V 3B2
Penguin Books (N.Z.) Ltd, 182–190 Wairau Road, Auckland 10, New Zealand

Penguin Books Ltd, Registered Offices:
Harmondsworth, Middlesex, England

First published by Plume, an imprint of Dutton Signet,
a division of Penguin Books USA Inc.

First Printing, August, 1996
1   3   5   7   9   10   8   6   4   2

 REGISTERED TRADEMARK—MARCA REGISTRADA

LIBRARY OF CONGRESS CATALOGING-IN-PUBLICATION DATA:

Cao, Lan.
Everything you need to know about Asian American history / Lan Cao and Himilce Novas.
p.   cm.
Includes bibliographical references.
ISBN 0-452-27315-3
1. Asian Americans—History—Miscellanea.   I. Novas, Himilce.
II. Title.
E184.O6C36   1996
973'.0495—dc20   96-1942
CIP

Printed in the United States of America
Set in New Baskerville
Designed by Steven N. Stathakis

Contents

Contents

Acknowledgments

Our thanks go to Rosemary Silva, a gifted writer, editor, and researcher, for her work on this book, to the Library of Congress, the Smithsonian Institution, the New York Public Library, Brooklyn Law School, Mount Holyoke College, the University of California at Santa Barbara, and all the people, public libraries, universities, and cultural institutions across the United States that enabled us to unearth information on these diverse, rich, and fascinating cultures.

We also extend our gratitude to Herminia del Portal, Lino Novas Calvo, Guillermo Cabrera Infante, Carola Ash, Ruth Elizabeth Jenks, Susan Herner, Deb Brody, Theresa Mantenfel, Professor Joan Cocks and Professor Penny Gill, General John Fritz Freund and Margaret Freund, Tuan Anh Cao, Lisa Bloom, Carolyn Howe, Marilyn Gilbert, Gail and Steve Humphreys, Jack and Teri Lindsey. Our thanks are also owed to the American Program Bureau, research students Eun Yeong Kim and Jane Kim of Wellesley College, to Professor Lorraine Elena Roses of Wellesley College, professors Arthur Pinto, Anthony Sebok and Spencer Weber Waller of Brooklyn Law School, and Professor Beryl Jones.

And to all Asian Americans, sung and unsung, across our blessed homeland.

How to Read This Book

We have organized this book for "interactive reading," meaning that the information between the covers is encapsulated in a modular, question-and-answer format. As such, you can select at random the aspects of Asian American history and culture that may interest you at any given time. However, if you read it straight through, from cover to cover, a larger and more fascinating picture will emerge than if you just pick, "cafeteria-style."

The group known as Asian Americans covers a vast and colorful variety of peoples with distinct histories and traditions. We have devoted one chapter to each group, from Chinese Americans to Pacific Islanders.

This book is not intended to serve as a mere accounting

of boring dates and historical happenings and mishaps. Rather, our aim is to share with you some of the richest and most interesting cultures that make up the ever-expanding universe known as the American experience. We have taken aim at some troublesome stereotypes, given credit where credit was long overdue, and turned the high beams on some of the real goings-on in the hundred-year civil rights struggle of Asian Americans. Most of all, we have made this a fun journey, a celebration and a tribute to a peoples whose extraordinary contributions and power of example bring joy to the hearts and minds of Americans everywhere.

Lan Cao, New York City
Himilce Novas, Santa Barbara, California
1996

Introduction:
Asian Americans:
As Diverse as Dim Sum

Who are the Asian Americans?

The term *Asian American* refers to any person of Asian descent, either foreign born or native, living in the United States. Persons of Asian descent in the United States also identify themselves strongly with their country of origin, thus Americans of Chinese ancestry are as likely—and often more likely if they are foreign born—to refer to themselves as Chinese or Chinese American, as they are to use the term Asian American.

If Asian Americans were described in one word, that word would be diversity. Chinese, Japanese, Koreans, Filipinos, Vietnamese, Cambodians, ethnic Lao, Hmong, Thai, Samoans,

Tongans, and Asian Indians are just some of the distinct ethnic groups that fall into the category of Asian American. Each has added a unique history, language, and culture to the American mosaic.

Even a cursory glance at Asian Americans reveals a storehouse of multiculturalism. The ancestral tongues of Asian Americans range from Tagalog to Mandarin, Japanese to Hindi, Vietnamese to Khmer, Cantonese to Korean. Asian Americans practice multifarious religions as well: from Hinduism to Buddhism and Jainism, from Roman Catholicism to Shintoism, from Cao Daism to Taoism.

Today half of the 600,000 or so legal immigrants who make their way to American shores annually are Asian. As a result, Asian Americans are one of the fastest-growing minority groups in the United States.

In 1990 the U.S. Census Bureau counted 7,273,662 Asian Americans. By the year 2000, the Asian American population is expected to reach the ten million mark. And according to several projections, this segment of the population will hit 20.2 million by 2020. Chinese, Filipinos, Japanese, Asian Indians, Koreans, and Vietnamese will continue to constitute nearly 90 percent of all Asian Americans, as they have in the past. But smaller Asian immigrant groups, such as the ethnic Lao, Hmong, Cambodians, Samoans, Tongans, Indonesians, and Thai will gain ground on the American landscape.

When did Asians first come to America and did they all have the same reason for coming?

According to historians, the first Asians to set foot on American land were Filipinos manning Spanish galleons. They jumped ship at Acapulco in the mid-1700s and headed north to the bayous of Louisiana, where they gave the communities they founded such names as Manila Village and Bayou Cholas.

When James Marshall discovered gold at Sutter's Mill in

California in 1848, unbeknownst to him he unleashed the first significant wave of Asian immigration to America. Chinese adventurers and fortune-seekers descended upon the gold fields of California within a month after Marshall struck gold, and in the early 1850s a Chinatown was born in San Francisco.

Nineteenth-century America was not only crazy for gold, it was hearing the call of Manifest Destiny, of aggressive territorial expansion "for the free development of our multiplying millions." The nation needed thousands upon thousands of laborers to work cheaply in the fields, in the factories, and on the railroads—and it found willing multitudes among the Chinese, the Japanese, the Koreans, the Filipinos, and, at the turn of the century, the Asian Indians. These laborers were used by their bosses and then abused by nativist mobs and white supremacists, who believed their jobs and way of life were "under siege."

When America decided it could do the work without Chinese, Japanese, Koreans, Filipinos, and Asian Indians, it slammed shut the doors of immigration with reams of legislation: the Chinese Exclusion Act of 1882, the Gentlemen's Agreement of 1908, the Tydings-McDuffie Act of 1934—the list goes on and on. Asians already in America struggled not only for equality and dignity, but for the right to bring loved ones across America's borders, and sometimes even for the right to stay.

The Hart-Celler Act of 1965 swung open the door to immigration for Asians once again. From the 1960s and 1970s on, immigrating Chinese, Filipinos, Japanese, Koreans, Asian Indians, and Pacific Islanders were joined by Southeast Asian refugees fleeing wars and destruction.

Why don't Asian Americans want to be called Orientals?

Because the word *Orient* has strayed too far from its roots. Derived from the Latin *oriens*, the noun *Orient* once referred strictly to "the east" (the compass direction) or "the East" (essentially, Asia); later arose a verb, *to orient*, whose original meaning was "to situate something, like a church or a grave, facing east."

But the word *Orient* came to connote an exotic and perilous faraway place of geishas, Fu Manchus, hidden bordellos, opium dens, and rare jewels, connotations at odds with the reality of Asia, the largest continent on the planet and home to half the world's population. The word *Oriental* referred to the inhabitants of that exotic and perilous place and ultimately to any American of Asian ancestry, whether foreign-born or native. In the American psyche *Orientals* both here and in Asia were the alluring yet sinister alter egos of "model minority" Asians, and possessed negative traits like "Oriental inscrutability," "Oriental passivity," and "Oriental despotism."

During the heyday of the Civil Rights Movement in the late 1960s, Asian American activists and students began to reevaluate their place in American society. They did away with the term *Oriental*, a term imposed upon them that insinuated that they were not only inscrutable, passive, and despotic, but that they were foreign since the peoples of Asia were Orientals as well. And so nowadays, in this age of multicultural enlightenment, "Orientals" exist only in the Western imagination of yesteryear. Now, an Oriental is a kind of rug.

To rid themselves once and for all of the stamp "Oriental," and to combat discrimination and hatred aimed at them, most Americans of Asian background, either foreign born or native, have embraced the umbrella term *Asian American*. In so doing, they have forged a common identity from disparate pasts and places, an identity that promises political clout—if, indeed, sheer numbers alone can deliver power, or at least fair representation.

Of course, Asian Americans who have adopted the umbrella term *Asian*, continue to identify themselves as most other Americans do, that is, with their or their forebears' country of origin, and refer to themselves as Japanese Americans or Chinese Americans or Korean Americans, and so on, who pledge allegiance to the flag of the United States of America along with Irish Americans, Polish Americans, Italian Americans, American Jews, and all other citizens.

What are some of the particularly flagrant myths about Asian Americans?

The myth of Asians as "the yellow peril" developed soon after the first Chinese laborers came ashore to pursue their dreams of riches during the California Gold Rush. By the 1870s, "Chinamen" bore the full brunt of racist hatred at the hands of nativist Americans, who called them names like "heathen Chinee" and "stolid Asiatics" and who, indeed, threw sticks and stones, too. In 1877 the California legislature even released a report, *Address to the People of the United States upon the Evils of Chinese Immigration,* and sirens sounded across the nation warning of the Chinese threat.

Only when American writer and Nobel Laureate Pearl S. Buck and Pearl Harbor came along and made heroes out the Chinese in America were the Chinese able to pass the baton of scapegoat to the Japanese—or, as white Americans liked to call them, "the dirty Japs," "the goddamn Japs," or the "yellow Japs." ("Jap" became so rooted in the vernacular that it lost its venom, and friendly whites began greeting the Japanese with "Hello, Mr. Jap.")

In the 1950s, when the country fell under the spell of McCarthyism, no Asians were exempt from institutionalized discrimination. Since the mid-1960s, Asian Americans have endured their share of racism, but it has been more at the hands of private citizens, educational institutions, small businesses, and corporate America than by legislators in government.

The myth of the "model minority" arose in the mid-1960s. Originally it applied only to Japanese Americans, but soon it spread to encompass all Asian Americans. The myth is entrenched in the American psyche to this day. Asian American youths are viewed as Albert Einsteins who outperform all other kids, including wealthy white preppies, especially in math and the sciences. And Asian Americans in the workforce are considered superhumans who work longer, harder, and better than anyone else. Hollywood has contributed to the stereotyping of Asian Americans by presenting image after image of nerdy Asian American adolescent math geniuses and brainy Asian American scientists who speak fortune-cookie English.

While Asian American accomplishments should not be underestimated by any means, the myth of the "model minority" is terribly misleading. At best it ignores the "lost generation" of Asian American youths who are failing in America's classrooms, and at its worst, it fans the flames of racism in mainstream American society by raising fears of unfair competition.

A third myth that Asian Americans have had to contend with is that their communities are crawling with ganglords, evil drug rings, brothels, and hidden lives. Of course, this myth completely contradicts the "model minority" myth, and merely attempts to shift the blame from American society at large to Asian Americans for the decay, demise, and demoralization of urban America.

FACTS AND FIGURES

1. By the year 2000, the Asian American population will reach ten million, making Asians the fastest-growing minority in the nation.

2. By the year 2050, Asian Americans will constitute 10.7 percent of the U.S. population.

3. Between 1980 and 1992, the Asian American population increased 123 percent.

4. By the year 2020, Asian Americans in California will number 8.5 million, or 20 percent of the state's population.

5. More Asian Americans earn over $50,000 than any other demographic group. By 1989, 35 percent of Asian Americans had an annual income of $50,000 or more.

6. In 1990, 54 percent of Asian Americans owned their own homes. This figure has barely changed over the past decade.

7. Entrepreneurship among Asian Americans is twice that of any other minority group: 5.7 percent of Asian American adults are entrepreneurs.

8. From 1977 to 1987, the number of businesses owned by Asian Americans increased 328 percent.

9. Between 1982 and 1987, new Asian American businesses grew 162 percent. The average national growth rate for new businesses was just 14 percent.

10. Eighty-two percent of Asian Americans age twenty-five and older have received a high school education.

11. In the fall of 1990, more Asian Americans entered the University of California at Los Angeles than Caucasians for the first time. Asian Americans made up 41 percent of the freshman class that year.

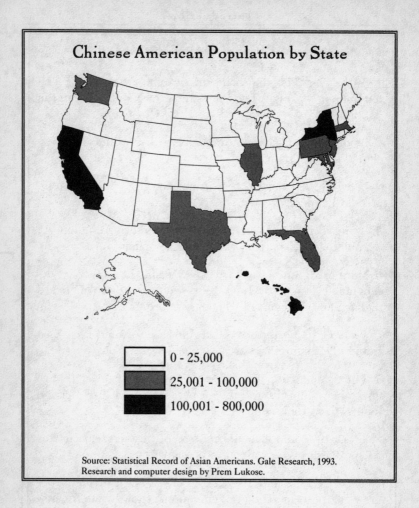

Chinese American Population by State

0 - 25,000

25,001 - 100,000

100,001 - 800,000

Source: Statistical Record of Asian Americans. Gale Research, 1993.
Research and computer design by Prem Lukose.

ONE

Chinese Americans

Where does the history of Chinese America begin?

Could the Chinese have discovered the New World before the Europeans did?

What's Gam Saan and how did it bring about the first significant wave of Chinese immigration to America?

Why were so many Chinese invited to participate in President Taylor's funeral service in 1850?

"California for Americans"?

1

What did the Chinese and the Latinos working in the gold mines have in common?

Why did the Chinese go on "California dreaming" in the face of all this nativist hatred?

How did rapid expansion into the Wild West create jobs for the Chinese in post-Gold Rush America?

How did the Fourteenth Amendment to the United States Constitution impact on the Chinese?

What's a coolie?

But were any of the Chinese laborers in America actually coolies?

Why did the Chinese settle in Chinatowns?

What were the Chinese Six Companies?

What are tongs and why have they been labeled the Chinese Mafia?

Is it true that the Chinese helped build the transcontinental railroad?

Were the Chinese given credit at the time for their part in building the transcontinental railroad?

Where did these thousands of ex-railroad workers go?

How did the Chinese help build California's agricultural industry?

How did the Bing cherry get its name and why does the Florida orange owe a debt of gratitude to a Chinese American?

How was Chinese labor used in the South after the Civil War?

Is it true that P. T. Barnum put Chinese people on display in his carnival in New York?

Why did Californians consider the Chinese evil?

Did San Franciscans harass the Chinese for their hairstyles?

How did the Chinese in America get started in the laundry business?

What was the Laundry Ordinance?

Why did the Chinese begin to head east in significant numbers?

Who was called "a hundred men's wife"?

What was the Page Law of 1875 and why was it an insult to Chinese women?

What was the Chinese Exclusion Act?

What effect did the Chinese Exclusion Act have on the Chinese community?

Why were there more Chinese women in Hawaii than in the United States in the late nineteenth century?

Since the Page Law and the Chinese Exclusion Act made it nearly impossible for Chinese women to come to America, did Chinese bachelors marry "out"?

What was the Scott Act of 1888 and how was it yet another setback for Chinese in America?

Where does the term "a Chinaman's chance" come from?

What was the Geary Act of 1892 and how did it manage to further demean Chinese immigrants?

Who were the "paper sons" and how did the San Francisco earthquake of 1906 actually facilitate Chinese immigration?

To what lengths did the federal government go in attempting to counter the "paper son" phenomenon?

Why did so many "paper sons" cling to their fake names long after they had assimilated into America?

What happened to those Chinese who got caught at immigration in San Francisco?

Where did some of the first civil rights protests by Chinese in America take place?

Why were Pearl S. Buck and Pearl Harbor considered blessings for the Chinese in America?

How did Time magazine teach Americans to distinguish the Chinese ally from the Japanese foe shortly after the bombing of Pearl Harbor?

How did America's affection for the Chinese translate into the repeal of the Chinese Exclusion Act?

When was the Chinese Exclusion Act finally repealed?

What was Franklin Delano Roosevelt's opinion of the Chinese?

Why were so many Chinese in America drafted during World War II?

How else did America's Chinese contribute to the war effort?

How was the seed for a Chinese American middle class planted on the East Coast during World War II?

Why did the Communist takeover of China put the Chinese in America on red alert?

How did McCarthyism intensify Chinese fears of a new era of persecution?

How did World War II and the Cold War lead to a change in U.S. immigration policies?

How did President Truman and President Eisenhower view the National Origins Quota System?

What was the Confession System?

What was the Hart-Celler Act and who were the san yi man?

How did the Chinese American community change radically after 1965?

What are the "new" Chinatowns of the 1980s and 1990s?

Who murdered Vincent Chin and why was the murderer given probation?

Who are some great Chinese Americans?

Who is Fu Manchu?

Who is Charlie Chan and why is he so unpopular among most Asian Americans?

What is the dragon lady/lotus blossom dichotomy?

Why are Americans so "gung-ho"?

Why does Chinese writing resemble drawings rather than letters?

What is Taoism?

How has Confucius contributed both to Chinese and Chinese American society's devotion to order and respect and to its patriarchy?

What variety of Buddhism did the Chinese bring to the United States and what religions do they now practice?

What Chinese holidays do Chinese Americans typically celebrate?

Do Chinese Americans really eat everything?

How did chow mein and chop suey come to America?

What is the origin of the fortune cookie?

Why do the Chinese use chopsticks?

How is traditional Chinese medicine different from Western medicine?

What is Chinese acupuncture and what is moxibustion?

What are traditional Chinese medicines derived from?

What is t'ai chi ch'uan?

What is kung fu?

According to the 1990 U.S. Census, of the 7,273,662 Asian Americans in the United States, 1,645,472 are of Chinese ancestry.

The Chinese first ventured to America in 1849, soon after the news that James Marshall had struck gold in the hills around San Francisco had reached Kwangtung Province. In the decades to come, the hardworking Chinese made invaluable contributions to the development of the mining, railroad, agricultural, and manufacturing industries in America. Yet they encountered severe hostility from nativist Americans, who went to extreme ends to rid the country of the "heathen Chinee."

Unbeknownst to many Americans, Chinese immigrants in America struggled in and out of the courts, with patience and perseverance, for the right to become Americans—a right that was granted them as recently as 1952 with the passage of the Immigration and Nationality Act, which eliminated racial and ethnic constraints on naturalization. In recent decades Americans of Chinese ancestry and newcomers from mainland China have been joined by their rich cousins from Taiwan, Hong Kong, and Singapore, who have been driven to the U.S. by fears of an economic and political crisis resulting from the transfer of Hong Kong from Great Britain to the People's Republic of China scheduled for 1997.

Where does the history of Chinese America begin?

You might say it begins in the late 1700s when Chinese men were first sighted on board sailing ships cruising the Pacific Coast. European merchants making a living in the China fur trade had hired these Chinese as tailors, blacksmiths, metal workers, and carpenters.

The first Chinese known to have stepped on American soil were three sailors from the Chinese trading vessel the *Pallas*, which sailed into Baltimore harbor in 1785. The ship's captain, American John O'Donnell did not schedule a return voyage to China, and so the three Chinese sailors were left stranded in the United States.

Could the Chinese have discovered the New World before the Europeans did?

Even before the eighth century A.D., Chinese vessels had navigated the waters of the Red Sea and the Persian Gulf.

In 1405, at the height of the Ming dynasty, the Chinese Imperial Palace dispatched Cheng Ho, known as "Three Jewel Eunuch," on a mission westward, the first of seven major voyages he would undertake between 1405 and 1433. The Chinese emperor commissioned Cheng Ho and the Imperial Fleet of sixty-two vessels to search for one of his relatives who had allegedly fled west in 1403. Whatever the original motive for the voyages, it is clear that they served a diplomatic purpose—that is, to exact "tributes" from other countries for presentment to the Chinese emperor.

The Imperial Fleet contained the largest sailing ships known to the world at the time. Several vessels measured over 134 meters in length; sported three or four superimposed decks, nine masts, a rudder about six meters long; and could carry cannons and a crew of over four hundred.

From 1405 to 1433, Cheng Ho and the Imperial Fleet diligently dropped anchor in Champa, Java, Sumatra, Ceylon, Siam, Bengal, Brunei, South Arabia, Mecca, Malindi, and at other ports of call to collect tributes for the Chinese emperor. Unbeknownst to Cheng Ho, the emperor had since passed away, and his successor, in an abrupt switch in foreign policy, did away with the tributes and ended China's policy of maritime exploration in the 1420s. The new emperor was so isolationist that he issued an order to halt the building of oceangoing vessels. By 1500, the Imperial Palace had made it a crime to build an oceangoing ship with more than two masts, and in 1551, going to sea in a multimasted ship was declared an act of treason.

At about the time that the Imperial Fleet was exploring

the east coast of Africa, the Portuguese were sailing along the continent's west coast. They rounded the Cape of Good Hope to the east coast in 1488, sixty years after the Chinese had been there. Although it is pure conjecture, many historians assert that if successive Chinese emperors had pursued maritime exploration during the Ming dynasty, China would not only have discovered Europe before Europe discovered China, but would have had a strong foothold in the New World by the time the Europeans ventured along.

What's Gam Saan and how did it bring about the first significant wave of Chinese immigration to America?

Gam Saan, which is Cantonese for "Gold Mountain," is the name the Chinese gave to California in the mid-1800s. In fact, the Chinese ideogram for "California" is "Golden Mountain."

The Chinese nicknamed California "Gold Mountain" after James W. Marshall discovered the precious metal at Sutter's Mill in the hills surrounding San Francisco on January 24, 1848.

In the early eighteenth century, the Chinese emperor had banned emigration under penalty of death. Then in the era of China's Open Door Policy, the Imperial Palace lifted the ban, enabling Chinese adventurers, excited by the news that the Americans had struck gold in California, to set sail for San Francisco. The first Chinese prospectors, mainly from the poor rural areas of south China, reached Sutter's Mill just one month after Marshall's discovery.

As time passed, more and more Chinese peasants caught gold fever and left China to pursue their dream of striking it rich in the New World. By 1851, some 2,716 Chinese had braved the rough ocean crossing to America; by 1852 that figure had increased nearly tenfold, to 20,026; and by 1870, fully 63,000 Chinese labored in America. Historians are divided in their opinion as to how the Chinese financed their voyage to the New World. Some argue that the majority of Chinese entered into credit contracts that essentially turned them into slaves. Other historians speculate that some Chinese paid their own way and that even those who had credit contracts could exercise free will. Seventy-seven percent of the Chinese lived in California, while the remainder found their way to the American Southwest, the South, and even up into New England.

Why were so many *Chinese invited to participate in* *President Taylor's funeral service in 1850?*

The Californians didn't seem to mind when in 1849 more than eighty thousand fortune seekers from every corner of the globe, not just China, descended on the gold mines around Sutter's Mill.

Euphoric over gold, the state of California rolled out the welcome mat. In 1850 the Chinese were invited to join American citizens at ceremonies marking California's admission into the Union. At the celebration Justice Nathaniel Bennett directed comments toward the Chinese: "You stand among us in all respects equals. . . . Henceforth we have one country, one hope, one destiny."

In August of 1850, San Francisco's mayor John White Geary and a group of citizens presented the Chinese in the city with gifts of books and papers printed in Chinese, and with an invitation to attend commemorative funeral services for President Zachary Taylor.

Two years later, in 1852, California governor John McDougal recommended that a system of land grants be put in place to encourage the Chinese to immigrate and settle in California. Little did he realize that Californians' good will toward the Chinese was swiftly turning to rancor.

"California for Americans"?

By 1852 gold fever had caused the population of California to swell to 250,000, of whom 10 percent were Chinese. White miners began to feel the pinch as foreigners poured into the gold mines, and exclusionist cries of "California for Americans!" were heard across the state. General P. F. Smith, in charge of military forces in California, expressed typical nativist discontent when he proclaimed that he would treat every non-citizen he found in the mines as a trespasser.

Despite the squawking in California over the "invaders" from distant lands who had caused wages to sink, Congress refused to pass laws forbidding foreigners from mining for gold in California, and the California legislature seconded the motion by insisting that decisions about regulations be left up to local authorities.

With little sympathy from the national and state governments, Californians vented their outrage directly on foreign miners and dispensed "justice" as they saw fit. Chinese people were dispossessed of property, violently attacked, and murdered. Many of the mining camps passed hateful resolutions outlawing mining by foreigners. In the eyes of these "patriotic" Americans, the category "foreigner" also included Native Americans and Mexicans, never mind that they and their ancestors had lived in California for centuries before the state was even American territory.

What did the Chinese and the Latinos working in the gold mines have in common?

In mid-1852 the California legislature responded, egged on by California governor John Bigler and the nativists, by passing the Foreign Miners' License Tax Law, which required persons who were neither native-born American citizens nor naturalized citizens under the United States–Mexico Treaty of Guadalupe Hidalgo to purchase pricey mining licenses. Aimed primarily at stopping the immigration of Latino and Asian laborers, the Foreign Miners' License Tax Law succeeded in driving out all foreign miners who could not afford to pay the exorbitant amount.

The Chinese struggled to pay the tax and stay on in the gold mines. From 1855 until the law was voided by the federal Civil Rights Act of 1870, virtually all the license tax collected in California—a sum of almost $5 million—came out of Chinese pockets.

Since the Chinese had bowed but had not broken from the weight of the tax legislation, California nativists became even more enraged and searched frantically for a way to stem the tide of Chinese immigration. The Committee on Mines and Mining Interest clutched at straws, charging that since the Chinese had come to the United States under credit contracts, such contracts should be declared null and void and the Chinese should be forbidden to work as miners. Although the committee and Governor Bigler favored such legislation, it did not pass. Thus angry Californians intensified their efforts to oust the Chinese from their state.

Not everyone was against the Chinese. In fact, when the Foreign Miners' License Tax was increased, numerous petitions, supported by major newspapers in the mining districts, were presented to the California legislature in 1856, asking that the tax on the Chinese be reduced. Nativist Californians fought back, and in 1858 they managed to stem the flow of Chinese immigrants into the state with the passage of legislation that forbade the Chinese from disembarking from ships on the Pacific coast except in cases of extreme emergency. The captain of any ship carrying Chinese docking along the coast could be fined up to $600 or imprisoned for up to one year.

Why did the Chinese go on "California dreaming" in the face of all this nativist hatred?

China's Qing dynasty (1644–1912) was reduced to a state of abject poverty after battling the British in the Opium Wars from 1839 to 1842 and from 1859 to 1860, and struggling to quell the Taiping Rebellion from 1850 to 1864, during which an estimated twenty million Chinese lost their lives.

Chinese peasants suffered horribly during this era of military defeat; many lost their homes, their land, and their meager savings. Tax increases and continued unrest at home were the final tug that uncorked mass emigration from China to the United States. The Chinese looked in particular to California, "Golden Mountain," for a way out of the economic morass.

How did rapid expansion into the Wild West create jobs for the Chinese in post-Gold Rush America?

In the heady days of the California Gold Rush, the young American republic was pursuing a dream of "Manifest Destiny," of stretching its borders in every direction for "the free development of our multiplying millions." To fulfill its Manifest Destiny, America needed strong, reliable workers. And the nation found them in the Chinese.

As America rushed to develop its industries and as the gold fields "dried up" in the mid-1860s, mining for gold gave way to mining for quartz, and Chinese laborers were singled out as the most dependable and hardworking, with little impetus to "make trouble." The Chinese were willing to do the dirty work—namely, construction and hard-rock mining—and they were willing to do it for meager wages.

Rather than return home to impoverished China, most Chinese laborers took Americans up on their job offers. After all, in the 1860s, a Chinese laborer could make thirty dollars a month in America compared to just three to five dollars a month in China. America was still the land of golden opportunity to the Chinese.

Still, most Chinese considered themselves "sojourners" abroad: they sought to make an honest living toiling in America and then to return home to pay off their debts and forge a better life on Chinese soil. That America denied them eligibility for U.S. citizenship made the Chinese feel even more like strangers in a strange land and intensified their desire to one day set sail for home.

How did the Fourteenth Amendment to the United States Constitution impact on the Chinese?

The Naturalization Law of 1790 specified that only "whites" were eligible for naturalized citizenship. However, the ratification of the Fourteenth Amendment to the United States Constitution after the Civil War meant that the naturalization statute had to be edited to include "persons of African descent" on the short list of those eligible for naturalization. At that time, Congress also took up the issue of whether Asians should enjoy naturalization rights.

Senator Charles Sumner of Massachusetts argued in vain that the Chinese should be eligible for naturalization; his bill was defeated by a vote of 30 to 14. A subsequent attempt by Senator Lyman Trumbull of Illinois to include persons "born in the Chinese Empire" also failed 31 to 9. The question of Asian naturalization would not be solved for many decades to come.

What's a coolie?

The word *coolie* is derived from the Hindi *k'u-li*, meaning "bitter labor" or "unskilled labor." In the mid–nineteenth century, *coolie* entered the vocabulary of foreigners at the ports in China who were overseeing the emigration of Chinese. The word crossed the seas on the tongues of foreigners, and found its way into the English language, where *coolie* came to mean "a servile laborer" and then "a servant."

With the abolition of the African slave trade in the 1800s in the midst of Europe's Age of Enlightenment, the use of Chinese and Indian contract labor in British, French, and Spanish colonies increased exponentially. In about 1845, a network for the export of coolie labor destined for Guiana, the silver mines of Peru, and the sugarcane plantations of Cuba emerged along the coast of China, in the port cities in Fukien, Shan-tou, and Kwangtung Provinces. Chinese coolies were disproportionately inhabitants of southeastern China, which, during the mid-1800s, had been ravaged by famine and the Taiping Rebellion.

The Europeans bartered for the coolies using a system the Chinese called "the buying and selling of pigs." The coolies were stripped of their clothes and then a letter symbolizing their final destination, such as "P" for Peru, was painted on their chests. The indenture of Chinese coolies was usually for a term of seven or eight years, at a fixed wage of about four dollars a month, plus food and clothing, and the cost of passage. Historical accounts show that conditions were horrendous for the coolies: overcrowding, abuse, and even kidnapping were rampant. Thousands died in Cuba and Peru.

In 1862, the United States made coolie trade illegal on American vessels and in American ports. Great Britain looked the other way for the most part until 1885, when the British Chinese Passenger Act went into effect, regulating British ships involved in the trade. It resulted in diverting coolie traffic to Portuguese ports.

But were any of the Chinese laborers in America actually coolies?

Historical records offer conflicting evidence of the existence of the coolie trade in the United States. For instance, the 1862 House of Representatives report on the coolie trade indicates that Chinese laborers voluntarily came to the United States and Australia, while coolies were bound for the tropical plantations of the West Indies, Cuba, and South America. Chinese benevolent associations in the United States, popularly known as the Chinese Six Companies (see *"What were the Chinese Six Companies?"* below), insisted that the Chinese indeed volunteered for immigration as paid laborers.

Nonetheless, President Ulysses S. Grant's Annual Message of 1874 specifically called to Congress's attention reports of the forcible emigration of Chinese to the United States. According to President Grant, "the great proportion of the Chinese immigrants who come to our shores do not come voluntarily. . . . Hardly a perceptible percentage of them perform any honorable labor, but they are brought for shameful purposes, to the disgrace of the communities where settled and to the great demoralization of the youth of those localities. If this evil practice can be legislated against, it will be my pleasure as well as duty."

In 1876, a committee of the California legislature investigating Chinese immigration concluded that the Chinese in California were in servitude. And reports circulated that the Chinese had in fact been bought and held in bondage by the Chinese Six Companies, the very organization that had insisted the Chinese had volunteered to emigrate from China.

Why did the Chinese settle in Chinatowns?

In the early days most Chinese settled in rural areas across the West. Some congregated in small enclaves that grew into self-sufficient Chinatowns. In the 1850s, a Chinatown took shape in the heart of San Francisco around what was then Portsmouth Square. In 1870, 24 percent of the Chinese in California lived in San Francisco's Chinatown, known as Dai Fou, or "Big City," and found employment in industrial production elsewhere in the city. Three decades later, two-thirds of the Chinese in California dwelled in cities, 45 percent in the San Francisco Bay area.

Under the 1870 Nationality Act, the Chinese were specifically denied the right to become naturalized American citizens. Americans took further steps to alienate the Chinese by passing legislation aimed at segregating them from the community at large. In 1879, the California legislature passed a law, subsequently struck down as unconstitutional, which required towns and cities to remove the Chinese from their streets. In 1885, the citizens of Tucson organized a petition drive to require Chinese to settle in a Chinatown, where they could be better monitored. In San Francisco, few landlords outside of Chinatown dared rent to Chinese.

Many Chinese who had previously lived in rural areas among America's citizenry had no choice but to flee to Chinatowns, where they could secure housing and set up stores and other businesses. By the 1880s, the Chinese had begun to migrate in significant numbers from California to the East, where they settled in nascent Chinatowns in large cities such as Boston and New York. By the end of the nineteenth century, only half of all Chinese in the United States lived in the state of California.

What were the Chinese Six Companies?

By the late 1850s the Chinese in America were forming associations geared at assisting newcomers and shielding them from xenophobia. Clan associations protected all those with a common ancestral lineage, while district associations looked out for Chinese from the same districts of Kwangtung Province, whence most of the immigrants had come.

As their numbers grew, district associations came under the jurisdiction of an umbrella organization called the Chinese Consolidated Benevolent Association, later called the "Chinese Six Companies" or "Six Companies."

Formed in the 1860s and headquartered in San Francisco, the Chinese Six Companies and its branches operated like mini–welfare states in every Chinese quarter. They fulfilled benevolent functions on behalf of newcomers and members of the community. For instance, they sent agents to greet incoming ships with Chinese passengers; helped with housing arrangements for newcomers; aided the elderly, the sick, and the unemployed; and arranged for the shipment back to China of the bones of the deceased for burial in ancestral grounds. The Chinese Six Companies also served as representatives of their community before the California legislature.

They hired white attorneys to represent Chinese interests during periods of anti-Chinese sentiment and agitation.

The chief beneficiaries of the Chinese Six Companies were merchants, who had enjoyed little prestige in Confucian China (which had always valued scholars above merchants) but whose influence increased enormously in the United States. The merchants acted to ensure that individuals in the community contributed their fair share to the Chinese Six Companies to keep its welfare programs up and running. All Chinese who returned to China had to pay a tax to the association and had to submit to a credit check to ensure that debts incurred in the United States had been paid off.

What are tongs and why have they been labeled the Chinese Mafia?

Whereas the Chinese Six Companies were aboveboard, community-oriented organizations, tongs functioned in total anti-establishment secrecy in Chinatowns. Most Chinese belonged to a district association in their community, but only a select and unknown few belonged to a tong.

The tong was modeled along the lines of the Triad Society, a fiercely political, anti-foreign, anti-Qing secret organization that originated in Kwangtung Province. The tongs were deprived of access to the political arena and were unsuccessful in their attempts to wrest control of Chinatowns from the Chinese Six Companies, so they turned to criminal activity, running brothels, gambling joints, and opium dens. The tongs ruled by terrorizing the Chinese and demanding protection money from businesses.

By the early 1900s, warring tongs had taken control of streets in almost every Chinatown in America. In New York's Chinatown, the tongs battled with knives and guns for territory, and the Hip Sings took over Pell and Doyer Streets, while the On Leongs claimed Mott Street. These gruesome battles stole the headlines of New York papers from the 1910s until the 1930s, when rival tongs finally drew a turf boundary down the middle of Mott Street.

The tongs were not only secret societies, but also Chinese trade unions. The cigarmakers and laundrymen constituted two of the largest tongs in California. Older Chinese immigrants also set up tongs that regulated Chinese businesses so as to avoid needless competition.

To this day, tongs in New York City are involved in both legitimate and illicit enterprises. Today they extort money from 80 percent of the restaurants and 66 percent of other businesses in New York's Chinatown. They also control approximately 70 percent of the heroin traffic in New York City, which they supply through links with drug rings in Southeast Asia.

Is it true that the Chinese helped build the transcontinental railroad?

In 1862, as the Civil War raged between the North and South, Congress enacted legislation providing for the construction of the transcontinental railroad to link the country from east to west. The U.S. government gave federal land grants to the Union Pacific Railroad to break ground at Omaha, Nebraska, and build westward to Promontory Point, Utah, and to the Central Pacific Railroad to begin construction at Sacramento, California, and build eastward to Utah.

Thousands of Chinese, many fresh from China, were hired by the Central Pacific Railroad as its main source of labor for the transcontinental railroad in the early 1860s, after doubts about the ability of the Chinese to handle strenuous labor due to their slight stature had been put to rest.

Employers with the Central Pacific Railroad soon realized that the Chinese were the most dependable workers around. Under pressure to complete construction in the time frame Congress had specified, the Central Pacific sent an agent to China to recruit Chinese laborers. Most Chinese could not afford the high fare of forty dollars for passage, so their future employers prepaid the sum. In return the Chinese signed contracts that committed them to working for no pay for a specified time period. Unfortunately, many workers could not read the contracts they signed and their employers cheated them out of pay, forcing them to work for free well beyond their contracts. When they were paid, the Chinese made far less than white laborers doing equivalent work.

Were the Chinese given credit at the time for their part in building the transcontinental railroad?

The construction of the Central Pacific Railroad line was a feat accomplished mainly by the Chinese. Of the 10,000 laborers in the Central Pacific's construction gangs, 9,000 were Chinese. They cleared the trees, blasted rock with explosives, shoveled and carted away debris, and laid the tracks. And 1,000 Chinese lost their lives in the effort.

Yet on May 10, 1869, when the two railways linking east and west were finally joined at Promontory Point, Utah, before a crowd of fifteen hundred, and a golden spike was driven in to commemorate the momentous occasion, the Chinese were absent. Despite their invaluable contributions to the building of the transcontinental railroad, the Chinese had been purposely excluded from the ceremonies and from the famous photograph of the Americans who drove the golden spike. Then to add insult to injury, the Central Pacific laid off almost all of the Chinese.

Where did these thousands of ex-railroad workers go?

After they were released by the Central Pacific Railroad, thousands of Chinese poured into San Francisco, where they joined Chinese ex-miners in manufacturing. The Chinese were clustered in low-paying jobs in knitting mills, woolen mills, paper mills, tanneries, garment factories, and cigar factories, and even when they did the same work as whites, their wages were less.

Had it not been for the Chinese, who were willing to work hard for rock-bottom pay, San Francisco might never have become the ninth-leading manufacturing city in America.

How did the Chinese help build California's agricultural industry?

While some of the Chinese built San Francisco's manufacturing industries, others who had been farmers in the Pearl River delta in Kwangtung Province, toiled away in rural California, imparting their expertise to American farmers who were turning their wheat fields into fruit orchards and vegetable croplands.

The Chinese were also hard at work transforming countless undeveloped acres in the state into fertile farmland. Near the confluence of the San Joaquin and Sacramento Rivers at Suisun Bay, the Chinese turned marshes into arable land by constructing an intricate system of drainage channels. Chinese laborers also dug six miles of ditches to drain the Salinas Valley and, in the process, raised the value of the land from twenty-eight dollars an acre in 1875 to one hundred dollars an acre in 1877.

In 1870 only 18 percent of farmworkers in California were Chinese. Once California farmers saw how effective the Chinese were in their agricultural methods—and how willing they were to work for low wages—virtually all of the state's farmland was "turned over" to the care of the Chinese. By 1880 the Chinese represented 86 percent of farmworkers in Sacramento County, 85 percent in Yuba County, and 67 percent in Solano.

Some Chinese farmers quickly tired of digging ditches and taking orders; they hungered for a piece of land to cultivate on their own terms. Through a system of tenancy, these Chinese signed contracts with white landowners which allowed them to cultivate the land with borrowed farm equipment and then split the profits.

How did the Bing cherry get its name and why does the Florida orange owe a debt of gratitude to a Chinese American?

Chinese farm laborers also made invaluable contributions to the development of agriculture in the Pacific Northwest and elsewhere. In Oregon, the horticulturalist **Ah Bing** developed the popular Bing cherry, and in Florida **Lue Gim Gong** bred oranges that were resistant to frost, thus enabling Florida's nascent citrus industry to get off the ground.

How was Chinese labor used in the South after the Civil War?

Even though the majority of Chinese stayed west of the Rockies, some headed south in the months after President Abraham Lincoln issued the Emancipation Proclamation freeing the slaves on January 1, 1863.

The reason was simple. During the era of Reconstruction, plantation owners lost control of their former slaves, who were no longer as willing to break their backs in the fields. So plantation owners hired Chinese laborers to compete with the blacks. In the 1870s, Louisiana and Mississippi planters brought hundreds of Chinese laborers to work on their land, pitting them against freed slaves, whom they deemed too uppity for their own good. Some planters also imported Chinese laborers directly from Hong Kong.

The Chinese, however, did not stick around on the Southern plantations for very long. They preferred to work in manufacturing in the cities rather than toil in the hot fields. By 1880, many Chinese in the South had gravitated to New Orleans to work as laundry operators, cooks, cigar makers, domestic servants, and gardeners. And planters contributed to this trend by laying off Chinese laborers once they regained control of the former slaves.

Is it true that P. T. Barnum put Chinese people on display in his carnival in New York?

Regrettably, yes. By the 1870s Americans in the West had long grown accustomed to the sight of Chinese, but for New Yorkers Asians were the epitome of exoticism. They were such a curiosity that P. T. Barnum attracted huge throngs to his carnival when he put Chinese people on display in a sideshow entitled the American Museum.

New Yorkers were insatiable in their desire to gape at the Chinese people, and when a Chinese sailor jumped ship in New York Harbor, crowds turned out to marvel at him.

Why did Californians consider the Chinese evil?

While curious Manhattanites gaped at the Chinese, other parts of the country, including California, were reciting lines to Bret Harte's poem "The Heathen Chinee," published first in the *Overland Monthly* in 1870: "That for ways that are dark/And for tricks that are vain/The heathen Chinee is peculiar." Newspapers reprinted the poem again and again, and before long the phrase "heathen Chinee" was on the tongue of every American.

In 1873 the exorbitant price of waging the Civil War, extensive railroad construction, inflated credit, and losses from high-risk commercial ventures threw America into an economic depression.

California's boom turned to doom, unemployment soared, and the state's anti-Chinese nativist cries of "California for Americans!" reached a feverish pitch as unemployed citizens looked around for a convenient scapegoat to blame their troubles on. Even though the Irish, German, and Scandinavian workers far outnumbered Asians, the unfortunate Chinese, with their queues, basket hats, loose-fitting clothes, and "yellow skin and almond eyes," couldn't fade into the background as easily, and again bore the brunt of nativist Californians' hostility.

In 1877, the California Senate appointed a committee to ascertain the extent to which Chinese immigrants threatened the welfare of the state. The committee published and distributed a report entitled *Address to the People of the United States upon the Evils of Chinese Immigration*, designed to alert Congress about how the Chinese had put California in jeopardy.

The report claimed that the Chinese were chiefly engaged in prostitution, criminal rings, and coolie traffic, and were not equipped to assimilate into the American mainstream:

> During their entire settlement in California, they have never adapted themselves to our habits . . . never discovered the difference between right and wrong, never ceased the worship of their idol gods, or advanced a step beyond the traditions of their native hive. Impregnable to all the influences of our Anglo-Saxon life, they remain the same stolid Asiatics that have floated on the rivers and slaved in the fields of China for thirty centuries of time.

On the subject of the Chinese and Christianity, the report stated that

> [o]f the vast horde not four hundred have been brought to a realization of the truths of Christianity. . . . It is safe to say that where no Chinese soul has been saved . . . a hundred white have been lost by the contamination of their presence.

Exclusionist Californians were so sure that the "stolid Asiatics" had displaced them and caused their economic troubles that a tune published in 1877 defaming the Chinese caught on like wildfire. One refrain went:

> *O' California's coming down,*
> *As you can plainly see.*
> *They are hiring all the Chinamen*

> *and discharging you and me;*
> *But strife will be in every town*
> *Throughout the Pacific shore,*
> *And the cry of old and young shall be,*
> *"O' damn, 'Twelve Hundred More.' "*

California's hostility toward the Chinese took more vicious forms than songs. In the late 1870s anti-Chinese riots erupted all over the state. In 1877 irate mobs set twenty-five Chinese laundries ablaze in San Francisco, and in 1878 citizens in Truckee chased out all the Chinese. All over California, signs reading "No Chinese Need Apply" cropped up, and restaurants, hotels, and barbershops commonly turned Chinese away at the door. Such episodes of violence and discrimination were repeated across the West.

Attacks on the Chinese became so commonplace that a San Francisco newspaper warned: "It is scarcely safe for a Chinaman to walk the streets in certain parts of this city. When seen, whether by day or night, they are mercilessly pelted with stones by the young scapegraces. . . . A Chinaman apparently has no rights which a white hoodlum, big or little, is bound to respect."

Did San Franciscans harass the Chinese for their hairstyles?

After the *Address to the Peoples of the United States upon the Evils of Chinese Immigration* was issued, anti-Chinese ordinances were passed with startling regularity in California. San Francisco even put ordinances into effect to do away with Chinese men's habit of wearing their hair in a queue, or braid hanging from the back of the head, a custom dating back to the seventeenth century. In 1873 the state of California passed the Queue Ordinance, which ordered that all Chinese prisoners have their queues cut off.

In addition, inane and malicious ordinances were written

into the books that made it illegal for Chinese people to carry vegetable baskets on the sidewalks, stage theatrical performances, and play the gong. An ordinance was even passed forbidding the Chinese from sending the bones of the deceased back to China for burial, a sacred gesture symbolizing the return of the spirit to its home.

How did the Chinese in America get started in the laundry business?

While 77 percent of all Chinese in America were in California in 1870, others had ventured to the Western states of Idaho, Montana, and Nevada in search of jobs in mining.

In 1862 the mining industry was established in Butte, Montana, and first the mining of gold, then the mining of silver, dominated the local economy. When copper was discovered in Butte in 1880, and the Anaconda Copper Mining Company talked of exploiting the "richest hill on earth," young adventurers answering the call "go west, young man" swarmed to the pioneer town with hopes of getting rich quick. Young Chinese men were among them in large numbers. In 1880, for example, the Chinese constituted 21.1 percent of the town's population.

However, mining in Butte lost its charm for the Chinese when the Montana Territorial Supreme Court declared in 1883 that all mining claims held by aliens ineligible for citizenship, such as the Chinese, would be void.

A number of Chinese miners in Butte and other frontier towns followed the example of Chinese laborers, who faced intense hostility in fields, mills, and factories across the nation, and turned to other occupations. Since towns like Butte had very few women to do the cooking and cleaning, the Chinese found a niche doing "women's work." In the 1880s they hired themselves out as domestic servants or set up restaurants, tailor shops, and laundries.

The laundry business was an especially suitable venture

for the Chinese, since it required only a minimal knowledge of English and a relatively small capital investment, and could be mastered in a short time through an apprenticeship with a clansman. Moreover, the laundry business was easy to exit should a Chinese "sojourner" desire to return home to China.

By 1905 the citizens of Butte, Montana, had their choice of thirty-two Chinese laundries. This trend caught on beyond the frontier towns. By the turn of the century, nearly every city in America had its share of Chinese laundries, and 25 percent of all employed Chinese men worked in a laundry. In the state of California, 69 percent of all laundrymen were Chinese by 1890.

What was the Laundry Ordinance?

Before the Chinese opened laundries in San Francisco, it was quite common for people to send their laundry by boat to Honolulu or Canton and then wait for its return a few months later. Thus local laundries started up by the Chinese filled a desperate need.

Yet San Franciscans quickly responded to the proliferation of Chinese laundries in their city by passing numerous discriminatory ordinances, with the self-professed intent to "drive [the Chinese] to other states." The Laundry Ordinance established exorbitant licensing fees targeted specifically against Chinese laundries: a $2 fee if the laundry depended on one horse for delivery; a $4 licensing fee if two horses were used; and a $15 fee if no horses were used. Because Chinese laundries did not use horses for delivery, they were saddled with the heaviest taxes.

Why did the Chinese begin to head east in significant numbers?

Some Chinese could no longer take the stress of living in the exclusionist West. In the 1880s, significant numbers of Chinese headed to cities on the eastern seaboard, where they joined Chinese already living in small enclaves.

In New York, a little Chinese neighborhood had sprung up on Doyer's Farm near the Bowery in Lower Manhattan. The first Chinese person to move into the area was a Kwangtung merchant by the name of **Wo Kee**, who took up residence at 8 Mott Street in 1858. The fewer than fifty Chinese who lived in this neighborhood in Lower Manhattan in 1870 inhabited uncomfortable attics and dank, dimly lit cellars, and sold cigars and newspapers on the streets to eke out a meager living.

Thanks to migration across the Rockies, Manhattan's Chinese population swelled to three thousand by 1890, and a self-sufficient Chinatown took shape around Mott Street. These early Chinese New Yorkers opened restaurants, noodle shops, tea parlors, laundries, and garment sweatshops in Chinatown, and kept mostly to themselves. A few ventured out of the neighborhood by day to hawk tickets to the popular Chinatown lottery.

Who was called "a hundred men's wife"?

A Chinese prostitute, known colloquially as a singsong girl, was. According to 1870 U.S. Census records, 61 percent of the 3,536 Chinese women in California made a living on the streets as prostitutes, mainly in mining and railroad towns across the state and in the Chinatowns of Sacramento and San Francisco. Almost all Chinese prostitutes were slaves to madams or pimps, who paid extortion money to the tongs. Many of the women had been kidnapped or had been sold into prostitution by their families.

What was the Page Law of 1875 and why was it an insult to Chinese women?

In 1875 Congress passed a statute commonly referred to as the Page Law, which prohibited the immigration of Chinese contract laborers and the importation of Chinese women for immoral purposes—purportedly in response to law-enforcement claims that an organized network was trafficking Chinese prostitutes into the United States. While the Page Law did cut down on Chinese prostitution, it unfortunately cast doubt on the virtue of all Chinese women seeking to immigrate to the United States.

Many Chinese women were forced to secure certificates of good character, but even such certificates did not ensure entrance into the United States. The overall effect of the Page Law was to restrict further the immigration of Chinese women into the United States; between 1875 and 1882 one-third fewer Chinese women immigrated to the United States than in the years just prior to the enactment of the Page Law.

As for the law's effect on Chinese prostitution, it was profound. By 1880, only 24 percent of the 3,171 Chinese women in the United States worked as prostitutes, while 46 percent had jobs as housekeepers, up from 21 percent in 1870. Many of these housekeepers were former prostitutes who had paid off their debts or escaped the vicious tongs, and moved on to less volatile employment.

What was the Chinese Exclusion Act?

The Chinese Exclusion Act of 1882 was nativist Americans' first major victory in their campaign to rid the United States of Chinese immigrants.

In a treaty with China ratified by the U.S. Senate in October 1881, the United States had earned the unilateral right to "regulate, limit or suspend" the entry of Chinese laborers into the United States. However, this same treaty permitted Chinese people to enter the United States "as teachers, students, merchants or from curiosity, together with their body and household servants, and Chinese laborers now in the United States to go and come of their own free will and accord."

Against the background of this international treaty, the U.S. Congress caved in to pressure from powerful labor unions in 1882 by enacting a bill entitled the Chinese Exclusion Act, the first and only immigration law in American history to target a specific nationality. Among other things, the Chinese Exclusion Act of 1882 prohibited the immigration of "lunatics," "idiots," and all "Chinese laborers" into the United States for ten years.

Merchants, students, and diplomats seeking to immigrate were exempt from the law. Those Chinese already on American soil were free to come and go provided they obtain special certificates confirming their legal status, as stipulated in the act's Section 6. The certificates were widely known as Section 6 certificates.

The vote in the House over the Chinese Exclusion Act was a resounding 201 in favor, 37 against, with 51 absent or abstaining. Support for exclusion came not only from the Western states but also from Eastern and Midwestern states, where relatively few Chinese had settled.

In 1888, the United States and China negotiated yet another treaty, this time extending the ban on Chinese laborers to twenty years, and an additional twenty years if neither party lodged a protest. The U.S. Senate attempted to insert additional provisions barring those Chinese who had previously been in the United States and held certificates entitling them to re-enter the country. These provisions were unacceptable to the Chinese government, and the treaty was never signed.

The Chinese Exclusion Act was renewed in 1892 and again in 1902, this time without an expiration date. It was not repealed until 1943, when by a curious twist of fate, China allied itself with the United States in World War II. The repeal of Chinese exclusion laws was necessary to ensure the success of the alliance.

What effect did the Chinese Exclusion Act have on the Chinese community?

The 1882 Chinese Exclusion Act shocked the Chinese community in America—and dampened the spirits of many Chinese bachelors. In 1880, for example, there were 70,000 Chinese men documented in California but fewer than 4,000 Chinese women.

Outside of California, the imbalance was even greater that year—30,000 Chinese men to fewer than 1,000 Chinese women. The ban on immigration meant that Chinese bachelors had little chance of finding a mate in America. Those men who were married or engaged could no longer send for their wives or fiancées. To be reunited with loved ones, they were forced to return home, and families they had started in China could not be brought to America.

The lopsided male-female ratio among Chinese in the United States accounts for the very small numbers of Chinese Americans born in the late 1800s and early 1900s.

Why were there more Chinese women in Hawaii than in the United States in the late nineteenth century?

Although in the 1880s Hawaii had also placed severe restrictions on Chinese immigration—by allowing only 2,400 Chinese to enter annually—the Hawaiian government exempted Chinese women from the quota. Plantation owners preferred a balanced ratio of men and women among their workers, believing that married men, and particularly men with families, worked more efficiently and were more reliable than bachelors.

Since Chinese laborers were permitted to bring their wives from China, there were few Chinese prostitutes in Hawaii. Chinese bachelors were allowed to marry Hawaiian women, another deterrent to prostitution.

Since the Page Law and the Chinese Exclusion Act made it nearly impossible for Chinese women to come to America, did Chinese bachelors marry "out"?

Chinese men in nineteenth-century America rarely courted women of other ethnicities. In the first place, most non-Chinese women shunned their company, and secondly, the Chinese felt that their race was superior to all others and did not want to jeopardize the ethnic purity of their lineage.

Over the course of time, as Chinese men assimilated to American life as best they could and tired of living as bachelors, many adopted more liberal attitudes about fraternizing with women of other ethnicities and abandoned the Chinese bachelor community. Some were enticed by the added benefits of marrying American citizens: as the spouses of citizens they could skirt anti-Asian laws that made it impossible for them to own land and thus they could finally drive roots into American soil and build families. Opportunities also opened up for Chinese women who married American citizens: they could get around naturalization and become American citizens.

By the 1920s, as more and more children were born to Chinese alien parents in America, and thus were automatically citizens, and as Chinese aliens married American citizens and achieved citizenship, the U.S. government decided that America's Anglo-Saxon way of life was in jeopardy and passed the draconian Cable Act in 1922. The Cable Act, an anti-miscegenation law, punished American women marrying aliens ineligible for citizenship by revoking the women's citizenship and prohibited women aliens ineligible for citizenship to bypass naturalization laws by marrying American citizens. Until the Cable Act was repealed in 1936, American women, for the most part, steered clear of eligible Chinese bachelors.

The Cable Act was preceded by a host of state laws aimed at stopping interracial marriage. In 1866, Oregon's anti-miscegenation law, originally aimed at African Americans, was extended to include Hawaiians, Native Americans, and persons more than half Chinese. California's anti-miscegenation law of 1880 prohibited marriage between a white and a "negro, mulatto, or Mongolian."

What was the Scott Act of 1888 and how was it yet another setback for Chinese in America?

The Scott Act, passed by Congress in October 1888, was designed to void the Section 6 certificates Chinese laborers were issued as stipulated in the 1882 Chinese Exclusion Act, which had guaranteed them the right to re-enter the United States after a trip to China. The Scott Act barred Chinese laborers from returning to the United States after visiting China unless they had relatives in America or owned real estate valued at over one thousand dollars. Since most Chinese in America were bachelors who lived from paycheck to paycheck, few met these requirements.

President Grover Cleveland signed the Scott Act into law and declared that the "experiment of blending the social habits and mutual race idiosyncrasies of the Chinese laboring classes with those of the great body of the people of the United States . . . proved . . . in every sense unwise, impolitic, and injurious to both nations."

At the time the Scott Act went into effect, approximately twenty thousand Chinese laborers holding certificates were out of the country, with every expectation of returning. Six hundred were already in transit, and when they reached the ports of San Francisco, they were denied entry.

Several U.S. senators protested that the Scott Act was a blatant violation of the 1881 treaty between the United States and China, which allowed for the free entry and exit of those Chinese laborers already in the United States. The Chinese in the United States were equally concerned and promptly raised one hundred thousand dollars to test the constitutionality of the Scott Act in the courts. Numerous constitutional challenges got them nowhere, and the Scott Act was upheld by lower federal courts as well as the U.S. Supreme Court. China also protested and pointed out that the Scott Act was a violation of the treaty of 1881, but to no avail.

Where does the term "a Chinaman's chance" come from?

In 1849, a California statute modeled after the slave codes of the South was enacted and provided that "No Black or

Mulatto person, or Indian, shall be allowed to give evidence for or against a white man."

In 1853, **George W. Hall** and two others were tried for murdering a Chinese named **Ling Sing**, and one white and three Chinese witnesses testified on behalf of the prosecution. The jury found Hall guilty of murder, and the judge sentenced him to death by hanging. However, Hall's lawyer appealed the case, arguing that the restrictions in the 1849 California statute should also apply to the Chinese.

In 1854, the California Supreme Court, in *People v. Hall*, reversed Hall's conviction on the grounds that the words "Indian, Negro, Black, and White" were "generic terms," and therefore non-whites like the Chinese could not testify against whites. In his opinion, Chief Justice **Hugh G. Murray** reasoned that "Indian as commonly used refers only to the North American Indian, yet in the days of Columbus all shores washed by Chinese waters were called the Indies. In the second place the word 'white' necessarily excludes all races other than Caucasian; and in the third place, even if this were not so, I would decide against the testimony of Chinese on grounds of public policy."

Thus the Chinese were stripped of legal protection, and they became easy prey for white attackers. When the Civil War ended in 1865, the California legislature removed the restrictions on the testimony of African Americans called for in the 1849 California statute, but those on the testimony of Mongolians, Chinese, and Indians were left intact.

The Chinese Exclusion Act of 1882 tightened the restrictions on Chinese offering testimony. A special provision in the act ensured that teachers, students, merchants, and diplomats would not be barred from entering the United States, and the U.S. government looked for a way to somehow exert control on the flow of merchants into the United States. They did so by forcing the Chinese merchants to provide proof that they indeed were merchants.

The government made matters even more difficult for Chinese merchants by deeming the testimony of other Chinese as an unacceptable form of proof: "[w]hen an application is made by a Chinaman for entrance into the United States on the ground that he was formerly engaged in this country as a merchant, he shall establish by the testimony of two credible witnesses other than Chinese the fact that he conducted such business as hereinbefore defined for at least one year before his departure from the United States."

"A Chinaman's chance," therefore, means no chance at all.

What was the Geary Act of 1892 and how did it manage to further demean Chinese immigrants?

In 1892, succumbing to complaints that all Chinese looked and sounded alike, Congress passed the Geary Act. The Geary Act instituted a national registration system so that Americans could distinguish legal Chinese aliens from illegal aliens. Every Chinese person in America was required to register by providing a photograph and a description of their unique characteristics. The individual was then issued a residence certificate, essentially an internal passport, which he had to keep on his person at all times, and present whenever asked.

All Chinese who failed to register were liable to be deported, no matter if they were lawful residents. Many Chinese refused to register, and challenged the Geary Act on the grounds that it was unconstitutionally selective and discriminatory. The United States Supreme Court, however, held that it was within Congress's power to exclude and expel aliens.

The Geary Act was considered a more draconian measure than the Scott Act because it placed the burden of proving the legality of a Chinese person's presence in the United States on the Chinese person himself, denied bail to those arrested for Geary Act violations, required that white witnesses testify in a case involving Chinese, and allowed for arrests without warrants. As Congressman James Bennett McCreary of Kentucky proclaimed in 1893, "[T]he acts . . . deny to the Chinese the right conceded to all other persons, of indictment and trial before conviction. The law also denies the universal rule of presumption of innocence. . . . There is no good reason for our Government to still further violate the treaty between the United States and China by requiring [Chinese resident aliens] to be tagged, marked, and photographed."

The Geary Act also extended the limit on the exclusion of the Chinese an additional ten years, so that only Chinese diplomats or their servants were permitted to enter the United States.

Who were the "paper sons" and how did the San Francisco earthquake of 1906 actually facilitate Chinese immigration?

After the Chinese Exclusion Act of 1882 was passed, many Chinese began to devise ways to enter the United States illegally. The Chinese were well aware that merchants (as opposed to laborers who were viewed as a threat to organized labor in the United States) were exempt from the Chinese Exclusion Act. Thus Chinese laborers often tried to pry open the door of immigration by bribing merchants to claim that they were partners in joint ventures.

The San Francisco earthquake and fires of 1906 ruined most of the city's official records, providing a unique opportunity for Chinese people to claim fraudulently that they were American-born, and hence were U.S. citizens. As "U.S. citizens" these Chinese enjoyed unrestricted entry to the United States, and any children they fathered back in China could come to America and claim U.S. citizenship (these were always sons, since patriarchal Chinese society placed no value on daughters).

This gave rise to a new enterprise in China—the business of creating fake documentation making it possible for Chinese to enter the United States as other men's sons, popularly known "paper sons."

To what lengths did the federal government go in attempting to counter the "paper son" phenomenon?

San Francisco immigration officials caught on to the fraudulent claims of U.S. citizenship by Chinese in San Francisco and the "paper son" scam soon enough. Ultimately the entire matter was brought to the attention of the State Department. As a State Department report from that time period noted, if every claim submitted were true, then "every known Chinese woman in San Francisco before the earthquake would have to have had 800 children." Ironically, some of the first federal jobs offered to Chinese required them to "sniff out" illegal Chinese immigrants.

Immigration officials responded to the surge in "paper sons" claims of citizenship by subjecting all prospective Chinese immigrants, even those eligible for exemption under the Chinese Exclusion Act, such as students, scholars and merchants, to detailed interrogations about their family history. The "paper sons" responded by memorizing facts and figures from their so-called family and village history in order to dodge any traps laid by immigration officials.

Transcripts of some of these interviews reveal that some of the questions covered details so minute that not even a real son could have known the answers: "Who occupied the house on the fifth lot of your row in your native village?" "How many water buffaloes does your village have?" "How many of the water buffaloes were male and how many were female?"

As a result, all immigrants, "paper sons" or not, had to learn a dizzying array of details to get through interrogations at U.S. immigration.

Why did so many "paper sons" cling to their fake names long after they had assimilated into America?

"Paper sons" safeguarded their true identities because in the first decade of the twentieth century a nativist immigration service raided Chinatowns across America in search of illegals. A good number of "paper sons" lived in fear over their identity long after nativist threats had diminished, and clung all their lives to their fake names. Some "paper sons" expressed wishes that their real names be inscribed on their tombstones, and thus their true identities were revealed only posthumously. As an added measure of protection, some "paper sons" requested that their real names be inscribed on their tombstones only in Chinese, next to an inscription of their fake names in English.

What happened to those Chinese who got caught at immigration in San Francisco?

In 1910, a special immigration facility was set up in the North Garrison on Angel Island in San Francisco Bay. It was designed expressly as a holding area for Chinese immigrants whose right to enter the United States was under question. Between 1910 and 1940, approximately fifty thousand Chinese were held, often for months and even years at a time, in barracks on Angel Island, until they could somehow convince American authorities that they were eligible for entry into the United States. Most endured session after session of humiliating interrogations by inspectors on even the most minute details of their family history, and then out of the blue they were let go.

Although Angel Island has been called "Ellis Island of the West," the comparison is terribly misleading. The average immigrant who came ashore at Ellis Island spent three to five hours being processed by immigration authorities. Due primarily to American protectionism and anti-Chinese discrimination, the unfortunate Chinese at Angel Island were detained on average for two to seven weeks; some were incarcerated for as long as two years.

As the Chinese immigrants waited and waited, packed in unsanitary and crowded quarters, many vented their frustration and anger over emigration, exile, and incarceration by carving poems in the barracks walls, and these poems are still visible today. One unknown poet wrote,

For what reason must I sit in jail?
It is only because my country is weak and my family poor.
.   .   .   .   .
How many people ever return from battles?
.   .   .   .
Leaving behind my writing brush and removing my sword, I came to America.
Who was to know two streams of tears would flow upon arriving here?

Where did some of the first civil rights protests by Chinese in America take place?

It was in Butte, Montana, where in 1883 the Montana Territorial Supreme Court had passed legislation to void all mining claims held by aliens, that the Chinese gained one of the most significant victories in court. Between 1895 and 1906 labor unions in Butte, in conjunction with the local chamber of commerce, organized a boycott of Chinese businesses to drive the Chinese out of town. The Chinese retaliated by hiring a well-known white lawyer, Colonel Wilbur Fisk Sanders, once a U.S. senator from Montana, to initiate a lawsuit against the unions. As it turned out, Sanders won the case, and the Chinese held their ground in Butte. When news of the legal victory reached the Chinese Six Companies in San Francisco, they supposedly declared: "The Butte Chinese are the smartest anywhere in the United States."

The Chinese laundry owners also held their own in New York in the early 1930s. White laundry operators in the city had introduced washing machines and steam presses, and the Chinese, who could not afford cutting-edge machinery, responded by lowering prices and offering free mending or free pickup and delivery. The white laundry operators retaliated by successfully lobbying the New York Board of Aldermen to pass a laundry ordinance requiring one-person laundries to post a thousand-dollar bond when they applied for a license. In 1933, Chinese laundry operators formed the Chinese Hand Laundry Alliance, hired two lawyers, and challenged the bond ordinance. The Chinese Hand Laundry Alliance was able to convince the Board of Aldermen that the bond requirement discriminated against small laundries, and the bond was reduced from one thousand dollars to one hundred dollars.

Why were Pearl S. Buck and Pearl Harbor considered blessings for the Chinese in America?

In 1932 the novelist **Pearl Sydenstricker Buck** was awarded the Pulitzer Prize for *The Good Earth,* a compassionate and vivid portrayal of the hardships of Chinese peasants, and in 1938 she was honored for her efforts with the Nobel Prize in Literature. Pearl S. Buck captivated the American imagination with her striking images of Chinese peasants, and she went on to write many more popular novels of China, among them *Dragon Seed* (1942), *Peony* (1948), and *Imperial Woman* (1956). In 1949 the distinguished writer founded Welcome House, an adoption agency for the children of Asian mothers and American GIs. Pearl Buck's literary and humanitarian accomplishments served in the 1930s and 1940s to improve dramatically America's opinion of the Chinese people both at home and in China.

Having resisted Japanese aggression in the early stages of World War II, China emerged as a potential U.S. ally. The day after bombs rained down on the U.S. Pacific Fleet moored in Pearl Harbor, the United States and the Republic of China declared war on Japan. Nearly a century of insult and violence aimed at the "Chinamen," "heathen Chinee," and the "Chinks" in America, gave way to gratitude that the Chinese at home and abroad had united with Americans to fight the "dirty Japs."

In 1942, President Roosevelt sent public messages of praise to **Chiang Kai-shek** and the people of China which rebounded on America's Chinese: "We remember that the Chinese people were the first to stand up and fight against the aggressors in this war, and in the future a still unconquerable China will play its proper role . . . in the world."

How did Time magazine teach Americans to distinguish the Chinese ally from the Japanese foe shortly after the bombing of Pearl Harbor?

Lest Americans confuse their Asian friends and foes, the December 22, 1941, issue of *Time* magazine published an article, "How to Tell Your Friends from the Japs," filled with helpful tips for distinguishing Chinese and Japanese, and supplemented with a photograph of each ethnicity for purposes of illustration. The article urged readers to keep in mind that the "Japanese are likely to be stockier and broader-hipped than short Chinese. . . . The Chinese expression is likely to be more placid, kindly, open; the Japanese more positive, dogmatic, arrogant. Japanese are hesitant, nervous in conversation, laugh loudly at the wrong time. Japanese walk stiffly erect, hard heeled. Chinese, more relaxed, have an easy gait, sometimes shuffle."

How did America's affection for the Chinese translate into the repeal of the Chinese Exclusion Act?

In response to both America's newfound compassion for the Chinese (thanks to Pearl S. Buck and Pearl Harbor) and to Japan's pernicious campaign to unnerve China with stories of discrimination against its citizens in the United States, Congress began to seriously consider repealing the Chinese exclusion laws.

In 1943, the Citizens Committee to Repeal Chinese Exclusion and Place Immigration on a Quota Basis was formed to study the issue. Committee members were culled from the American intelligentsia and elite, among them Richard J. Walsh, publisher of the John Day Company and editor of *Collier's Weekly, Judge, Asia Magazine,* and *United Nations World,* and the husband of Pearl S. Buck; Roger Baldwin of the American Civil Liberties Union; the socialist academician Broadus Mitchell; Henry R. Luce, the legendary founder of *Time, Fortune, Life,* and *Sports Illustrated* magazines; and retired admiral Harry R. Yarnell.

In an effort to appeal to the average American, the Citizens Committee argued that the elimination of exclusion in favor of a quota system would grant the Chinese equality as far as immigration was concerned, and at the same time would actually reduce the number of Chinese laborers in the United States, since such an egalitarian policy would induce Chinese emigration authorities to cooperate with the United States and crack down on illegals leaving China.

When was the Chinese Exclusion Act finally repealed?

In 1943 nine bills modifying the Chinese Exclusion Act came up for debate in Congress. New York City congressman Vito Marcantonio, a leftist, introduced the most liberal bill, which advocated that naturalization statutes be completely color-blind. The law repealing Chinese exclusion finally enacted in late 1943 was based on a more moderate bill introduced by Democratic congressman Warren Magnuson of Washington.

The law repealed all or part of the fifteen exclusionary statutes passed between 1882 and 1913; amended the nationality act to allow "Chinese persons or persons of Chinese descent" to become eligible for naturalization; and instituted an annual quota of 105 for "persons of the Chinese race." Although the law was a step forward for the Chinese, it still discriminated based on race. For instance, persons of Chinese ancestry, regardless of their country of origin, were categorized under the quota as "persons of Chinese race." Thus Chinese born in Canada fell into this special category, while persons of European ancestry born in Canada could enter the United States as non-quota Canadian immigrants.

What was Franklin Delano Roosevelt's opinion of the Chinese?

President Roosevelt's motive for improving the lot of the Chinese in America had everything to do with strengthening U.S. ties with China, and nothing to do with social progress. Roosevelt argued that China's war efforts depended on "the spirit of her people and her faith in her allies." In a special message to the Congress, he asserted that the United States "owe[d] it to the Chinese to strengthen that faith. One step in this direction is to wipe from the statute books those anachronisms in our laws which forbid the immigration of Chinese people into this country and which bar Chinese residents from American citizenship."

Thus, President Roosevelt stressed that "[w]hile [repeal] would give the Chinese a preferred status over certain other Oriental people, their great contribution to the cause of decency and freedom entitles them to such preference." Upon signing the bill into law, Roosevelt declared that "[a]n unfortunate barrier between allies has been removed. The war effort in the Far East can now be carried on with a greater vigor and a larger understanding of our common purpose."

The Republic of China gave the repeal its stamp of approval, as evidenced by a press statement the Chinese consul in Seattle issued: "repeal of the Chinese Exclusions Acts places the Chinese people on a footing of actual equality with races of Caucasian or colored descent and it will constitute a milestone in the futherance of friendship and mutual understanding between our two peoples."

The concerns of the Chinese, and of other Asian groups in America, were irrelevant to the deliberation and passage of the repeal of the Chinese Exclusion Act. Thus a bill introduced in 1943 by Congressman John Lesinski of Michigan, which would have granted the right to the non-citizen wives of Chinese American citizens to enter the United States without regard to the yearly ceiling of 105, was completely ignored by President Roosevelt. Three more years would pass before this bill, so critical to the issue of family unification, would become law and Chinese men could petition to have their spouses join them in America.

Why were so many Chinese in America drafted during World War II?

Until 1946 generations of Chinese men lived in a state of perpetual bachelorhood, thanks to the Page Law and the Chinese Exclusion Act. Since most of these men had no families and no dependents in America, they were among the first to be drafted. Altogether, 13,499 Chinese—22 percent of all adult Chinese males in the United States—were drafted or enlisted in the United States armed forces.

How else did America's Chinese contribute to the war effort?

The Chinese contributed to the American war effort in countless ways. Eager to help their homeland fight Japanese imperialism, the Chinese community of Portland, Oregon, sent thirty-three trained pilots to serve under Generalissimo Chiang Kai-shek. In San Francisco, Chinese people raised $18,000 for the war campaign and bought $30,000 worth of bonds in the Defense Bond Drive.

Like their mainstream American counterparts, Chinese women entered the defense industry in droves. The exquisite actress **Anna May Wong** volunteered as an air-raid warden in

Santa Monica. In the Boston Navy Yard, Chinese women ran light lathes, grinders, planers, and other machine tools. Chinese women also took jobs building aircraft. And **Emily Lee Shek** became the first woman of Chinese ancestry to join the WACs. Apparently, she had tried to join at the very beginning of the war, but was ineligible due to the 105-pound minimum weight. When the minimum was dropped to 100 pounds, she jumped at the chance to be a WAC.

The Chinese in America even put their children to work collecting tin cans and tin foil as scrap materials for the war effort.

How was the seed for a Chinese American middle class planted on the East Coast during World War II?

In 1880 a mere 3 percent of all Chinese people in America lived in the East, but by 1940 that figure had risen to 40 percent, and New York's Chinatown boasted the country's largest Chinese population after that of San Francisco.

When Japanese troops invaded the northern provinces of China in 1937 and Chinese resistance unleashed the Second Sino-Japanese War, numerous Chinese professionals, scientists, and engineers visiting the United States were stranded abroad. Many settled in New York's Chinatown, where they laid the foundation for the emergence of a middle class. This process was helped along by Chinese high school students in New York City, who in the 1940s outperformed their non-Asian peers, and went on to college in greater numbers than any other ethnic group in the city.

The war also provided a unique opportunity for the Chinese to break out of small businesses such as restaurants and laundries. A number of them found higher-paying defense industry jobs in shipyards, manufacturing plants, and airplane factories. The job market also opened up for college-educated Chinese, who were able to find great employment in certain fields of specialization, such as engineering.

Why did the Communist takeover of China put the Chinese in America on red alert?

In the aftermath of World War II, hostilities between Chinese Nationalists and Communists escalated into a full-fledged war as both factions tried desperately to secure areas evacuated by the Japanese. In 1947 the Communists gained the upper hand, and by April 1950, they had overrun all of mainland China. A few months later Communist Chinese forces intervened in the Korean War to intercept United Nations forces headed toward the Manchurian border. As "Red China" took center stage, the pro-Chinese sentiment of 1930s and 1940s America rapidly gave way to suspicion.

In 1950 Congress passed the McCarran Internal Security Act, authorizing the internment of Communists during a state of national emergency. The U.S. attorney general was vested with the authority to detain anyone if there was "reasonable ground" to believe that he or she was engaged in espionage or sabotage.

Again the Chinese in America had cause for alarm, for they knew by now that their status rested on U.S. foreign policy toward China. Furthermore they had witnessed how Japanese hostility toward the United States in World War II had devastated the Japanese community in America and landed honest, hardworking Japanese in internment camps.

The Chinese Consolidated Benevolent Association of New York and the Chinese Six Companies headquarters in San Francisco swiftly organized anti-Communist campaigns across the nation to combat rumors that Chinese Communists had infiltrated America. The year 1951 saw the formation of the Anti-Communist Committee for Free China, which immediately declared its loyalty to the United States and condemned communism as un-Chinese. In 1954 the Chinese in New York organized the All-American Overseas Chinese Anti-Communist League to combat misperceptions that Chinese Americans and Chinese residents in the United States were Communists.

How did McCarthyism intensify Chinese fears of a new era of persecution?

In 1953 Senator **Joseph McCarthy** was selected chair of the Senate permanent investigations subcommittee, and he exploited the enormous power of the post to unleash a Red Scare. Through unsubstantiated accusations of wrongdoing, unidentified informers, and widely publicized hearings, McCarthy pursued anyone he cared to classify as a Communist and a subversive. McCarthy's whims destroyed many bright careers.

In this atmosphere of nationalism gone haywire, Joseph McCarthy had Americans convinced that Communist infiltrators were all around them, and across the nation citizens were on guard for signs of espionage and sabotage activities. In late 1955 the American consul general in Hong Kong, **Everett F. Drumwright**, warned the U.S. government that Chinese Communist agents were infiltrating the United States by presenting fraudulent citizenship papers at customs. In early 1956 agents with the Immigration and Naturalization Service launched an investigation of "suspect" Chinese in America, and raided Chinatowns on both coasts to take illegal immigrants—and potential Communists—into custody.

Chinese American communities were shrouded in fear, and everyone, most of all "paper sons" and others who entered the United States by fraudulent means, worried that the past would come back to haunt them.

How did World War II and the Cold War lead to a change in U.S. immigration policies?

America's desire to emerge from World War II and the Cold War as the leader of the free world led the country to rethink its domestic policies, including Asian immigration and naturalization, which had stirred so much trouble in the past.

In 1952, the U.S. Congress enacted the Immigration and

Nationality Act—also called the McCarran-Walter Act—which dropped racial and ethnic barriers to naturalization while preserving the race-based National Origins Quota System. Thus statutory discrimination against Asians became a thing of history. At the same time, the McCarran-Walter Act created an Asia-Pacific restrictive zone and allotted each of the nineteen countries in the zone a quota of two thousand immigrants.

How did President Truman and President Eisenhower view the National Origins Quota System?

Congress passed the McCarran-Walter Act over the veto of President Harry S. Truman, who believed that the race-based National Origins Quota System should have been completely abolished. After the passage of the McCarran-Walter Act, President Truman appointed a Special Commission on Immigration and Naturalization to study the immigration system. The commission's report, issued in 1953, urged that the National Origins Quota System be abolished and replaced with a system of allocating visas without regard to national origin, race, creed, or color.

Although President Dwight D. Eisenhower endorsed the findings of the report, he was unable to eliminate the quota system.

What was the Confession System?

After the McCarran-Walter Act was passed, the U.S. government put in place a mechanism to allow illegal immigrants such as "paper sons" and others to obtain legal status. The Confession System became a statute in 1957 and allowed illegal Chinese aliens to regularize their status if they had a close relative who was a permanent resident alien or an American citizen.

As it turned out, the majority of illegal Chinese aliens were too afraid of the INS to step from the shadows. They remembered all too well how INS agents had raided Chinatowns in

1956 in search of illegal aliens and Communist infiltrators. They also knew that the INS and the FBI had, on occasion, used information gathered from confessions, intelligence reports, and loyalty tests to deport or exclude Chinese people who supposedly sympathized with "Red China."

What was the Hart-Celler Act and who were the san yi man?

In 1965 Congress passed the Hart-Celler Act, which abolished the National Origins Quota System of the Immigration and Nationality Act, which had favored immigrants of Western European descent. This legislation was designed to unite families and to prevent any one country from enjoying special preferences. Occupational preference categories were established for professionals who filled jobs for which there was no qualified U.S. worker.

The Hart-Celler Act also allotted 170,000 visas to immigrants from the Eastern Hemisphere, with no more than 20,000 visas going to a single country regardless of its size. A new refugee category favoring persons fleeing a Communist or Communist-dominated country benefited those Chinese who fled mainland China after 1949. However, the annual limitation of 10,200 for the entire category meant that this allotment went largely to refugees from other Communist-dominated countries.

The Hart-Celler Act essentially opened wide the gates of immigration for the Chinese *san yi man*, or "new immigrants," as these post-1965 immigrants are called. Approximately 711,000 *san yi man* made their way to the United States between 1965 and 1990, almost double the number of Chinese who reached America's shores between the gold rush of 1849 and 1930.

How did the Chinese American community change radically after 1965?

While the Chinese who ventured to America from 1849 until after World War II (the *lo wa kiu*, meaning "old overseas Chinese") were generally poorly educated peasants from rural areas of China, the *san yi man* have been mostly blue-collar and white-collar workers from urban areas who speak either Mandarin or Cantonese. Nearly half of all Chinese immigrants who came to America between 1966 and 1975 were professionals, managers, and technical workers.

Like the *lo wa kiu* before them, a good number of *san yi man* have fled political upheaval in China. Before the normalization of relations between the United States and China in 1979, many *san yi man* escaping the persecution of the Cultural Revolution found their way from mainland China to Hong Kong or Taiwan, and then on to the United States.

Unlike the early Chinese bachelor sojourners who were cut off from their families and dreamed of getting rich quick and going home, *san yi man* men and women have come to the United States with their children in tow and with the intention of making it in America. Fearless before the U.S. government, they have taken the bull by the horns and have fought for social reforms in Chinatowns, for much needed legal aid, long overdue funds for housing, and essential educational programs.

San yi man white-collar and blue-collar workers have created a dichotomized Chinese American community. *San yi man* professionals, shocked by the unemployment, poverty, and crowded conditions in America's Chinatowns, have swelled the ranks of upwardly mobile Chinese Americans. They have assimilated swiftly into the mainstream and have left Chinatowns behind for middle- and upper-middle-class neighborhoods and suburbs. Their children go to the finest universities, such as Yale, Harvard, and the University of California at Berkeley.

At the same time, *san yi man* blue-collar workers have settled in the Chinatowns, where the men secure low-paying jobs as dishwashers and cooks in restaurants and the women slave away as seamstresses in the garment industry by day and as housewives in the evenings. These *san yi man* work hard, pressure their children to excel in school, and dream of owning their own businesses and one day leaving Chinatown for the middle-class suburbs. Yet the future looks rather dim for most of these workers. More than half are trapped in the Chinese ethnic economy by a lack of English-language fluency and education. Many earn less than minimum wage with no health benefits or job security, and live below the poverty line.

This dichotomy in the Chinese American community is readily apparent in New York City, where the "Uptown Chinese," wealthy professionals and business owners who have totally acculturated, rarely rub elbows with the "Downtown Chinese," who work at low-paying jobs in Chinatown.

Both sides of the Chinese American community help preserve the vitality of the Chinatowns. Blue-collar workers in need of cheap housing and social programs supply the service sector, which in turn attracts upwardly mobile Chinese Americans who flock to Chinatowns to shop, dine, and do business, and thus lend financial stability to a way of life that is a step closer to China.

What are the "new" Chinatowns of the 1980s and 1990s?

In the 1980s, wealthy Chinese from Taiwan and Hong Kong became increasingly concerned about the transfer of the British colony to the People's Republic of China in 1997, and the economic turmoil that may result despite promises from Beijing that China and Hong Kong will operate as "one country, two systems." The Taiwanese also fear the reversion of Hong Kong to Chinese rule because it represents a first step toward possible reabsorption of Taiwan by China, a vision Chinese Communists have nurtured ever since their victory in a bitter civil war that forced Chinese Nationalists to set up a rival government in Taiwan in 1949. If China were to reclaim Taiwan it would take control of Taiwanese investments. As a result, the peoples of Taiwan and Hong Kong began shifting their capital to Monterey Park, California. Before the eighties were over, the Chinese had become the largest ethnic minority in Monterey Park, and the city had elected **Lily Lee Chen** its first Chinese mayor. When Chen was elected in September 1984 she became the first Chinese American woman mayor of a U.S. city. The Chinese command such a presence in Monterey Park that the city has earned the titles "Chinese Beverly Hills" and "Little Taipei."

At the same time, Chinese big business from Taiwan and Hong Kong have been buying up New York's Chinatown, setting off a real estate boom and attracting large amounts of capital. In response to demand, professional and business service companies have set up shop in Chinatown: the neighborhood now boasts an estimated two hundred law practices and one hundred accounting practices, in addition to numerous advertising and real estate agencies. As a result of the influx of Hong Kong and Taiwan investors, New York's Chinatown doubled in size between 1980 and 1990. Its borders now encompass areas that had been part of Little Italy and the Jewish Lower East Side.

Who murdered Vincent Chin and why was the murderer given probation?

On June 19, 1982, **Vincent Chin**, a twenty-seven-year-old Chinese American engineering student, went with three friends to the Fancy Pants Tavern, a topless bar in Highland Park, Michigan. **Ronald Ebens**, an unemployed auto worker at the bar, thought Chin was Japanese and began hurling racial epithets at him, blaming him for the auto industry's plight. A fight broke out and both sides were asked to leave the bar.

Later that night Ebens and his stepson, **Michael Nitz**, spotted Vincent Chin at a nearby fast-food restaurant. The two men attacked Chin and beat him badly with a baseball bat. Seriously injured, Vincent Chin died four days later.

Ebens and Nitz were charged with second-degree murder. In a plea bargain, both agreed to plead guilty to the lesser charge of manslaughter. At sentencing, Wayne County circuit judge Charles Kaufman merely fined Ebens and Nitz $3,750 each and placed both on probation for three years.

The Chinese American community reacted to the light sentence with disbelief and outrage, and formed the Justice for Vincent Chin Committee to see that justice would prevail. The federal government stepped in to investigate the case, and indicted Ebens for allegedly committing a racially motivated crime and, therefore, depriving Vincent Chin of his civil rights. A federal jury found Ronald Ebens guilty, and he was sentenced to twenty-five years in prison. Citing judicial errors, an appellate court reversed the conviction on appeal in May 1987. In a civil settlement, Ronald Ebens agreed to pay the Chin estate $1.5 million, but this may not come to pass, since he has been unemployed for many years.

The case was retried in 1987 in a different venue. Ebens's lawyer successfully convinced the jury that the murder was not racially motivated. Ebens was acquitted, and a subsequent civil suit against him was settled out of court for $1.5 million.

Who are some great Chinese Americans?

Chinese Americans have made valuable contributions to all spheres of American culture and life—from science to law; from the arts to sports; from education to business. However, the traditional Chinese love for scholarship and science has translated into a endless crop of brilliant Chinese American scientists. In 1957 **Chen Ning Yang** and **Tsung-Dao Lee** became the first Chinese Americans awarded the Nobel Prize for Physics, after they disproved a basic quantum-mechanics law known as conservation of parity.

Popular voices in Chinese American literature include **Chin Yang Lee**, best known for his witty first novel *Flower Drum Song* (1957), which Rodgers and Hammerstein adapted into a musical in 1959, and **Maxine Hong Kingston**, author of *The Woman Warrior* (1976), *China Men* (1980), and other best-selling books, and the first Chinese American to be named a "Living Treasure of Hawaii." More recently **Amy Tan** has captured the attention of the American readership with her runaway best-seller *The Joy Luck Club* (1989) (which was made into a hit movie) and her highly successful novels *The Kitchen God's Wife* (1991) and *A Hundred Secret Senses* (1995). The 1990s unleashed a powerful wave of interest in Asian American writers. **Gus Lee** made a splash on the literary scene with the publication of his semiautobiographical *China Boy* (1991), **David Wong Louie** won enthusiastic applause for his humorous tales in *Pangs of Love* (1991), and **Gish Jen** grabbed the critics' attention with her bittersweet *Typical American* (1991).

In music, the cellist **Yo-Yo Ma** has earned a place among the world's most gifted instrumentalists with his dynamic stage presence, extraordinary technique, and insightful interpretation.

Ruth Ann Koesun became the first Asian American woman to join a national ballet company and is currently a soloist with the American Ballet Theater. Also on stage but in a different medium, **David Henry Hwang**, the Chinese American playwright, captivated audiences and critics in the 1980s with his play *M. Butterfly*. The play went on to win the Tony Award for Best Broadway Play of 1988 and other awards, establishing Hwang as a leading playwright. Actor **B. D. Wong** also captured a Tony, the first for an Asian American, for his extraordinary performance as the mistress Song Li Ling in *M. Butterfly*.

On the big screen, film director **Wayne Wang** offered Americans fascinating glimpses of Chinese America with his critically acclaimed films *Chan Is Missing* (1981), *Dim Sum* (1987), and *Eat a Bowl of Tea* (1989). His greatest hit at the box office and with critics was *The Joy Luck Club* (1993), based on Amy Tan's best-selling novel of the same name. Actress **Joan Chen** distinguished herself on the TV screen in 1990 and 1991 in the series *Twin Peaks* and on the big screen in the motion pictures *Blade Runner* (1982), *The Last Emperor* (1987), *Heaven and Earth* (1993), and *Golden Gate* (1994). Born Chen Chong in the People's Republic of China, she earned a following there as a child film star. In the 1960s and 1970s **Bruce Lee**, the renowned martial artist and founder of Jeet Kune Do, popularized the Wing Chun style of kung fu in his books and Hong Kong films. He captivated viewers here and abroad with his performance in the 1973 Warner Brothers film *Enter the Dragon*. Bruce Lee never saw the film's release. He died suddenly of a cerebral edema; filmgoers and martial arts fans around the globe mourned the passing of the great martial artist.

In broadcast journalism, **Kaity Tong**, a New York City anchorwoman, and **Connie Chung**, the first woman to anchor a weeknight network news broadcast, have won plaudits from American viewers for their fine reportage.

Chinese Americans have distinguished themselves in the field of architecture. **I. M. Pei**, one of America's most famous architects, has designed, among other structures, the glass pyramid in the courtyard of the Louvre Museum in Paris, the John F. Kennedy Library in Boston, the National Gallery of Art in Washington, D.C., and the seventy-two-story Bank of China in Hong Kong, the tallest building in Asia. And the architect **Maya Ying Lin** has won a place in the hearts of millions of Americans for her designs of both the Vietnam Veterans Memorial and the Civil Rights Memorial, both in Washington, D.C. **Dong Kingman** is a critically acclaimed illustrator and painter.

In politics, **Herbert Y. C. Choy** was the first Asian American appointed to a U.S. federal court; **Hiram Leong Fong** became the first Chinese American elected to the U.S. Senate in 1959 and until his retirement in 1976 encouraged trade and good will between the United States and Pacific Rim nations; and in 1974 **March Kong Fong Eu** became the first Asian American woman elected secretary of state in California. In

1984 **S. B. Woo**, a Chinese American physicist, captured the lieutenant governorship of Delaware, proving that an Asian could compete for an elected post in a state with a small Asian American population.

In education, **Chang-Lin Tien**, a mechanical engineer born in China, became the first Asian American to head a major research university when he was appointed chancellor of the University of California at Berkeley in 1990.

Chinese Americans have distinguished themselves in business. **Dr. An Wang** founded the billion-dollar computer company Wang Laboratories in 1951 with a $600 investment; **Dr. Gerald Tsai** is chairman of Primerica Company, one of the leading world corporations; **Winston Chen** is chairman and CEO of Solectron Corporation; entrepreneur **Gene Lu** founded Advanced Logic Research before the age of thirty; and **David Lam** started the multimillion-dollar software company Expert Edge.

In sports, tennis champ **Michael Chang** amazed the tennis world in 1987 at the tender age of fifteen by becoming the youngest player to win the French Open. And football fans are keeping a close watch on one of the few Chinese Americans in the sport, **Eugene Chung**, the celebrated offensive line guard for the New England Patriots.

The list goes on and on. Hundreds of other Chinese Americans over the past century and a half have contributed significantly to the rich mosaic of American life, from California's Redwood Forests to Mott Street in New York's Chinatown.

Who is Fu Manchu?

The fictional fiend Dr. Fu Manchu was created in 1911 by **Sax Rohmer**, whose thirteen Fu Manchu novels have been translated into more than a dozen languages and Braille. In each of the books, Dr. Fu Manchu plots to conquer the world and resorts to kidnapping, mind control, and extortion to get his way. Fu Manchu is the perfect embodiment of America's past perceptions of Asians as cruel and cunning criminals. He is, in fact, as his creator described him in *The Insidious Dr. Fu Manchu*, "the yellow peril incarnate in one man."

Novelist **Jack London** once made the outrageous claim that the Anglo-Saxon possesses "a certain integrity, a comradeship and warm human feeling, which is ours, indubitably ours, and which we cannot teach to the Orientals as we would teach logarithms or the trajectory of projectiles." Fu Manchu is Jack London's worst nightmare, for he is all brain and no heart. In Sax Rohmer's words, Fu Manchu is "superman, Satan materalized and equipped with knowledge which few had ever achieved; a cold, dominating intellect, untrammeled by fleshly ties, a great mind unbound by the laws of man."

In the 1920s a series of British silent films were made based on the Fu Manchu novels. A string of talkies followed, beginning in 1929 with *The Mysterious Dr. Fu Manchu*, starring **Warner Oland**, and ending in 1970 with the release of *The Castle of Fu Manchu*.

Who is Charlie Chan and why is he so unpopular among most Asian Americans?

Charlie Chan, the good-natured Chinese detective, was the creation of **Earl Derr Biggers**, who got his inspiration for the character from a real-life detective by the name of **Chang Apana**. Between 1925 and 1932, Biggers wrote a total of six Charlie Chan novels; all were serialized in the *Saturday Evening Post* and several were translated into as many as ten foreign languages.

Charlie Chan made his debut on the silver screen as a minor character in the 1926 serial *House Without a Key*. Two more minor appearances followed, and then in 1931 the Charlie Chan phenomenon began, and before it ended the Chinese detective would be the centerpiece of more than forty-five Hollywood motion pictures. The pudgy sleuth delighted American audiences as he trotted the globe solving crime puzzles, as in *Charlie Chan in Reno* (1939) and *Charlie Chan in Panama* (1940). Charlie Chan was played primarily by the Swedish actor Warner Oland and the non-Asian American actors Sidney Toler and Roland Winters, but filmgoers didn't seem to mind, and Earl Biggers made a huge profit from Hollywood's adaptations and the sale of his books. In the 1950s, television tried to get in on the act and resurrected Charlie Chan in a half-hour series starring **J. Carrol Naish**, but the show bombed. Universal's efforts to revive Chan in 1971 in the pilot film *Happiness Is a Warm Clue* were just as futile. In 1981 Hollywood attempted one last time to reignite interest in Charlie Chan with the release of *Charlie Chan and the Curse of the Dragon Queen*, but filmgoers and critics gave the film a thumbs-down.

According to John Stone, producer of the first Charlie Chan film, the Charlie Chan books were made into movies "as a refutation of the unfortunate Fu Manchu characterization of the Chinese, and partly as a demonstration of [the] idea that any minority group could be sympathetically portrayed on the screen with the right story and approach."

Many Asian Americans refute the notion that the affable Charlie Chan is the perfect antidote to the evil Fu Manchu. At first glance he appears so. He is a portly Chinese detective who roams the exotic streets of Chinatown and other international locales, solving murder mysteries and aiding white men in their fight against crime.

But a closer look reveals that Charlie Chan walks daintily, and in "fortune cookie English" spouts "Confucius-say" aphorisms, supposed nuggets of Chinese wisdom. A sampling of Chan aphorisms might include "Woman's intuition like feather on arrow. May help flight to truth." "Necessity mother of invention, but sometimes stepmother of deception." "If strength were all, tiger would not fear scorpion." These aphorisms were so popular with the public that they were collected and published in a book.

In the eyes of many Asian Americans, Charlie Chan is in essence an effeminate, wimpy, nerdy, inscrutable Asian male, who helped plant the seed of the pervasive racist stereotype of Asian Americans as the "model minority." Even kung fu superman Bruce Lee was not able to abolish this stereotype decades later.

What is the dragon lady/lotus blossom dichotomy?

This term was coined by filmmaker **Renee Tajima** to describe the two stock images of Asian women on the silver screen: the cunning and deceitful temptress and the innocent girl who is always ready to please.

For instance, in the 1931 Fu Manchu thriller *Daughter of the Dragon*, **Anna May Wong** plays the deceptive dragon lady and sexual temptress. By contrast, Suzie, the Hong Kong prostitute played by **Nancy Kwan** in the 1960 motion picture melodrama *The World of Suzie Wong*, epitomizes the "naive innocent Asian girl" stereotype when she falls in love with William Holden and tells him in typical good-girl fashion: "I not important," and "I'll be with you until you say—Suzie, go away."

Why are Americans so "gung-ho"?

Gung-ho is a Mandarin word meaning "to work together." The word meandered into the English language where it underwent a major overhaul. To Americans it does not denote communal labor, but rather "a naive spirit of enthusiasm and cooperation," as in being "really gung-ho about" something or other.

Why does Chinese writing resemble drawings rather than letters?

China is spread out over three and a half million square miles, extending from south of the tropic of Cancer to the border of Siberia, from the Pacific to the center of the Eurasian continent. The peoples who inhabit this vast landmass are diverse culturally and linguistically. The language spoken in China is so diverse, in fact, that Chinese from different regions often cannot understand each other. Some linguists classify all the variants of the Chinese language as dialects, while others categorize them as different languages, since many are mutually unintelligible.

While the spoken languages and dialects in China have little in common, the written language is universal and acts as a unifying element. Chinese writing consists of a character, or ideogram, for every word, instead of a group of symbols representing sounds, and therefore indicates no phonetic property of the word. Thus, though Chinese from different regions may not be able to converse, Chinese from all regions can read each other's writing. One major drawback with this system, however, is that the reader needs to know several thousand characters even to read the newspaper. This has proved a challenging obstacle to mass literacy.

What is Taoism?

Taoism, which has a following in Chinese America, is a philosophy developed by **Lao-tzu** in the sixth century B.C. Lao-tzu saw a tragic perversity in the human pursuit of superfluous and temporal matters, and decided to withdraw from society and government service. He put down in writing, in an obscure and poetic style, what he considered to be the correct path. His short treatise was entitled *Tao-te ching*, or *The Way of Virtue*, in which he called for a return to nature and a rejection of civilization.

Tao-te ching has been subject to numerous interpretations. However, the essence of Taoism is quite simple. Artificial divisions in society, codes of conduct, and so forth, are contrary to the *Tao* (literally, "way"), the underlying pattern of the universe; and simplicity, not accumulation, is what is harmonious with the true rhythm of life. In Taoism, distinctions are arbitrary, and life and death are simply two faces of the same reality.

The natural way, the Tao, according to Taoist philosophy, mimics the properties of water, which flows and seeks the lowest point until it can merge again with the seas. To follow the natural way and to live like water, then, is to live by "non-action," or "non-striving." "Non-action," though, does not mean doing nothing. It means avoiding actions to force events to unfold in a certain way. It means being quiet and tuning in to the natural flow. Contemplation and harmony with this flow, not willfulness, bring contentment, dissolve conflict, and promote peace.

Thus, while the firmness of rock is praised in the West, the softness of water is extolled in China. "As the soft yield of water cleaves obstinate stone, so to yield with life solves the insoluble: to yield, I have learned, is to come back again."

How has Confucius contributed both to Chinese and Chinese American society's devotion to order and respect and to its patriarchy?

The founder of Confucian philosophy, **K'ung Ch'iu**—known as K'ung Fu-tzu ("Master K'ung"), hence the Latinized name **Confucius**—lived from approximately 551 to 479 B.C. The abuses of the feudal system led Confucius to develop a system of instruction designed to heal the breaches of society. Confucian teachings underscore ethical precepts such as righteousness, benevolent love, decorum, sincerity, and wise leadership. Family, society, and government should abide diligently by these precepts. Thus, according to Confucius, a monarch must rule his subjects with benevolence and in the same way a father must rule his children. The monarch's subjects, in turn, like a father's children, must show respect, abiding loyalty, and reverence.

In a male-dominated world, Confucian teaching inevitably demands men's virtue with regard to women and women's loyal obedience to men. In fact, the Confucian principles of the Five Human Relationships refer to ruler and subject, father and son, husband and wife, elder brother and younger brother, and friend and friend.

What variety of Buddhism did the Chinese bring to the United States and what religions do they now practice?

Buddhism was founded in India at the end of the sixth century B.C. by **Siddhartha Gautama**, called the Buddha ("the Enlightened One"). Buddhism moved east from India along trade routes, reaching China about the first century A.D. It was not until the fifth and sixth centuries A.D., though, that Buddhism emerged as a popular and established religion in China.

Mahayana Buddhism, as opposed to the Hinayana, Theravada, and related Buddhist schools, was embraced in China. The main philosophical tenets of Mahayana Buddhism—that good deeds lead to a better life in future reincarnations and that the Buddha is but one incarnation in a series—appealed to all layers of Chinese society, including the common people. Buddhism was essentially transformed in China into a religion bringing enlightenment only to the mystic or the learned, but capable of bestowing universal salvation on the masses.

Buddhism managed to coexist with a wealth of native religions and philosophies in China by providing insights into salvation, rather than being a rigid and monolithic system of absolutes. Certain aspects of Buddhism were already present in Chinese traditions, and these were emphasized. Thus, Buddhist meditation was practiced intensively by the Chinese because of its resemblance to the Taoist *kuan*, or "mystical vision." For Chinese consumption, the Buddhist *dharma*, or "teaching," was likened to the Tao, or "the Way," while the Buddhist concept of *nirvana,* or "enlightenment," was equated with the Taoist notion of "non-action." Early Chinese immigrants brought Mahayana Buddhism to the United States, erecting numerous temples in California, twenty of which still stand today. Other Chinese immigrants practiced Taoism and Confucianism in the New World, and still others were converted to Christianity by American missionaries who set up social-welfare programs in Chinatowns. Chinese Christians, particularly the foreign-born, however, tended to adhere both to the teachings of Christianity and to Buddhist, Taoist, or Confucian practices. To this day Chinese Americans worship religions brought from China as well as the Christian religions they or their forebears came in contact with in the United States.

What Chinese holidays do Chinese Americans typically celebrate?

The Chinese New Year is perhaps the Chinese holiday most often observed by Chinese Americans. It begins with the second new moon after the winter solstice, usually between January 21 and February 19. Just as there are twelve months in the Chinese calendar year, there are also twelve years in a cycle. In the Han dynasty each year in the Chinese cycle was matched with a different animal, beginning with the rat, then the ox, tiger, hare, dragon, serpent, horse, ram, monkey, rooster, dog, and pig. Everyone, according to the Chinese, possesses qualities of the animal whose year he or she was born in. Thus an individual born in the Year of the Rat will exhibit persistence, "gnawing away" until a goal is achieved. Chinese New Year celebrations incorporate the "animal of the year." The year 2000 of the Gregorian calendar will be the Year of the Dragon, the most beloved creature in Chinese mythology.

In preparation for the Chinese New Year, Chinese Americans traditionally repay all their debts, clean and repair their houses, and stock up on foods for a sumptuous feast. Oranges and fish are especially good luck for the new year. During this time the Chinese do their best to avoid conflict in order to ensure that the new year will be full of prosperity and harmony. Chinese Americans believe that even a single bad word uttered or the accidental breaking of a dish will bring bad luck in the coming year.

As a preliminary to the New Year's celebration, on the twenty-fourth day of the twelfth moon, Chinese Americans traditionally honor the Kitchen God as he departs for Heaven to report to the Emperor about the activities of the household. To help the Kitchen God on his way, the family usually burns incense and candles, and places cakes and candy on the family altar or by the Kitchen God's portrait near the stove. Often, family members will coat the Kitchen God's lips with honey to ensure a positive report.

On New Year's Eve the family comes together for a feast; even the deceased are considered present in spirit, and a bowl and chopsticks are laid out for them. After dinner, parents typically give their children *bao*—red envelopes with lucky money inside—and perform rites before the family altar. The elder in the family may light incense and candles and perform rites asking that the Heaven, the Earth, and ancestors bestow blessings on the family in the new year. The family might also set off firecrackers to drive away evil spirits.

In Chinatowns across America, Chinese Americans from all walks of life, and tourists too, gather to watch and participate in the colorful and noisy New Year's Parade. In San Francisco a three-hour procession winds down Grant Street, in the heart of Chinatown, while in Lower Manhattan a parade twists and turns through Mott, Pell, and Bayard Streets. Lion dancing, other folk dancing, and martial arts demonstrations entertain the crowds, but everyone thrills at the sight of the *gum lung*, the ceremonial golden dragon, often made in Hong Kong and shipped to America expressly for the celebration. This most beneficent creature, a symbol of strength and longevity for the Chinese, floats through the streets held aloft by dozens of dragon-bearers. It bespeaks *Gung hay fat choy!*—Happy New Year!

Another of the many Chinese holidays celebrated by Chinese Americans is the Mid-Autumn Festival, or Moon Festival. It is associated with yin, the female element of life, and hence is a celebration of fertility and the harvest. The Mid-Autumn Festival takes place on the fifteenth day of the eighth lunar month, when the moon, considered a female deity, shines brightest. During this festival, young girls burn incense in the temple, and ask Yueh Lao, the man in the moon, for a vision of their future husbands. Moon cakes—rich pastries traditionally filled with sweet red bean paste—are eaten during the Chinese Moon Festival.

Do Chinese Americans really eat everything?

According to a popular saying, "The Chinese eat everything in the sky except an airplane, everything in the sea except a submarine, and everything with four legs except a table."

A list of the more unusual Chinese delicacies available in America's Chinatowns might include one-hundred-year-old eggs—also called thousand-year eggs, century eggs, and Ming dynasty eggs—which are chicken, duck, or goose eggs preserved in a mixture of lime, salt, and ash for approximately one hundred days until the yolk turns gray. One-hundred-year-old eggs are often added to rice gruel or eaten with soy sauce, minced ginger, or pickles.

Shark's fins, actually just the cartilage of the shark's dorsal fin, pectoral fin, and a portion of the tail fin, are a rare delicacy with a reputation as an aphrodisiac. When cooked, the shark's fin cartilage releases a gelatin that is used to thicken and flavor soups, particularly shark's fin soup. The highest-quality fins are those five inches in length.

Birds' nests built by swallows are also highly prized by chefs in China and in Chinese American communities. The swallows construct their nests in dark caves. The nests are held together with layers of a gelatin-like substance that the male swallows secrete from swollen salivary glands. Nest collectors must carry lights into pitch-black caves (which are also usually home to bats), climb to the top of bamboo scaffolding, and gently pry the nests from the cave walls with a special tool. Chinese Americans go through all this trouble because they believe that bird's nests contain properties which strengthen all the vital organs of the body. "Raw" bird's nests are tasteless, but like shark's fins, they impart a delicious flavor when boiled in stocks.

How did chow mein and chop suey come to America?

Contrary to popular belief, early Chinese immigrants did not bring recipes for chow mein and chop suey with them from China. Rather, these popular dishes were invented by Chinese Americans.

Chow mein came into existence purely by accident. According to popular lore, a cook in China accidentally dropped some noodles into a frying pan filled with fat. Much to his surprise, he had invented a tasty dish. Other cooks perfected the recipe over time by adding meat, vegetables, and shrimp to the fried noodles. Voilà, chow mein.

Chop suey, a dish that is not prepared in China, is Cantonese for "miscellaneous mixture." Theories abound as to the origins of chop suey. A popular explanation is that Chinese Americans invented the recipe in the nineteenth century to please a Chinese viceroy visiting the United States as the Chinese emperor's emissary. Apparently Viceroy Li Hung-chang suffered from indigestion during his visit and requested a bland assortment of vegetables with a little bit of meat. The dish was concocted and quickly coined "chop suey."

What is the origin of the fortune cookie?

The fortune cookie originated as part of a plan in the early 1900s to transform San Francisco's Chinatown from a ghetto of "inassimilable" and "undesirable" Chinamen into a "quaint" tourist attraction. Advertisements for Chinatown promised tourists an "Oriental experience" in the Occident; a tour of Canton and the distant and magnificent land of Cathay. Exoticism was necessary to attract tourists, and when San Francisco's Chinatown was destroyed by the 1906 earthquake, it was rebuilt, and though modern, was designed to retain its "Oriental charm and attractiveness," as the *San Francisco Chronicle* put it in 1917. Chinese pageantry, styles of architecture, and decorations were promoted. The Grayline bus company participated in the campaign and brought more than ten thousand tourists to San Francisco's Chinatown in 1935.

Increased tourism led to the invention of the Chinese fortune cookie. Tourists expected a dessert course in Chinese restaurants, and the fortune cookie was designed to satisfy their demands. In the 1930s a worker in San Francisco's Kay Heong Noodle Factory invented a plain flat cookie, which, while still warm, was folded around a little slip of paper on which a prediction or pearl of wisdom had been written.

Why do the Chinese use chopsticks?

Throughout its history, China has been plagued by chronic fuel shortages. As a way to conserve fuel in cooking, the ancient Chinese chopped and shredded food into bite-size pieces so that it would cook faster, and they depended on stir-frying as a speedier method of preparation than baking.

The ancient Chinese found it easiest to eat bite-size morsels of food with chopsticks; they had no reason to develop the fork and knife to spear and cut food at the table. The earliest chopsticks in China date back to the Shang dynasty (1700–1050 B.C.) and were invariably fashioned from bamboo. Nowadays wealthy Chinese employ chopsticks made from a variety of materials such as agate, jade, and silver, but average Chinese and Chinese Americans stick with hardwood, lacquered wood, and bamboo. In Chinatowns across America, as in China, wood and bamboo chopsticks are frequently sold in packets of ten pairs, since no more than ten people may sit at one table at a Chinese banquet.

How is traditional Chinese medicine different from Western medicine?

Chinese medicine is based on the fundamental Taoist concepts of yin and yang. Yin emblematizes the passive principle of life, which includes the female, the moon, earth, water, while yang represents the active principle, the male, the sun, heaven, and fire. Yin and yang do not clash, but in fact interact in a balanced and all-embracing circle, representing the Tao, the universal harmonizing force of nature.

Harmony with the Tao results in good health. When the balance between the forces of yin and yang has been disturbed, illness results. The purpose then of medicine is to restore this balance. Diagnosis by a traditional Chinese doctor consists of a thorough examination of the pulse of the left and right wrists, which give clues as to the condition of internal organs. Over fifty-two kinds of pulses have been recorded, seven of which signify imminent death.

Through the use of herbs, massage, acupuncture, and moxibustion, a traditional Chinese physician aims to restore the balance of yin and yang in the patient's body. Chinese Americans, particularly those who reside in Chinatowns, are apt to turn to traditional Chinese medicine rather than Western medicine.

What is Chinese acupuncture and what is moxibustion?

Acupuncture is a method used to release and stimulate the yin and yang in the human body, thereby preventing and curing disease. Using needles made of either gold, silver, copper, brass, or iron and ranging from three to twenty-four centimeters in length, Chinese physicians excite the appropriate acupuncture points in the body (there are 365 in all) and in this way restore health in the diseased organ or prevent the manifestation of an ailment.

Often used in conjunction with acupuncture, moxibustion is a technique of burning plant substances, often mugwort leaves, on the human skin after the acupuncture needle has been withdrawn. The heat released in the process is believed to further stimulate the flow of yin and yang.

The World Health Organization has compiled a list of fifty common disorders that it believes acupuncture is effective in treating. Acupuncture is one of the most sought after courses of treatment in America today, and over five thousand qualified acupuncturists, many of them Chinese Americans, currently practice in the United States to meet the high demand.

What are traditional Chinese medicines derived from?

A *Catalog of Native Herbs*, the foremost Chinese pharmacopoeia, was completed in 1578 and presented to Emperor **Wan Li** of the Ming dynasty in 1596. The complete catalog encompasses 52 volumes with 8,160 prescriptions and details on 1,892 medicinal herbs and substances derived from metal, stone, insects, mollusks, reptiles, birds, and mammals. Ginseng, angelica root, dried sea horse, cicada shells, dried red lizard, snake, bear gallbladder, tiger bone, and rhinoceros horn are just some of the medicines listed in *A Catalog of Native Herbs*.

Ginseng, a sweet root with a slightly bitter taste, is the quintessential Chinese herb and a veritable panacea. It is commonly taken to lower fevers, enhance visual acuity, stop hemorrhages, and promote overall good health. Wild ginseng from Manchuria and Korean ginseng are considered the most effective, while Japanese and American ginseng are generally deemed far inferior.

Dried sea horse is used to treat neck tumors and to loosen phlegm. Dried gecko, a kind of lizard, is used as a cure for asthma and tuberculosis and impotence, while snake is often prescribed as a treatment for syphilis. Rhinoceros horn is considered an effective remedy to counteract fevers and convulsions in children. Tiger bone and bear gallbladder contain properties believed to ease aches and pains, and cicada shells are used to cure headaches and the common cold.

Unfortunately, many of these medicines are derived from endangered animals and plants, and their continued production may lead to the extinction of certain species. In the twentieth century, Chinese American healers following millennia-old medical procedures now find themselves on the wrong side of United States and international endangered-species law.

What is t'ai chi ch'uan?

T'ai chi ch'uan ("supreme ultimate fist") is the most popular of the three "internal" or "soft" martial arts of China, the other two being hsing-i and pakua. At the core of t'ai chi ch'uan is form, a meditative sequence of postures and circular actions that flow from one to the next without interruption. The end result is a kind of ballet or slow dance. For this reason, t'ai chi ch'uan is one of the most difficult martial arts to master and requires a long apprenticeship.

An important aspect of t'ai chi ch'uan is *chi*, the universal energy that runs through the body. Chinese medicine strives to keep a person's *chi* in balance to maintain good health. If there is too much or too little *chi* in the body, it must be rebalanced. Chinese and Chinese American physicians regard the study of t'ai chi ch'uan as a form of "physical therapy," which, through its tranquil movements, restores balance to the body.

Another facet of t'ai chi ch'uan is the practice of "push hands," a complex technique of pushing a partner and yielding to a partner's pushes with attention given to balance. Some schools of t'ai chi ch'uan have transformed "push hands" into a fighting technique by concentrating *chi* to unleash hard pushes on the opponent.

What is kung fu?

In contrast to t'ai chi ch'uan, *kung fu* is an "external," meaning more physical, system of self-defense like karate, but with circular rather than linear movements. Theories abound as to the origins of kung fu. It is widely accepted that this system of martial arts dates back to about 2600 B.C., and that it gained popularity in China during the Han dynasty. As it developed, kung fu incorporated various fighting styles based on the movements of such animals as the monkey, the white crane, the tiger, and the praying mantis.

Monkey-style kung fu is one of the most fascinating. It demands that the student mimic the monkey, adopting its leaps, rolls, and alertness. Praying mantis kung fu was founded by Master **Wong Long** in the seventeenth century. The most striking feature of the praying mantis style is the "mantis claw," which entails shaping the fist to imitate the claws the insect uses to seize prey. The "mantis claw" is supplemented with throwing moves, locking joints, and grasping and pulling.

Kung fu has become enormously popular in the United States thanks to Bruce Lee and to the two *Kung Fu* television series starring David Carradine.

CLASSIC ASIAN AMERICAN FILMS

1. *Shanghai Express* (1932)

2. *Mr. Moto's Gamble* (1938)

3. *The Crimson Kimono* (1959)

4. *Enter the Dragon* (1973)

5. *Chan Is Missing* (1981)

6. *The Killing Fields* (1984)

7. *The Karate Kid* (1984)

---

8. *Alamo Bay* (1985)

9. *Year of the Dragon* (1985)

10. *The Great Wall Is the Great Wall* (1985)

11. *The Karate Kid Part II* (1986)

12. *Dim Sum* (1987)

13. *China Girl* (1987)

14. *The Last Emperor* (1987)

15. *The Color of Honor* (1987)

16. *The Wash* (1988)

17. *True Believer* (1988)

18. *The Karate Kid III* (1989)

19. *Eat a Bowl of Tea* (1989)

20. *Come See the Paradise* (1990)

21. *Lonely in America* (1990)

22. *Iron Maze* (1991)

23. *Pushing Hands* (1991)

24. *Rapid Fire* (1992)

25. *The Joy Luck Club* (1993)

26. *The Wedding Banquet* (1993)

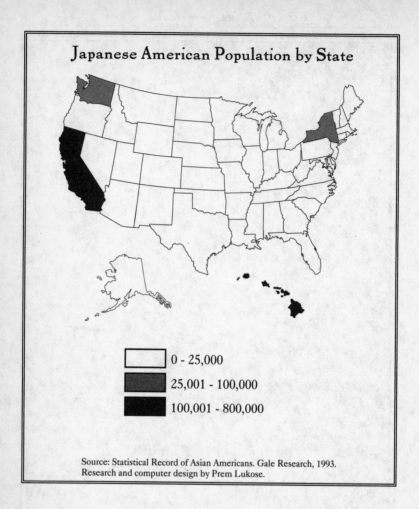

Japanese American Population by State

☐ 0 - 25,000

▨ 25,001 - 100,000

■ 100,001 - 800,000

Source: Statistical Record of Asian Americans. Gale Research, 1993.
Research and computer design by Prem Lukose.

TWO

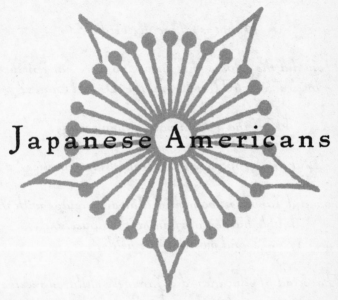

Japanese Americans

Why are Japanese Americans called Issei, Nisei, Kibei, Sansei, and Yonsei?

When did the first Japanese come to the United States and why were they "labornapped"?

Where was the first Japanese colony in the United States and what happened to it?

When did larger numbers of Japanese start to emigrate, and how did Senator Daniel K. Inouye's family end up in Hawaii?

Why were so many Japanese willing to leave Japan for the Hawaiian plantations?

How did pride play a role in the Japanese government's selection of workers for emigration?

What is a "picture bride"?

How did the Japanese women who were not "picture brides" reach Hawaii and the United States?

Were the women paid a living wage?

Did these Japanese immigrants start families?

How did Japanese women in Hawaii manage with the double burden of running the household and working the fields?

What kind of education did Japanese children receive in those days?

How did the Japanese laborers fare compared with other ethnic minorities?

How did the Japanese deal with this inequity?

Where did the Japanese settle in the continental United States?

What was the most popular California destination for Japanese immigrants?

*What impact did the 1906 earthquake
in San Francisco have
on the Japanese community there?*

*How did the Japanese become such successful farmers
in California?*

*If the Japanese were such great farmers, why were laws
passed forbidding them from owning land?*

*What was the Alien Land Act and how did it target
Japanese Americans?*

How did the Japanese outsmart the Alien Land Act?

*A "yellow peril"? Just how severe was discrimination
against Japanese after the turn of the century?*

*Why did the San Francisco school board want to
segregate Japanese students?*

*How did Teddy Roosevelt intervene
to stop segregation?*

*Why was Roosevelt so afraid that discrimination
against the Japanese in America would escalate into an
international incident?*

*Having appeased Japan, what did Roosevelt do about
pressure at home from anti-Japanese groups? What was
the Gentleman's Agreement?*

How did Teddy Roosevelt go about enforcing the Gentlemen's Agreement and why did more Japanese than ever manage to get into the United States?

What was the Immigration Act of 1924?

How large was the Japanese immigration anyway?

What was the Japanese Association and the Japanese American Citizens League?

How was Pearl Harbor a "lifetime of infamy" for Japanese Americans?

So did things work out the "American Way"?

What was Executive Order 9066?

How was Executive Order 9066 implemented?

How did the proclamations against Japanese Americans strip them of their civil rights?

When was the evacuation finally complete?

How did the United States Army decide who was "Japanese"?

How were Americans taught to distinguish Japanese enemies from Chinese allies during World War II?

Did any Japanese Americans resist evacuation orders?

What effect did Executive Order 9066 have on the American people?

Why were Hawaiians of Japanese descent not evacuated and interned?

If America was also at war with Germany and Italy, why were Americans of German and Italian descent spared internment?

What were the costs of evacuation for Japanese Americans?

What was the War Relocation Authority?

How were the Japanese Americans organized and what were the living conditions like in the assembly centers and the internment camps?

What did the Japanese Americans do all day long in the camps?

What kind of loyalty tests did the internees have to take, and who were the No-No Boys?

Did the interned children receive any schooling?

Is it true that Nisei served in the U.S. military in World War II?

Why is the 442nd Regimental Combat Team famous?

Who was Private First Class Sadao S. Munemori?

*Did Nisei serve in the Military Intelligence
Service too?*

Were Nisei ever drafted?

*Other than military volunteers and draftees, were any
other Japanese Americans allowed to leave the camps
during the years of internment?*

*Did the students just pack their bags
and go off to college?*

Who else got to leave the camps?

Who is Mitsuye Endo?

*Why did the Supreme Court rule for Endo but
against Korematsu and Hirabayashi
in the two prior cases?*

*What impact did the Endo decision have
on the evacuation?*

Who was Tokyo Rose?

*Where did internees go after the war
and how did they fare?*

*Have the Sansei and Yonsei managed to achieve the
American dream despite the setbacks
their forebears faced?*

*Who are some prominent Japanese American
political figures?*

*Why was the passage of the Hart-Cellar Act of 1965
important for Japanese Americans?*

*Did the U.S. government provide redress to those
Japanese Americans interned during World War II?*

What is "economic Pearl Harbor"?

What is Rafu Shimpo?

*Besides politicians, who are some prominent
Japanese Americans?*

Who are some great Japanese American athletes?

What religions do Japanese Americans follow?

What is Zen?

*How did tea drinking become so popular
with the Japanese?*

*How has Zen influenced the Japanese sense
of aesthetics?*

What's an akari lamp?

What is Nisei Week?

Where's the beef in Japanese cooking?

What is sukiyaki?

What is sake?

What is fugu and why has it been called Japanese roulette?

What are some of the more popular Japanese systems of martial arts practiced by Japanese Americans?

Why is there so much yelling in karate?

How do judo and aikido differ from karate?

Today, 847,562 Japanese Americans reside in the United States, the majority still concentrated in regions where their ancestors settled generations ago. Japanese Americans in contemporary society, like Chinese Americans, have inherited a history that stretches back more than a century in the New World and embodies the relentless human struggle from persecution to acceptance. Generations of Japanese Americans suffered decade after decade of overt discrimination in America—which even took the form of internment in the aftermath of the bombing raid on Pearl Harbor.

Against the odds, Japanese Americans have emerged as

one of the most economically successful minority groups in the United States and as an integral part of a society where sushi and Toyota are now as American as apple pie and Chevrolet. The Japanese American success story in the United States is nothing short of remarkable.

Why are Japanese Americans called Issei, Nisei, Kibei, Sansei, and Yonsei?

Issei is the name used to describe first-generation Japanese Americans, especially those who immigrated to Hawaii and the United States at the end of the eighteenth century. The Naturalization Law of 1790 prevented these immigrants from becoming naturalized citizens, a law which remained in effect until 1952.

Nisei refers to Issei offspring, Japanese of the second generation, who were born in the United States. Nisei were granted United States citizenship in keeping with the Fourteenth Amendment. The term *Nisei* has also been used to refer to all Japanese Americans.

Kibei are Nisei educated in Japan. *Sansei* is the name given to third-generation Japanese Americans, born in the United States to Nisei parents, while *Yonsei* are fourth-generation Japanese Americans.

When did the first Japanese come to the United States and why were they "labornapped"?

With the exception of a few shipwrecked sailors, and students and diplomats abroad, the first Japanese to land on American shores were farm laborers who ventured to the New World in 1868. Since the Japanese government had long before placed a ban on emigration, **Eugene M. Van Reed**, Hawaii's consul general in Japan, had to negotiate with Japanese authorities for the privileges of transporting 149 Japanese laborers to the Hawaiian Islands (then the Kingdom of Hawaii), where they would work as contract laborers on sugar plantations. After negotiations failed, Van Reed resorted to "labornapping," that is, arranging the unlawful transportation of the workers willing to be recruited.

As it turned out, many of Van Reed's recruits did not take a liking to plantation work (many were city dwellers who had no prior farming experience). When reports of the mistreatment of these laborers reached Japan, the alarmed Japanese government arranged for the return of forty of these "labornapped" immigrants.

Where was the first Japanese colony in the United States and what happened to it?

In 1869, Japanese pioneers came to America to establish a permanent settlement. Approximately thirty immigrants were illegally recruited, and they arrived in America with **John Henry Schnell** as their leader, a European who had been in Japan during the Meiji struggle to overthrow the Tokugawa shogun, who had more power than the emperor. The immigrants established their colony, soon christened the Wakamatsu Tea and Silk Colony, at Granger ranch in Gold Hill, north of San Francisco.

The colonists had high hopes of cultivating mulberries (perhaps for silkworm production), tangerines, grapes, and tea. However, an inhospitable climate and financial trouble plagued their efforts. In this time of troubles, Schnell abandoned the colony, and the immigrants dispersed, leaving little trace. The records of only three Japanese members of the colony have been unearthed. One was a woman named Okei, probably the nanny of Schnell's children, who some speculate was the first Japanese woman to die on American soil when she succumbed to a fever in 1871.

The Wakamatsu Tea and Silk Colony became known as the lost colony, whose failure was attributed to the same afflictions that had thwarted many English colonists in America: bad luck, failed crops, internal dissension, and starvation.

When did larger numbers of Japanese start to emigrate, and how did Senator Daniel K. Inouye's family end up in Hawaii?

In the 1880s the Japanese government finally lifted its ban on emigration. Thousands of Japanese, mostly from the countryside, clamored to emigrate to Hawaii and later to the United States.

Most Japanese were lured to Hawaii by the prospect of a brighter financial future. Many planned to "sojourn," that is, stay temporarily, working hard and saving enough money to return to Japan to pay off family debts or regain lost farmland. This is precisely the dream that brought the grandfather of Daniel Inouye, the Democratic senator from Hawaii, to Hawaii. Like many of the immigrants, however, Senator Inouye's forebears opted in the end to make Hawaii their permanent address.

Hawaii was in desperate need of labor, especially on sugar plantations, due in part to the 1876 Reciprocity Treaty the island nation had signed with the United States government, which allowed for the duty-free importation of Hawaiian sugar into the United States to satisfy the American sweet tooth. The sugar industry in Hawaii experienced a boom after the signing of this treaty, and sugar plantation owners scurried to find field hands.

Sugar plantation owners focused on Japan as one of the sources of cheap labor. It was thus that Hawaii became first a magnet for migration from rural Japan, and later, a springboard for migration to North America.

Why were so many Japanese willing to leave Japan for the Hawaiian plantations?

Interpreting the presence of Western colonial powers in China as a threat to Japanese sovereignty, Japan restored the Meiji emperor in 1868 and instituted a system of centralized government as a buttress against colonization by the West. The Japanese government made industrialization and militarization its new goals and began to levy high taxes to finance these pursuits.

Japanese farmers bore the brunt of the government's new taxation program. Many lost their land in the upheaval, and thus the fabulous stories of riches in the Kingdom of Hawaii, where a plantation worker could earn six times more than the average wage in Japan, was music to their ears. In pursuit of the American dream, 200,000 Japanese left for Hawaii and 180,000 for the United States between 1885 and 1925.

How did pride play a role in the Japanese government's selection of workers for emigration?

In an effort to safeguard Japan's honor, the Japanese government strictly supervised the flow of emigrants from Japan until 1894. Japanese officials viewed its workers abroad as diplomats who had a responsibility to preserve Japan's fine reputation. Thus the Japanese carefully screened out lowly, illiterate workers and other such undesirables who might jeopardize Japan's honor. Only literate, healthy, strong, and relatively well educated Japanese made the grade for emigration. Japanese officials were determined that the fate of Chinese workers, whom the United States barred from immigration with the Chinese Exclusion Act of 1882, would not befall Japan's subjects.

What is a "picture bride"?

In Japan, as in many Asian countries, marriage was a serious family matter, and romance and courtship, individualistic notions, were out of the question. Marriage was so serious, in fact, that elders frequently sought outside help, from the equivalent of a matchmaker, in arranging meetings for their sons and daughters that hopefully would end in matrimony.

When it happened that a man and a woman lived a considerable distance apart, they exchanged pictures and information in lieu of meeting. The "picture bride" method suited eligible Japanese bachelors in Hawaii and the United States who desired to marry Japanese women but who were too far from home to meet any. Japanese women willing to sail to the New World were often swamped with marriage offers, and the family had to decide which bachelor it would be.

Before the "picture bride" left Japan, she took part in a traditional wedding ceremony with a curious twist: she exchanged vows with a man who substituted for her fiancé during the ceremony. Then, armed with a picture of her betrothed, the "picture bride" sailed to the much glorified lands of the West.

For many "picture brides" their new husbands and new homes were a letdown. Some Japanese men misled their brides by sending them pictures of themselves dressed in classy clothes they had rented to disguise their status as laborers. Still, most of the imposed-upon picture brides overcame their disappointment and forged a married life in the foreign land. If they had complained they would have shamed their families. This method of matrimony flourished in Hawaii and in America; rough estimates indicate that one in four Issei women were "picture brides."

How did the Japanese women who were not "picture brides" reach Hawaii and the United States?

The Japanese government encouraged "picture brides" to go to the New World in an effort to avoid the problems plaguing Chinese immigrant communities in America with a surplus of bachelors, namely prostitution and gambling. However, in 1921, the U.S. government prohibited picture brides from immigrating, but by then women could leave Japan by other avenues.

Motivated by economic development, the Japanese government made it a policy to educate its female citizens and allow them entry into the labor force as wage earners in the late 1800s. Educational and employment opportunities empowered Japanese women and allowed them greater mobility at home' and abroad. They increasingly left family farms to find employment in the construction industry, textile mills, and coal mines. By 1900, women constituted 60 percent of Japan's industrial workforce. By this time, too, Japanese women were permitted to emigrate to Hawaii as laborers, and in 1908, with Teddy Roosevelt's signing of the Gentlemen's Agreement, they were allowed into America.

The Hawaiian sugar plantation owners happily hired single Japanese women as field-workers, contending that they increased the productivity of the men. After all, women performed certain tasks men found abhorrent, such as nursing the sick, cooking, cleaning, and sewing and mending clothes, and they also contributed to men's sense of well-being. By 1920, the Japanese population of Hawaii was 46 percent female, and in California, it was 35 percent.

Were the women paid a living wage?

Issei women performed the same strenuous fieldwork as men, such as hoeing and harvesting, usually for ten hours a day, six days a week, but they were paid less than male workers. For instance, in 1915, the going rate for female field-workers was 55 cents per day, compared to 78 cents per day for male workers.

While the sugar plantation remained the most important source of employment for Japanese women in Hawaii until 1920, beginning in 1900 many women began to branch out into urban jobs, working in the pineapple and garment industries, and providing domestic and personal services. In these jobs they were also underpaid and eventually had to fight for better wages.

Did these Japanese immigrants start families?

During the early days of immigration, the birthrate in the Japanese community in America and Hawaii was rather low. Families depended on two breadwinners and simply could not afford for women to raise children. Japanese women received no pay during maternity leaves, and once they went back to work, the family was saddled with the cost of day care. With such a heavy financial burden, only 50.8 percent of Japanese couples in the United States had children, and in fewer numbers than any other ethnic group at the time. Women's income was so critical to the family's survival that some mothers worked until their last month of pregnancy. Some also took their babies along to the fields, carrying them on their backs or in crude cribs, to save on day care.

More families were formed as picture brides arrived in greater numbers or wives in Japan rejoined husbands, and slowly the birthrate rose. The sight of childless couples and single Issei sojourners gradually gave way to families with children.

How did Japanese women in Hawaii manage with the double burden of running the household and working the fields?

Like most women on the planet, they were run ragged. As if they didn't have enough on their plate, lower wages forced many women to work extra jobs, ironing and cooking for the bachelor laborers on the plantations. Before long they began to fight for equal pay for equal work and for improved conditions, and they took part in the labor strikes against plantation owners. In the Great Japanese Strike of 1909, the women demanded among other things that the plantations provide paid maternity leave.

What kind of education did Japanese children receive in those days?

Having undergone four years of compulsory schooling in Japan, many Issei prized education as a stepping-stone to advancement in American society.

The Issei often supplemented their children's education by sending them to Japanese-language schools as well as regular schools. The first Japanese schools were established in Hawaii in 1896, and soon they began to proliferate in the Western states. The teachers, usually recruited from Japan, taught Nisei children Japanese language and tradition as well as morality.

Many Issei parents saw these schools as a means of preserving Japanese traditions and instilling Japanese values in their children, who were rapidly acculturating to Hawaii and the United States. They were also grateful that while they toiled long hours in the fields, the schools provided supervision for their children. Nisei children appreciated the close friendships they made at Japanese-language schools and the absence of the taunting that they endured in regular schools.

How did the Japanese laborers fare compared with other ethnic minorities?

Due to a labor shortage and other pitfalls on the way to prosperity, Hawaiian businesses actively recruited cheap labor from China, Portugal, Puerto Rico, Korea, and the Philippines, as well as Japan. While this diversity bred a climate of tolerance in Hawaii that worked in favor of the Japanese during World War II, at first it was to their absolute disadvantage. Hawaiian businesses tied the laborers' earning power to their ethnicity, with the Japanese receiving the lowest wages.

In 1904, the Japanese lost out again when the Hawaiian Sugar Planters' Association passed a resolution limiting access to skilled positions to "American citizens, or those eligible for citizenship." Under U.S. law, Asians were denied naturalization, and so Japanese workers, regardless of their experience, were kept from managerial positions until much later.

How did the Japanese deal with this inequity?

Workers of the same ethnicity formed "blood unions" to combat inequality. Protesting unfair wages, Japanese laborers went on strike in 1909, refusing to work in Oahu because they were paid only $18.00 a month, while Portuguese laborers took home $22.50. Japanese communities throughout Hawaii rallied in support of the striking laborers and sent food and money. Japanese businesses made contributions to a support fund, and Japanese doctors provided free medical services to strikers and their families.

By 1900, many Japanese workers had given up the idea of "sojourning" and had decided to settle permanently in Hawaii rather than return to Japan. In the 1909 strike they framed their argument in "American" terms, asserting that inequality was both undemocratic and un-American. The Americanization of the Japanese workers worried plantation owners, who realized they could no longer pull the wool over Japanese eyes and exploit them so readily. After the 1909 strike, plantation owners began a massive campaign to import Filipino workers, who were easier to control.

Where did the Japanese settle in the continental United States?

The Japanese immigrated to the United States in large numbers in the 1890s. The majority settled on the West Coast, particularly in California. Washington and Oregon also had their fair share of Japanese residents, with better job opportunities luring more Japanese to Washington. They found work on the railroads, in lumber mills, salmon canneries, and of course in agriculture.

Like the Chinese, many Japanese immigrants left the West

Coast to settle in places like Utah, Wyoming, and Colorado, where they were primarily engaged in work on the railroad and in the sugar beet industry as well as in the coal mines. Like the Japanese on the West Coast, the Issei in these states also began to engage in independent farming.

Japanese students often went to the East Coast to attend college, but their stay was not permanent. Upon graduating, almost all returned to Japan.

What was the most popular California destination for Japanese immigrants?

San Francisco was the most popular California and West Coast destination for Japanese immigrants during the early years. Many Issei settled in and near this port city, and a good number found jobs there as unskilled laborers. With the Exclusion Act of 1882, Chinese laborers were barred from entering the United States, so Japanese workers took their place.

As the Issei community grew, workers branched out into every conceivable sector of the economy. Many established small businesses, such as supply stores, restaurants, barbershops, boardinghouses, ice cream parlors, and banks to meet the needs of the growing Japanese population. Still others found employment as domestic workers, schoolteachers, tailors, physicians, and dentists. The Japanese also manned commercial fishing fleets throughout California.

What impact did the 1906 earthquake in San Francisco have on the Japanese community there?

After the devastating 1906 earthquake leveled San Francisco, Japanese chose to settle in Little Tokyos in other parts of California, particularly in Los Angeles County, where they worked on the railroad, in farming, and in small businesses. According to reports, only 36 Japanese resided in Los Angeles County in 1890; by 1910, the number had grown to 8,641.

How did the Japanese become such successful farmers in California?

The industrialization of America in the late nineteenth century created enormous demands for fresh produce in America's urban centers. This, coupled with the development of an improved irrigation system in California (which made intensive agricultural production feasible), led to a boom in farming in that state. Although job opportunities for the Japanese had begun to open up outside of agriculture, farming remained a way of life for the majority of the Issei and the growing number of Nisei, and they took advantage of the demand for produce.

If the Japanese were such great farmers, why were laws passed forbidding them from owning land?

The Japanese laborers knew that they were nobody until they owned their own farms, and often several Japanese laborers from the same *ken*, or clan, pooled their resources in order to lease or purchase land. In 1909, Issei and Nisei owned 16,449 acres of land in California and leased another 137,233 acres. That same year their crops were valued at $6,235,858.

While this seems like a lot, in reality the Japanese leased or owned less than 2 percent of all the farmland in California. Nonetheless, white landowners in California and other western states began to fear Japanese competition, a fear that has stayed with Americans to this day, and farm lobbies and union interests called for strict limits on land ownership by the Japanese.

What was the Alien Land Act and how did it target Japanese Americans?

In response to the growing tide of anti-Japanese sentiment, the California state legislature passed the Alien Land Act in 1913, prohibiting the ownership of property by "aliens ineligible to citizenship," which of course included not just the Chinese but also the Japanese. The law also barred Japanese and other Asian aliens from leasing agricultural land for more than three years, and from bequeathing any land they owned. Though the law did not specifically name the Japanese, it targeted them in order to undermine their successes in agriculture. By 1920 thirteen other western states had followed suit with their own alien land acts, some of which stayed in effect until 1947.

How did the Japanese outsmart the Alien Land Act?

The Japanese could not understand why they could not own land, much of which had been very difficult to reclaim in the first place. They refused to be thwarted by the Alien Land Act and capitalized on a loophole they discovered. They leased and purchased land in the name of their children born in the United States, who, thanks to the Fourteenth Amendment, were American citizens. As legal guardians, the Issei operated their children's land.

Infuriated, American farmers throughout the West mounted another offensive, and consequently, the California state legislature tightened the screws and passed even stricter alien land legislation in 1920 and 1923. The amended law deprived the Japanese of the right to lease land or to purchase it on behalf of minors. As a result, production on Japanese farms dropped from 12.3 percent of the total yield in 1921 to 9.3 percent in 1925.

A "yellow peril"? Just how severe was discrimination against Japanese after the turn of the century?

Discrimination against the Issei and Nisei was quite fierce. Around the time that the Alien Land Act was enacted, an epidemic of hatred for the Japanese was sweeping the land. Not only were the Issei considered aliens ineligible for citizenship, and barred from owning land, they often encountered a whole slew of Jim Crow–like hostilities in daily life. The Japanese were routinely refused service in barbershops, grocery stores, hotels, and restaurants. Often they were segregated from whites. In California, the Japanese were sometimes greeted by hatemongers carrying placards with messages such as "Japs keep moving: This is a white man's neighborhood."

Swayed by popular opinion, Republicans, Democrats, and Populists in California called for a halt to immigration from East Asia in 1900. The California state legislature could not stem immigration on its own, as this power was vested in the U.S. Congress. Tempers flared throughout California, where the press was especially harsh on the Japanese. Early in 1905, the *San Francisco Chronicle* published a series of inflammatory articles citing the threat, or "yellow peril," Japanese immigrants posed to America. The articles depicted the Japanese as spies, massive hordes (even though they were a small percentage of the population) plotting to take over white man's land, and criminals who preyed on white women. Some of the more frenzied headlines read: "Crime and Poverty Go Hand in Hand with Asiatic Labor," "The Yellow Peril: How Japanese Crowd Out the White Race," and "Brown Artisans Steal Brains of Whites."

With its racist articles, the *San Francisco Chronicle* fanned the flames of hatred against the Japanese. Fearing that an international incident would erupt over the discrimination against Japanese on American soil, President Theodore Roosevelt felt under mounting pressure to take matters into his own hands.

Why did the San Francisco school board want to segregate Japanese students?

The San Francisco school board claimed that the Nisei posed a threat of contaminating the white children, especially given the overcrowding in the schools following the 1906 earthquake. Separate schools had already been established for children of "Chinese or Mongolian descent," and the school board decided to pass a resolution in 1893 ordering Japanese children to attend Chinese and Mongolian schools. The school board ran into trouble when it was determined that Japanese children were not Mongolian, and therefore should be allowed to attend regular schools.

In 1906, having reversed the determination that the Japanese were not "Mongolian," the San Francisco school board ordered the segregation of all Chinese, Japanese, and Korean children from the white children. Japanese children would attend Chinese schools so that Caucasian children would not have to associate "with pupils of the Mongolian race."

How did Teddy Roosevelt intervene to stop segregation?

Concerned that the San Francisco school board's demands would be the straw that broke the camel's back and would plunge America into war, President Roosevelt sent Secretary of Commerce and Labor Victor H. Metcalf to intervene on behalf of the ninety-three Japanese students in San Francisco public schools.

Under attack from the president, school officials sensationalized their case by insisting to Metcalf that the Japanese with poor English-language proficiency who occupied classrooms with younger white students were a clear threat to the girls' safety. The Metcalf report revealed that indeed older Japanese kids mixed with younger white students, most notably, two nineteen-year-olds in a class of fourth graders.

Citing "fifty years of more or less close friendship with the Empire of Japan," Secretary Metcalf recommended that the school board deal with the issue by setting age limits rather than segregating students. He advised that students with poor language skills be sent to separate schools to learn English and later returned to regular classrooms. Public opinion on the issue was divided along regional lines, with the West and the South supporting California, and the rest of the nation behind the president.

Eager to have the school board retract its ruling and to persuade the California legislature to cease and desist with its anti-Japanese actions, President Roosevelt called the California congressional delegation and San Francisco officials to the White House to negotiate a settlement. After a week of tense talks, the San Francisco school board finally agreed to revoke the segregation after the federal government promised to halt immigration from Japan. President Roosevelt also wrote directly to California's governor requesting that he put a stop to anti-Japanese legislation.

Why was Roosevelt so afraid that discrimination against the Japanese in America would escalate into an international incident?

Unlike China in the mid-1800s, Japan was not a tottering nation rotting from within and under siege from without. Japan enjoyed enormous respect in the international arena, and its government deemed it part of the national agenda to monitor how Japanese citizens were treated abroad. For example, in 1888, the Japanese foreign minister to the United States stopped off in San Francisco to check on the local Japanese community, specifically to make sure that no Japanese undesirables were damaging Japan's national honor.

In 1891, the Japanese consul in San Francisco had investigated the conditions in the Japanese community and had been particularly disturbed by the presence of Japanese prostitutes and pimps, a problem that had befallen the Chinese in America and had contributed to their tarnished reputation. According to the consul, responsibility lay with Japan to adopt measures to prevent such undesirables from leaving Japan.

The Japanese government was so sensitive about its citizens' reputation abroad that when officials were told of derogatory accounts in San Francisco newspapers of the filthy and disheveled appearance of the Japanese, the government, rather than deride the American media, cracked down on Japanese going abroad. Before embarking on their journey, travelers and emigrants were given rigorous instruction at Japanese ports on hygiene and dress.

Japan's concern over the treatment of its subjects abroad, particularly on how it rebounded on the country's status as an international player, also registered with Washington. President Roosevelt was acutely aware of Japan's military prowess, as witnessed by its relatively easy defeat of Imperial Russia in the Russo-Japanese War of 1905. Roosevelt feared that while the Japanese government deemed America justified in some of its criticisms of the Japanese on U.S. soil (such as the way they dressed), it would not tolerate California's push for anti-Japanese legislation. In an effort to safeguard American-Japanese relations, Roosevelt reassured the Japanese government in 1905 that "the American Government and the American people at large have not the slightest sympathy with the outrageous agitation against the Japanese."

In his State of the Union Address in December 1905, President Roosevelt made a point of distinguishing between the Chinese, who got no respect, and the Japanese immigrants: "The entire Chinese coolie class were undesirable immigrants." By contrast, according to President Roosevelt, Japanese immigrants were worthy of America's admiration.

Having appeased Japan, what did Roosevelt do about pressure at home from anti-Japanese groups? What was the Gentlemen's Agreement?

By reassuring the Japanese government that the Japanese in America were in good hands, Teddy Roosevelt managed to buy himself some time to devise a plan to settle the immigration problem once and for all. He came up with a seemingly ingenious solution that would calm anti-Japanese zealots and at the same time assure Japan its national honor and that its citizens were respected. It was called the Gentlemen's Agreement.

The Gentlemen's Agreement, signed by the United States and Japan in 1908, prohibited Japan from issuing passports to Japanese laborers bound for the United States, and thus halted Japanese labor immigration. The United States in turn agreed to block legislation designed to harass Japanese Americans. With the Gentlemen's Agreement, President Roosevelt accomplished his goal of maintaining good relations with Japan, while satisfying the California-for-Americans nativists of California.

How did Teddy Roosevelt go about enforcing the Gentlemen's Agreement and why did more Japanese than ever manage to get into the United States?

First, by executive order, President Roosevelt issued a regulation preventing Japanese persons in American insular possessions—Hawaii—from migrating to the mainland United States. This order was carefully crafted to ensure that while the Japanese in Hawaii were barred from going to the mainland, Japanese laborers were still welcome in the Hawaiian chain to work the sugar plantations.

Although the Gentlemen's Agreement was designed to stem the tide of immigration from Japan, it inadvertently swung open the floodgates to Japanese immigration to the United States. A provision in the agreement allowed the parents, wives, and children of laborers already in residence in the United States to immigrate. As a result, the number of Japanese immigrating to the United States more than doubled.

Perhaps women benefited most from the agreement's loophole. Japanese immigration went from predominantly male to female as thousands of women were reunited with their husbands or met them for the first time as "picture brides." Had it not been for the Gentlemen's Agreement, the Japanese population in the United States probably would have remained 90 percent male, and many of the Nisei generation probably would not have been born. Instead, by 1924, the sexes were evenly represented among the Japanese.

What was the Immigration Act of 1924?

The increased flow of Issei immigrants into the United States outraged nativists and exclusionists, who felt betrayed by the Gentlemen's Agreement. Anti-Japanese lobbies clamored for a stricter immigration policy, and their efforts culminated in the passage of the 1924 Immigration Act, which brought immigration from Asia to a virtual standstill until after World War II.

The Immigration Act of 1924 prohibited foreigners ineligible for U.S. citizenship—by definition all Asians—from coming to American shores. The Naturalization Law of 1790 had allowed for the naturalization of only free white persons, but it was amended after the Civil War to allow persons of African ancestry to attain citizenship. The amendment did not include Asians; consequently, they continued to be denied the right to naturalize. Their alien status impeded their immigration for nearly thirty years.

How large was the Japanese immigration anyway?

Actually it was fairly small. In fact, other immigrant groups dwarfed the Japanese. For instance, 283,000 Italians entered the United States just between July 1, 1913, and June 30, 1914, while only 275,000 Japanese came to America during the entire period of Japanese immigration from the mid-1800s until 1924. In 1907, the year that Japanese immigration peaked, only 30,842 Japanese entered the United States, a mere 2.4 percent of the 1,285,349 immigrants who came from all countries. With the 1924 Immigration Act in place, only 7,000 came between 1925 and 1941.

What was the Japanese Association and the Japanese American Citizens League?

The Japanese Association was an organization formed by the Issei to aid in the assimilation process. Each Japanese American community had its own chapter, which sponsored lectures, social events, and athletic competition for the enhancement of the community, published helpful literature, and acted as a representative in labor disputes. The Japanese Association also fulfilled the role of community police, guarding against undesirable activities that might tarnish the reputation of the Japanese. Though its influence waned as the Nisei developed a stronger foothold in American society, the Japanese Association served a vital role in the early Japanese American communities.

The Japanese American Citizen's League (JACL) was a national organization founded in 1930 in Seattle by an educated and acculturated Nisei group to promote the collective interests of the Nisei in America. The league made U.S. citizenship a requirement for membership; thus Issei were excluded. From 1930 to 1940, the JACL spawned fifty chapters, and membership ballooned to 5,600. The JACL encouraged the Nisei to sever ties to Japan and its traditions, to embrace the American way as a means of overcoming discrimination and racism, and to find their niche in U.S. society.

Their Japanese American creed, written in 1940 by **Mike Masaru Masaoka**, a longtime leader of the JACL, demonstrated the superpatriotic views and optimism of JACL members in the face of discrimination: "I am proud that I am an American citizen of Japanese ancestry, for my very background makes me appreciate more fully the wonderful advantages of this nation. I believe in her institutions, ideas and traditions; I glory in her heritage; I boast of her history; I trust in her future."

The JACL trust in the American future would be sorely tested in the coming war years.

How was Pearl Harbor a "lifetime of infamy" for Japanese Americans?

Conflict erupting between Japan and the United States was a frightening thought for Japanese Americans, who watched in horror when Japan signed a military pact with Germany and Italy in 1940. Anti-Japanese propaganda, prevalent since the Japanese first set foot in America, could only intensify if a war with Japan broke out.

When Japan bombed Pearl Harbor on the island of Oahu on December 7, 1941, Japanese Americans were overcome with shock and shame, and with dread for what the future in America might hold.

In his autobiography *Journey to Washington*, Senator **Daniel K. Inouye** captured in writing the anger, disbelief, fear, and confusion he felt as he raced to a Red Cross station after the raid on Pearl Harbor: "In the marrow of my bones I knew that there was only deep trouble ahead.... My people were only a generation removed from the land that had spawned those bombers, the land that sent them to rain destruction on America, death on Americans. And choking with emotion, I looked up into the sky and called out, 'You dirty Japs!'"

Japanese Americans were right to feel great apprehension after the raid on Pearl Harbor. Navy secretary **Frank Knox** was immediately dispatched to Hawaii to assess the damages and investigate the circumstances surrounding the attack. Interestingly, Knox had once been general manager of the Hearst newspapers, which were famous for their fierce anti-Japanese stance. In Knox's assessment, Japanese Americans were involved in sabotage and espionage operations in Oahu, and he recommended that they be evacuated to another Hawaiian island. Many government officials, including **J. Edgar Hoover** of the FBI and Lieutenant General **Delos C. Emmons**, disagreed with Knox's findings. In a radio announcement, General Emmons reassured Japanese Americans in Hawaii that the government had no intention or desire "to operate mass concentration camps. . . . We must remember that this is America and we must do things the American Way."

So did things work out the "American Way"?

Not quite. The American government feared that the Japanese empire would invade the West Coast, and it decided to take proper security measures.

In other words, within a few days of the bombing, the FBI tracked down thousands of "suspicious" Japanese aliens, as well as persons of Italian and German descent. Many Issei and a handful of Nisei and Kibei citizens, among them Buddhist priests, Japanese-language teachers, business leaders, and senior citizens, were rounded up and interrogated. Most were found guilty by association with Japan and were shipped off to internment camps in Montana, New Mexico, North Dakota, and other states.

Newspapers such as those belonging to Hearst lost sight of the fact that two-thirds of the people of Japanese ancestry were American citizens. They spread wild rumors about Japanese saboteurs who had blocked traffic with their parked cars to hamper American efforts in the attack or had sent signals to enemy Japanese planes. On December 8, 1941, *The Los Angeles Times* commented: "We have thousands of Japanese here. . . . Some, perhaps many . . . are good Americans. What the rest may be we do not know, nor can we take a chance in the light of yesterday's demonstration that treachery and double dealing are major Japanese weapons."

Newspaper columnists commonly called Japanese Americans "Nips," "Japs," and "yellow vermin." Many went as far as demanding the evacuation of all Japanese Americans from the West Coast to the interior of the country. One such advocate was **Henry McLemore**, a columnist for the Hearst papers, who wrote on January 29, 1942: "I am for the immediate removal of every Japanese on the West Coast to a point deep in the interior. . . . Let 'em be pinched, hurt, hungry. Personally, I hate Japanese."

Even the liberal columnist **Walter Lippmann** wrote articles in favor of the evacuation. Times were bad for Japanese Americans.

What was Executive Order 9066?

In early February 1942, the Select Committee Investigating National Defense Migration was formed, headed by Representative **John H. Tolan** from California. The committee planned to hold hearings to determine whether an evacuation of Japanese Americans from the West Coast was necessary. However, before the hearings took place, President Franklin Delano Roosevelt signed Executive Order 9066, authorizing and ordering the relocation and internment of nearly 120,000 Japanese women, men, and children, two-thirds of whom were U.S. citizens. The hearings were held anyway in San Francisco on February 21, 1942, and became a convenient forum for advocates of the evacuation policy.

JACL leaders who were invited to testify at the hearings agreed to cooperate with the evacuation even though they knew it violated the civil liberties guaranteed by the Constitution to Nisei citizens. JACL leaders decided to cooperate with government orders for several compelling reasons, one being to confirm in no uncertain terms the loyalty of Japanese Americans to the United States. They realized that resistance would be misinterpreted as further evidence of their disloyalty, or even as an act of sabotage or an attempt to undermine the U.S. military.

They also hoped that cooperation would compel the government to carry out the evacuation in a humane manner. If the Nisei did not cooperate, the government would undoubtedly resort to a forcible evacuation and even bloodshed. Such violence would hurt both those involved directly and future generations of Japanese Americans. The alternatives being so bleak, the JACL leaders urged the Japanese American community to cooperate with the government and the military in the impending evacuation.

The attack on Pearl Harbor is often recounted in history books as a cataclysmic event that served to unify the American people against the Axis powers. However, for Japanese Americans, it was a time that they suffered through like no other Americans and for which they endured unspeakable consequences.

How was Executive Order 9066 implemented?

Convinced that the mere presence of Japanese on American soil threatened national security, Lieutenant General **John L. DeWitt**, the military commander appointed to carry out the evacuation, proposed a mass internment policy involving anyone of Japanese descent. Wartime exigencies meant that care could not be taken to sift through the entire Japanese population to find spies.

General DeWitt also advocated searches of Japanese homes, without search warrants, to confiscate any weapons or cameras that could be used in subversive activities. Reports of the seizure of 2,592 guns, 199,000 rounds of ammunition, 1,652 sticks of dynamite, 1,458 radio receivers, and 2,012 cameras belonging to Japanese were met with widespread approval. These reports misled the public because they failed to mention that many of the objects seized came from a gun shop and a warehouse for a general store, both of which were fully licensed and legitimate.

On March 2, 1942, General DeWitt announced Proclamation No. 1, the first in a series of proclamations as part of Executive Order 9066, which eventually led to the evacuation of all persons of Japanese ancestry on the West Coast and in parts of Arizona. Proclamation No. 1 designated the western halves of Washington, Oregon, and California, and the southern region of Arizona as Military Area No. 1, the area in the most danger, since enemy soldiers could launch a full-scale raid there. The remaining regions of the Pacific coast states and Arizona were labeled Military Area No. 2, a dangerous area, but not under immediate threat like Area No. 1.

The proclamation recommended that Japanese Americans move inland or risk internment, and did not advocate a forceful evacuation. Many Japanese Americans on the West Coast refused to move, because they feared the unknown and greater hostility inland. Many did not have the financial resources to pack up their homes and businesses and start over in a strange new place. Only 4,889 of the 107,500 Japanese in Military Area No. 1 decided to resettle away from the coast. As they predicted and feared, those who moved inland faced severe hostility and rejection. Fearing an outbreak of violence and even death, many simply moved back to the West Coast. They felt, as did those who chose not to resettle, that life in an internment camp, however bleak, was more appealing than death and mob violence.

Soon after, General DeWitt issued Proclamation No. 2, which designated the states of Idaho, Montana, Nevada, and Utah, and hundreds of other small zones as Military Area Nos. 3, 4, 5, and 6. DeWitt wanted to evacuate and intern Japanese Americans in these areas as well, but the War Department opposed him.

How did the proclamations against Japanese Americans strip them of their civil rights?

On March 21, 1942, President Roosevelt signed a bill giving the military the power to govern and monitor those areas designated as military zones. For example, Public Law No. 50 of the bill prescribed that if a civilian in the military zones violated orders, she or he would face fines and incarceration. Against this backdrop, General DeWitt issued Proclamation No. 3, which instituted a curfew restricting all "enemy" aliens and individuals of Japanese ancestry to designated areas: their workplace, their home, and an area five miles in circumference from their homes during the day. Between the hours of 8 P.M. to 6 A.M. Japanese Americans were restricted to their homes.

Proclamation No. 4 prohibited any movement out of Military Area No. 1. Now even those who wished to move inland were no longer allowed to do so.

On March 24, 1942, General DeWitt issued Civilian Exclusion Order No. 1 to remove fifty-four Japanese American families from Bainbridge Island in Puget Sound, near Bremerton Navy Yard in the state of Washington. On March 31, the families were led from their homes by armed soldiers and transported by train to Manzanar Relocation Camp in central California. More exclusion orders followed which covered the California localities of San Pedro, Long Beach, San Diego, and San Francisco. Eventually all those of Japanese ancestry living in Military Areas No. 1 and No. 2 within California were evacuated, as well as those residing in Military Area No. 1 within the states of Washington, Oregon, and Arizona.

When was the evacuation finally complete?

On August 7, 1942, a little over five months after it began, the evacuation was over. Nearly 120,000 Japanese alien residents and Japanese American citizens had been uprooted from their homes, businesses, and communities, and placed in assembly centers, which were temporary shelters, or sent directly to "relocation centers," a euphemism for the internment camps or concentration camps that were swiftly constructed expressly for the Japanese. The camps, holding on average 10,000 prisoners, were located in remote, uninhabited areas of several states.

Most of the evacuees would live in these internment camps until the final days of World War II.

How did the United States Army decide who was "Japanese"?

The army removed anyone one-eighth Japanese or more. However, even those who were one-sixteenth Japanese were forced to evacuate. Some of those evacuated were shocked to learn that they had Japanese blood.

The army did exempt from evacuation families with mixed children where the mother was of Japanese ancestry and the non-Japanese father was a citizen of the United States or of a friendly nation. Families with mixed children in which the mother was non-Japanese and a U.S. citizen or from a friendly nation, and the Japanese father was either deceased or separated from the family, were also exempt. Japanese children under the care of Caucasian foster parents were also spared, as were Japanese wives of non-Japanese servicemen in the armed forces of the United States.

How were Americans taught to distinguish Japanese enemies from Chinese allies during World War II?

On December 22, 1941, *Time* magazine ran an article entitled "How to Tell Your Friends from the Japs," with the intent of teaching readers how to tell the good guys from the bad guys, the Chinese from the Japanese. The article warned, however, that the process was not foolproof.

According to *Time* magazine, most Japanese are "stockier and broader-hipped then short Chinese" and tend to "dry up ... as they age." They exhibit nervousness and a tendency to laugh loudly at inappropriate moments. The Japanese are easily recognized because their facial expressions are "dogmatic" and "arrogant," while the Chinese are "more placid, kindly, open."

Did any Japanese Americans resist evacuation orders?

Yes. Most Japanese Americans cooperated fully with the evacuation, but a handful resisted orders on the justifiable grounds that their rights were being violated. One such resister was **Gordon K. Hirabayashi**, a college student, who violated both curfew and evacuation orders. He was consequently arrested and found guilty in the Seattle Federal District Court on both counts and was sentenced to six months in prison. He appealed his case, and *Hirabayashi v.*

United States was heard in the Supreme Court, which issued a unanimous decision on June 21, 1943, to uphold the original verdict. The Supreme Court did not rule on the legality of the evacuation order itself. It ruled only that the curfew imposed by the military to limit the movements of Japanese Americans was legal. Under pressure from his colleagues, Justice **Frank Murphy**, originally a dissenter, sided with the majority.

Another resister, **Minoru Yasui**, was a reserve officer in the U.S. Army who in 1939 had taken a job at the Japanese consulate's office in Chicago. After Pearl Harbor, Yasui resigned from his job and went to Oregon, where the Army informed him of his dismissal from the reserves. When Proclamation No. 3 was issued, Yasui blatantly violated the curfew in order to challenge, in court, the military's jurisdiction over civilians in such a manner.

Minori Yasui's case was heard in a federal court presided over by Judge **James Alger Fee**, who held that Dewitt's Proclamation No. 3, which instituted the curfew, was unconstitutional. However, Judge Fee decided that Yasui had given up his citizenship by working for the Japanese consulate. Without citizenship, Yasui was an "enemy alien," and hence the curfew was legal as it applied to him. Minoru Yasui was found guilty, fined $5,000, and sentenced to one year in prison.

Yasui appealed his case, and the Supreme Court ruled on June 21, 1943—the same day as the Hirabayashi ruling—that the curfew was legal and that Yasui was indeed guilty of violating a legal curfew. However, the Court disagreed with Judge Fee that Yasui had lost his citizenship due to his work with the Japanese consulate. Once again, however, the Court avoided the issue of evacuation, and ruled only on the constitutionality of the curfew order.

A third resister was **Fred Toyosaburo Korematsu**, a Nisei from Oakland, California, who violated the Civil Exclusion Order by going underground to avoid incarceration in a relocation center. He assumed a Mexican name and was working as a welder for the war effort when he was discovered and arrested by the FBI. In September 1942, a federal district court in San Francisco found Korematsu guilty of disobeying the evacuation orders and sentenced him to five years' probation. In accordance with the Civil Exclusion Order, Korematsu was also evacuated to a relocation center.

A civil rights lawyer, **Wayne M. Collins**, who represented Korematsu, appealed on the grounds that the evacuation order itself was unconstitutional. On October 11, 1944, the Supreme Court heard the case of *Korematsu v. United States*. Two months later, the Court returned with a six-to-three decision upholding the constitutionality of the evacuation order.

Although all three cases upheld the constitutionality of the various proclamations and orders at issue, the unanimous front the Supreme Court showcased in the *Hirabayashi* and *Yasui* cases was not present in the *Korematsu* case. This dissension in the Court regarding the constitutionality of the evacuation foreshadowed the outcome of the next challenge to the evacuation orders in the Supreme Court.

What effect did Executive Order 9066 have on the American people?

Executive Order 9066 imparted a large dose of legitimacy to the wartime hysteria and racism rampant in America. Since Americans bought the propaganda they were fed about how the Japanese Americans on the West Coast were enemy aliens loyal to Japan, they supported the government in its assault against Japanese Americans. Newspapers fed the hysteria by running articles with headlines that read: "Two Japs with Maps and Alien Literature Seized," "Map Reveals Jap Menace," "Jap and Camera Held in Bay City."

Why were Hawaiians of Japanese descent not evacuated and interned?

Hawaii was a wartime paradox. Geographically closer to Japan than California, and once attacked by the Japanese empire, Hawaii was more vulnerable to ambush than the United States. Yet all but 1,444 Japanese Hawaiians escaped evacuation and mass internment. The U.S. military surely did not believe that the Hawaiian Japanese were less likely to engage in subversive activities than Japanese Americans on the West Coast. Even so, "military necessity" was cited as the reason for leaving Japanese Hawaiians alone. The same "military necessity" meant that almost 120,000 Japanese in the continental U.S. were incarcerated.

The Japanese in Hawaii were not part of a massive internment campaign for a few simple reasons. One was that "military necessity" really meant economic necessity. Hawaiian Japanese were vital to keeping the economy of the island chain afloat. Numbering about 150,000, the Japanese constituted over one-third of Hawaii's population and a large chunk of the labor force. They provided labor resources not only for private industry in Hawaii but also for the military. Had a mass internment of Hawaii's Japanese occurred, the islands' economy would invariably have sunk to the bottom of the deep blue sea.

Another factor that weighed in favor of the Japanese was that the military governor of Hawaii, Lieutenant General **Delos C. Emmons**, opposed internment. He did not want to expend the limited resources of the military in Hawaii on mass incarceration. He did face some opposition from Secretary of the Navy **Frank Knox**, however, who urged the mass internment of Japanese Hawaiians to the island of Molokai, and from the Army, which favored their internment on the mainland. Nonetheless, plans to evacuate Japanese Hawaiians were never carried out. Again military necessity meant economic necessity. Such a military operation would have broken the Hawaiian bank.

That whites were in the minority in Hawaii also benefited Hawaiian Japanese. Although Hawaii was not an island paradise free of discrimination, the Japanese Hawaiians did not experience the unbridled racism of the mainland. With Hawaii's Asian population in the majority, the Japanese presence was tolerated by the ethnically diverse community at large.

This, of course, was not the case on the West Coast, where Japanese Americans constituted a small minority. Thus, economics did not act to check the anti-Japanese exclusionary groups that sprang up on the West Coast. Especially prevalent in California, such groups played a key role in pressuring the government to remove the West Coast Japanese to the interior parts of the country.

If America was also at war with Germany and Italy, why were Americans of German and Italian descent spared internment?

You could say that in the case of the Italians and Germans, familiarity did not breed contempt. Most government officials agreed that they knew enough about the habits and personalities of Germans and Italians to distinguish between the loyal and the disloyal. Many insisted that it was very difficult to recognize loyalty and disloyalty in Japanese Americans because their language and culture were so "strange." Simply put, it was a question of skin color.

What were the costs of evacuation for Japanese Americans?

The most quantifiable cost of evacuation for the Japanese Americans was financial. In a short time, they had to close down their businesses or find tenants, sell off their furniture and worldly possessions—in other words, liquidate their entire estates except for the few mementos they could carry with them into internment. Most were able to recoup only a fraction of the true value of their possessions. Signs like "Evacuation Sale: All Furniture Must Be Sold" were common during World War II.

Even in these desperate times, some prized the preservation of dignity more than making money on the sale of property. In her autobiography *Farewell to Manzanar*, **Jeanne Wakatsuki Houston** recounts how her mother threw the family's china set, worth over two hundred dollars, one dish at a time, at a dealer who had made a meager offer of seventeen dollars.

Aside from financial losses, the evacuation took a psychological toll. Many Japanese Americans felt betrayed by Imperial Japan for ruining their reputation with its assault on Pearl Harbor and by the United States for subjecting them to the humiliation of incarceration.

Japanese Americans also felt enormous uncertainty about what the future might hold. It was distressing to them that no one knew for sure how long they would be detained, or what sort of existence awaited them in the camps. Reports of the destruction of their property at home also distressed them. For instance, in 1942 news made it to the camps that many of the cemeteries where Japanese immigrants were buried had been desecrated, a shock for the Japanese, who so revere their ancestors. Many wondered how they could possibly reconstruct their former lives after such ruin.

What was the War Relocation Authority?

The War Relocation Authority (WRA) was established on March 18, 1942, by Executive Order 9102. As a civil agency, the WRA's job was to erect and run the internment camps set up around the country to house Japanese Americans. **Milton S. Eisenhower**, the brother of Dwight D. Eisenhower, was appointed the first director of the WRA.

Eisenhower envisioned the camps as temporary shelters, where the evacuees would stay until they were employed in the private sector away from the restricted zone. However, his idea was not well received by politicians from other states. On April 7, 1942, Eisenhower held a meeting in Salt Lake City with the governors and representatives from the states of Utah, Arizona, Nevada, Montana, Idaho, Colorado, New Mexico, Wyoming, Washington, and Oregon to discuss the relocation of the evacuees to their respective states. Tempers flared. One governor even threatened to have any Japanese brought into his state hanged. The only official receptive to the idea was **Ralph Carr**, the governor of Colorado, who maintained that aiding in the resettlement of the evacuees was a citizen's duty.

After this disheartening meeting, Eisenhower realized that his plan for the swift placement of evacuees in interior states was out of the question. Until wartime hysteria died down, Japanese evacuees would have to remain incarcerated and manage the best they could. Thus, the WRA examined various sites to construct ten permanent relocation camps, and by June 5, 1942, all the sites were selected. Under the direction of the Army, construction of the permanent camps was done hastily, though at a staggeringly high cost of $56,482,638. Evacuees, generally in groups of five hundred, began to arrive by train and bus to the relocation camps even before they were completed.

Eisenhower resigned as WRA director in June 1942 to become the assistant director for the Office of War Information. Before his departure, he wrote the following to the president: "I cannot help expressing the hope that the American people will grow toward a broader appreciation of the essential Americanism of a great majority of the evacuees and of the difficult sacrifice they are making." Eisenhower also recommended that a public statement supporting the loyal Nisei be issued, that Congress develop programs for the repatriation of those Japanese who wished to be repatriated, and that it enact special rehabilitation programs to help internees after the war.

Dillon S. Myer, a New Deal bureaucrat in the Department of Agriculture, was appointed the new WRA director by Franklin D. Roosevelt. He supported Eisenhower's proposal to move the evacuees out of the internment camps as quickly as possible so they could resume a normal life. Within a year, programs were created which allowed several groups of internees to leave the camps.

Project directors who headed the individual camps were soon selected to help Myer provide for the needs of the evacuees. They busied themselves with issues such as fire control, food production, army patrol, staffing the camps, and setting up schools. Myer and his staff worked to make internment more bearable for the evacuees, a difficult task given the suffocating confines of the camps.

How were the Japanese Americans organized and what were the living conditions like in the assembly centers and the internment camps?

The Army posted instructions for Japanese alien residents and Japanese Americans to report to control centers where families would be registered and given numbered tags in preparation for internment. With the tags attached to their bags and coat lapels, the families were organized, no longer by surname, but by number.

From the control centers, the evacuees reported to local assembly centers before moving on to one of the ten permanent internment camps or they went directly to the camps. Located on fair grounds and racetracks, most assembly centers consisted of filthy animal shelters hastily converted, if at all, into temporary living quarters. One evacuee compared the conditions to "a family of three thousand people camped out in a barn." Another woman described the toilet facilities as "one big row of seats, that is, one straight board with holes out about a foot apart with no partitions at all." The kitchens were also noted for their filthiness, and as a result, diarrhea was common among the internees. Still, such minimal facilities cost the Army and the taxpayers more than ten million dollars.

The Japanese Americans did not find conditions much improved once they reached the internment camps. Their new homes were surrounded by barbed-wire fences and watchtowers. The U.S. government claimed internment was necessary in part to protect Japanese Americans from a backlash from "patriotic" Americans. Curiously, though, the guns pointed *into* the camps, at the Japanese Americans, and armed military police patrolled the grounds *inside* the barbed wire.

The internment camps housed between 8,000 and 20,000 people, but most typically 10,000. They usually consisted of 36 blocks of barracks, each barrack measuring about 20 feet by 120 feet and partitioned into approximately six rooms. Cavernous, impersonal mess halls, bathroom and laundry facilities, and an empty recreation building also stood on the site.

Conditions improved as the Japanese Americans began to make the best of their situation and worked to make the camps more livable. Internees grew vegetables such as sweet potatoes and eggplants in front of their barracks. They also built furniture, such as chairs and bookshelves, and even constructed Buddhist altars from scrap lumber left over from construction. Also, as more clothing arrived, the internees could better protect themselves against the brutal cold of winter.

One of the most difficult adjustments for the internees concerned the communal nature of the camps. The Japanese Americans ate in large mess halls and lived in the barracks with minimal partitions, offering little privacy. The lavatories, with their unpartitioned toilet seats and communal showers, were the hardest of all to adjust to.

What did the Japanese Americans do all day long in the camps?

Many Japanese Americans found themselves employed with the government for the first time. Some worked as cooks, dishwashers, and pot scrubbers in the mess halls, others as seamsters and janitors. Physicians, nurses, and dentists worked in their area of expertise. Many also found themselves employed as teachers, librarians, administrators, supervisors in agriculture, and directors of warehouse supply distribution.

The internees had a great deal of leisure time in the camps. For the first time, they had the opportunity to take adult classes in such areas as American history and bookkeeping. Japanese flower-arrangement classes were offered, and arrangements created in such classes added a nice touch to the usually drab rooms of the barracks. The Japanese also organized makeshift libraries, and entertained and educated themselves with whatever books they could collect.

What kind of loyalty tests did the internees have to take, and who were the No-No Boys?

All internees over the age of seventeen were given a questionnaire designed to test their loyalty to the United States. Those with test results indicating loyalty would be allowed to serve in the military, while the disloyal would have to face the consequences.

The most controversial questions in the survey were "Are you willing to serve in the Armed Forces of the United States on combat duty, wherever ordered?" and "Will you swear unqualified allegiance to the United States of America and faithfully defend the United States from any or all attack by foreign or domestic forces, and forswear any form of allegiance to the Japanese emperor, to any other foreign government, power or organization?"

Although their constitutional rights had been blatantly violated, more than 65,000 evacuees answered "yes" to both questions, hoping that these answers would hasten their release from the camps. The U.S. government labeled most who answered "yes" loyal, while those who answered "no" were labeled disloyal and branded the No-No Boys.

Many of the "disloyal" were weeded out and sent to Tule Lake Camp, a camp specifically reserved for those the government found especially suspicious.

Did the interned children receive any schooling?

Yes. Among the nearly 120,000 Japanese Americans interned, roughly 30,000 were school-age children. The internees began to organize temporary schools at the assembly centers within days of their arrival. For instance, in the Santa Anita Assembly Center, as early as June 1942, 2,470 children attended classes and 125 preschoolers went to nursery school. Similar classes were found in the other assembly centers.

The children's education continued when they were relocated to the permanent camps. The War Relocation Authority recognized the need for public education and searched for funds to construct schools and purchase school supplies. However, even before the WRA sent in education directors and white teachers with credentials to the camps, the internees had created makeshift schools in the mess halls and recreation barracks. Though they hardly possessed the necessary classroom materials, and though Japanese teachers with credentials were hard to find (since they had been shut out of pedagogy in America), the Nisei did the best they could to educate their children.

Is it true that Nisei served in the U.S. military in World War II?

Yes, and they served with great distinction. The Selective Training and Service Act of 1940 ensured those who registered in the armed forces that they would not be discriminated against on the basis of race, creed, or color, or membership or activity in any labor, political, religious, or other organization. And so before the raid on Pearl Harbor, about 3,500 Nisei had already been drafted into the military.

After Pearl Harbor, the Army made an about-face and did not accept Nisei, with their suspect ancestral ties, into its ranks. The Nisei previously inducted were transferred to the enlisted reserve or were discharged from active duty. Even those who had been trained by the ROTC discovered that after the attack on Pearl Harbor the Army was no longer looking for a few good Japanese American men.

However, in 1943, the War Department once again experienced a change of heart and organized a segregated combat team consisting solely of Nisei soldiers, an action approved by President Franklin D. Roosevelt. In a letter addressed to Secretary of War **Henry L. Stimson**, dated February 1, 1943, Roosevelt explained his position regarding Nisei service in the war effort: "No loyal citizen of the United States should be denied the democratic right to exercise the responsibilities of citizenship, regardless of his ancestry. . . . Americanism is a matter of mind and heart; Americanism is not, and never was, a matter of race or ancestry."

The Army recruitment campaign in relocation camps met with great success. Many Japanese Americans jumped at the chance to serve their country and prove their loyalty to the United States. As one Japanese man in the Manzanar internment camp said: "All of us went because we knew we had a job to do to prove to the people of the United States and the government that we're not Japs. We are American citizens and should be treated as Americans."

In addition to the usual Application for Voluntary Induction, prospective Japanese American volunteers had to fill out a special form, the Statement of United States Citizen of Japanese Ancestry. On it they had to list all their political, religious, and social affiliations, as well as the newspapers and magazines they customarily read, and they were asked to provide five references from individuals other than employers. Prospective volunteers also had to indicate their willingness to serve on combat duty anywhere ordered, and to swear unqualified allegiance to the United States and forswear allegiance to Japan.

Hawaiian Nisei, few of whom were interned, were particularly enthusiastic about serving, and volunteered in great numbers. One such volunteer was **Daniel K. Inouye**, the future U.S. senator, who joined the now-famous "Go for Broke" 442nd Regimental Combat Team.

Nisei women also volunteered for service, many joining the Women's Army Corps, to contribute to the war effort. Eventually, 33,000 Japanese Americans served in World War II and helped the Allies achieve victory.

Why is the 442nd Regimental Combat Team famous?

The 442nd Regimental Combat Team was the segregated unit of Nisei from Hawaii and the West Coast that achieved fame for its bravery overseas. The 442nd Regimental Combat Team adopted its motto "Go for Broke" from a Hawaiian pidgin phrase, and go for broke is exactly what they did.

They fought courageously, on the front line in Italy, in the air invasion of Germany, and everywhere they were sent into combat. Among their most heroic accomplishments was saving 211 soldiers, mostly Texans, from the "Lost Battalion" of the 141st Infantry Regiment who were surrounded by the German enemy in France. The rescued men of the Lost Battalion later presented the 442nd with a silver plaque engraved with words of gratitude for their "gallant fight."

By the end of the war, the 442nd, which suffered 9,486 casualties, was one of the most decorated units in the history of the U.S. Army. Awards to individuals in the 442nd included a Congressional Medal of Honor, 52 Distinguished Service Crosses, a Distinguished Service Medal, almost 600 Silver Stars, and some 4,000 Bronze Star Medals. The 442nd earned laurels as a unit as well, winning 43 Division Commendations, 13 Army Commendations, 2 Meritorious Service Unit Plaques, and 7 Presidential Distinguished Unit Citations.

In recognition of their tremendous heroism and accomplishments, President Truman told the Japanese Americans of the 442nd: "You fought for the free nations of the world along with the rest of us. . . . You fought not only the enemy, but you fought prejudice and you won. Keep up that fight, and we will continue to win to make this great republic stand for what the Constitution says it stands for: 'The welfare of all the people all the time.' "

Who was Private First Class Sadao S. Munemori?

Private First Class **Sadao S. Munemori** was the first Japanese American to receive the military's highest award, the Medal of Honor. A member of the 442nd, Munemori was killed on April 5, 1945, near Seravezza, Italy, when he threw himself on top of an unexploded grenade to smother the blast and save the lives of two of his comrades.

Sadao S. Munemori was only twenty-one years old when he was killed. Ironically, Munemori was a Kibei, one of the Japanese Americans thought to be the most disloyal of all.

Did Nisei serve in the Military Intelligence Service too?

Remarkably, yes. Nisei, who were labeled a threat to national security, were taken into the Military Intelligence Service to work covertly for an end to the war. They were considered a secret weapon in the fight against Japan, and military officials estimated that their efforts shortened the war by two years.

The Military Intelligence Service, 6,000 Japanese Americans strong by the end of World War II, consisted of interpreters, translators, spies, and intelligence specialists. Their job was to intercept and monitor radio transmissions; translate confiscated maps, journals, letters, and other documents that revealed enemy tactics and operations; interpret for military officers; and interrogate Japanese taken prisoner. While these Japanese Americans were trusted to carry out some of the nation's top secret work, the American public was fiercely contesting their loyalty to the United States.

Were Nisei ever drafted?

Several thousand Nisei inside the internment camps were drafted by the U.S. military. Most went along with the draft, right or wrong, to prove their loyalty to the American flag. However, about three hundred Nisei refused to serve unless their civil rights were restored. Their refusal led to time in a jail cell.

The draft resisters were led by **Frank Emi**, a soft-spoken Nisei, who at the time of the draft had been relocated to Heart Mountain Camp, an internment camp in Wyoming. When the American government demanded that he serve in the military, he refused to budge, arguing that the democratic ideals of "liberty and justice for all" that America was fighting for overseas were being denied to Japanese Americans supposedly protected by the Constitution and the Bill of Rights.

Frank Emi organized several hundred draft resisters into the Fair Play Committee, but their arguments fell on deaf ears, and a total of 315 draft evaders were convicted and sent to prison. President Truman, however, pardoned the resisters after the war.

The draft caused much conflict within the relocation camps. Brawls occasionally broke out between the volunteers and the resisters. While the volunteers were generally honored by fellow Japanese Americans, draft evaders were usually ostracized and taunted as pro-Japanese.

The Japanese American community has always lauded the Nisei veterans of World War II, who are revered not only for fighting valiantly on the battlefields of Europe, but for winning the trust of the American people on the battlefield of racism. Nowadays, draft resisters are gaining the respect and support sorely missing in the internment camps, as the story of their defiant and courageous stance against injustice spreads in the Japanese American community.

Japanese American veterans of the war feel the portrayal

of resisters as heroes is a distortion of history. Many veterans insist that the Japanese American community would still be battling overt racism even today had it not been for Japanese Americans' willing service in the military.

Other than military volunteers and draftees, were any other Japanese Americans allowed to leave the camps during the years of internment?

One group of internees that were allowed to leave as early as the summer of 1942 were college students.

Respected educators, concerned with the interruption in the higher education of Nisei youth, formed the National Japanese American Student Relocation Council (NJASRC) in 1942. **Robert Sproul**, the president of the University of California, along with other concerned individuals, wrote a letter to President Roosevelt arguing that America could not afford to close the doors of higher education to loyal American-born Japanese who had the potential to one day be the country's most influential leaders.

The government agreed with this assessment and after some debate authorized the release of loyal Nisei students with letters of acceptance to institutions of higher learning. The NJASRC set about convincing universities to accept Nisei and preparing the students for the transition to university life. While the U.S. Office of Education promoted higher education for Nisei, it did not help subsidize tuition costs, and the War Relocation Authority was able to provide a travel allowance and a grant of only about $25 per student. The students were largely left to their own devices, and depended for financial assistance on private scholarships, their families, and the NJASRC, which raised funds for scholarships and other forms of financial aid.

The council also played an aggressive role in encouraging colleges and universities in inland states to accept Nisei students. Many academic institutions, including the Massachu-

setts Institute of Technology and Princeton University, refused to enroll Japanese Americans. But others opened their
doors, and between 1942 and 1946, 4,084 Nisei resettled in
various college and university towns throughout the Midwest
and the East.

Did the students just pack their bags and go off to college?

In spite of cooperation from the War Relocation Authority,
the students had to jump through a lot of hoops to obtain
clearance to leave the camps. They had to provide proof of acceptance to a college or university in America's interior, away
from the Western Defense Command, and they had to
demonstrate that they had the wherewithal to finance their
education. Also, a public official had to testify on each student's behalf that the student posed no threat to the community. The students also had to clear an FBI security check.

Despite the seemingly endless obstacles, the thought of
liberation from the camps sustained the Nisei students. With
the aid of the National Japanese American Student Relocation Council, thousands of young Nisei left the internment
camps for America's institutions of higher learning, where
they experienced some semblance of a normal life.

It has been estimated that 40 percent of the students who
resettled in academic institutions were women. Despite the
suffocating confines of the camps, going off to college was
not an easy decision for most Nisei women. Many felt in-
tensely an obligation to remain in the camps to care for elderly parents. Also, their uncertainty about resettlement and
how the outside world would treat them prevented many
from taking the leap. Favorable reports from students already
enrolled, however, allayed their worst fears and encouraged
many to follow suit.

Although the first few months outside the camps were a
frightening and awkward period of adjustment, most found

that the initial stages of relocation away from the camps were worth it.

Who else got to leave the camps?

Besides students, the War Relocation Authority also released laborers who pledged to contribute to the war effort. Labor was badly needed during the war, especially in agriculture, and the Japanese Americans were an ideal labor force. Fifteen laborers were withdrawn from an assembly center in May 1942 as a trial group to work on a farm in Oregon. The results from this experiment were positive, and 1,500 internees were released by the end of June 1942 to work the land in Idaho, Utah, and Montana. By the end of the year, approximately 10,000 more were granted seasonal releases to harvest crops. Others went to work in factories, which were also severely affected by labor shortages. Outbreaks of violence against the Japanese Americans occurred, but most were not that serious.

Labor shortages impacted dramatically on Nisei women who had been kept out of white-collar and even blue-collar jobs. Prior to the war, their main source of employment, other than in agriculture, had been in domestic service. Though they were predominantly in domestic service jobs during the war years, Nisei women also landed positions as secretaries, typists, file clerks, and factory workers. By 1950, only 10 percent of the Japanese American women in the labor force were engaged in domestic service, while 47 percent occupied clerical, sales, and operative positions.

The resettlement of students and workers helped to disperse the Japanese American population throughout the country. Illinois, and particularly Chicago, proved the most popular resettlement destination before January 1, 1945. Other popular states were Colorado, Ohio, Utah, Idaho, Michigan, Minnesota, and New York. The War Relocation Authority and President Roosevelt applauded the resettlement program. In a press conference around this time, Roosevelt stated: "A good deal of progress has been made in scattering them through the country. . . . They are American citizens. . . . 75,000 families scattered around the United States is not going to upset anybody."

Who is Mitsuye Endo?

Mitsuye Endo was a Nisei civil servant who was detained in the camps while her brother fought in the United States Army overseas. Although Endo could have applied for resettlement, since she was clearly employable in the civilian economy, she decided instead to challenge her unlawful detention.

In July 1942, **James Purcell**, a civil rights attorney, filed a writ of habeas corpus on Endo's behalf with the San Francisco federal courts challenging the constitutionality of incarceration. Purcell argued that Endo's detainment without trial was a violation of her civil rights. As in other cases challenging the authority of the military, the federal judge denied Endo's petition and upheld the rights of the military to detain Endo.

Endo's case was then appealed to the Supreme Court of the United States. On December 19, 1944, the Supreme Court issued a unanimous opinion holding that it was unlawful to detain a law-abiding U.S. citizen, and ordered the release of Mitsuye Endo. As the court stated, "A citizen who is concededly loyal presents no problem of espionage or sabotage. Loyalty is a matter of the heart and mind, not of race, creed or color. He who is loyal is by definition not a spy or a saboteur."

Why did the Supreme Court rule for Endo but against Korematsu and Hirabayashi in the two prior cases?

All three decisions rest on the premise that a citizen deprived of liberty and property without due process of law must, nonetheless, obey an unlawful order and then, as Justice

Douglas suggested in *Hirabayashi*, find the appropriate means to challenge it in court. Endo obeyed the military order of internment without resistance and then found the appropriate means to challenge its legality.

What impact did the Endo decision have on the evacuation?

Not surprisingly, following the *Endo* decision, the War Department announced that the evacuation orders would be rescinded effective January 2, 1945. With the Supreme Court's decision in the Endo case and the War Department's announcement, the evacuees began to move out of the camps as the end of the war approached. By March 1946, all the evacuees had left the relocation camps.

Who was Tokyo Rose?

American GIs in the Pacific theater pinned the name "Tokyo Rose" on all the English-speaking women broadcasters of Radio Tokyo, who announced popular music programs and war propaganda. Most GIs developed an affection for the American-sounding women who offered them the music they liked to hear. Journalists after a scoop caught the Tokyo Rose fever in 1944, and created the myth of one Tokyo Rose, a seductive and vicious teaser who undermined the morale of American soldiers. With the press fueling the hysteria, Tokyo Rose's celebrity spread like wildfire among the GIs, who had few amusements, no sex, and a lot of battle fatigue. Tokyo Rose became a pinup girl of the radio waves who lived in the imaginations of American soldiers and journalists.

Reporters, who exploited the news value of Tokyo Rose, constantly speculated on her identity. The most fantastic rumor was that she was Amelia Earhart, who had disappeared over the Pacific in 1937. In 1945 the myth fell on a naive Japanese American girl named **Iva Ikuko Toguri**.

A few weeks after graduating from UCLA in June 1941, Iva Toguri traveled to Japan to visit a critically ill aunt. Iva was disappointed with Japan, and complained about the poor Japanese diet that caused her to have bouts of scurvy and beriberi. She longed to go home, but much to her misfortune, war broke out between America and Japan. Trapped in Japan, Iva was continually pressured to revoke her U.S. citizenship, but she refused to abandon America, even though America would soon abandon her. With bills to pay, she took a job at Radio Tokyo, first as a typist, then as a broadcaster of Japanese propaganda and music until the Japanese surrender.

American reporters hoping to cash in on the Tokyo Rose story followed a few "leads" that took them to Iva Toguri in 1945. They offered her $2,000 for an interview about her alias—Tokyo Rose—and told her that if she agreed to do it, reporters would stop hounding her. Pleased to be among Americans again, delighted with the U.S. victory, and caught up in the carnivalesque search for Tokyo Rose, Iva Toguri foolishly did the interview and signed a contract saying she was Tokyo Rose, not realizing she was part of a massive Tokyo Rose witch-hunt. Before long, U.S. military police took Toguri into custody. She spent time in and out of prisons in Japan until August 26, 1948, when the U.S. government presented her with a formal arrest warrant. She was brought to San Francisco and tried for "treasonable conduct." The trial was essential for the satisfaction of the American people, and harassment, falsifications of the evidence, and distortions of the truth were used to build a case against Toguri. In an egregious miscarriage of justice, Iva Toguri was found guilty by an all-white jury in 1949, and remained behind bars until 1956. Months after her release, the Immigration Service, arguing that her conviction made her a stateless person, issued her a formal order to leave the country or face deportation. Toguri contested the order, and in 1958, the U.S. government canceled deportation proceedings, but refused to restore her American citizenship.

During her trial and long after, the Japanese American community distanced itself from Iva Toguri, whose indictment was viewed with shame. Japanese Americans largely ignored Toguri until the early 1970s, when reports surfaced that her prosecution had been based on testimony the Justice Department knew was false. **Dr. Clifford I. Uyeda**, a retired San Francisco pediatrician who was convinced that Iva Toguri had been terribly wronged, led the campaign for her pardon. The Japanese American community, which had grown more secure by the 1970s, finally showed its support for Toguri. Although requests had been denied by both the Eisenhower and Johnson administrations, on his last day in office, President Ford granted Toguri a presidential pardon.

Where did internees go after the war and how did they fare?

Most of the remaining 50,000 Issei and Nisei still in the camps in January 1945 were sent home, no doubt with some apprehension. Although the JACL urged the War Relocation Authority to take on a greater role in helping with the resettlement of Japanese Americans, the organization refused and provided only basic assistance. The War Relocation Authority issued $25 to individuals and $50 to families, and covered transportation costs. After that, the former evacuees were on their own.

Many Japanese Americans were shocked upon their return home to find their former lives in total ruin. Their homes and businesses had been vandalized, burned down, or neglected by tenants; their ancestors' graves had been desecrated; and their possessions had been picked clean. Some merchants refused to sell goods to the Japanese, and banks froze their accounts. Financial losses suffered by the Japanese Americans totaled an estimated $400,000,000.

Although racism was still prevalent on the West Coast, the attitudes of mainstream Americans were improving. In 1948, Congress passed the Evacuation Claims Act, which compensated for, albeit minimally, the damages the internees suffered. They recovered a dime for every dollar lost, and though this hardly made up for the heavy losses they endured, the act itself was symbolic of justice.

Another significant piece of legislation passed during the post-war period was the Immigration and Nationality Act, also called the McCarran-Walter Act, of 1952, which abolished racial qualifications for American citizenship. The JACL lobbied heavily for the passage of the act, which finally permitted the Issei to become naturalized Americans. The McCarran-Walter Act was the realization of the dreams of Japanese immigrants who had struggled for the same rights afforded to immigrants from places other than Asia. Many Issei quickly seized the opportunity to become citizens, and by 1965, 46,000 had been naturalized.

With laws discriminating against Japanese Americans no longer on the books, public opinion began to change. The widespread accusations of betrayal and treachery were largely proven wrong, and the heroic efforts of Japanese Americans, such as those on the 442nd Regimental Combat Team, became widely known. As barriers to opportunity fell, Japanese Americans entered white-collar professions in increasing numbers. Between 1940 and 1960, the percentage of Japanese males in professional occupations rose from 3.8 to 15. Many found employment in the post-war boom economy and broke new ground in fields such as architecture and civil service. The high demand for teachers in post-war America meant that even Nisei were able to find jobs in pedagogy, a field largely closed to them before the war. Ironically, many had learned to teach in the camps.

The war years robbed Japanese Americans of most of their material wealth and their dignity, but for the most part the community recovered remarkably.

From the autobiographical novel *Talking to High Monks in the Snow* (1992) by Japanese American writer Lydia Yuri Minatoya:

"Call it denial, but many Japanese Americans never quite understood that the promise of America was not meant for them. They lived in horse stalls at the Santa Anita racetrack and said the Pledge of Allegiance daily. They rode to relocation camps under armed guard, labeled with numbered tags, and sang 'The Star-Spangled Banner.' They lived in deserts or swamps, ludicrously imprisoned—where would they run if they ever escaped—and formed garden clubs, and yearbook staffs, and citizen town meetings. They even elected beauty queens. . . . Call it adaptive behavior. . . . Get along, work hard, and never quite see the things that can bring you pain. Against the tyranny of nature, of feudal lords, of wartime hysteria, the charm works equally well. And so my parents gave me an American name and hoped that I could pass. They nourished me with the American dream: Opportunity, Will, Transformation."

Have the Sansei and Yonsei managed to achieve the American dream despite the setbacks their forebears faced?

The Sansei and Yonsei have done extremely well for the most part. The average Japanese American family enjoys a standard of living higher than the national average. Japanese Americans are actively engaged in all white-collar professions, with many achieving a high degree of success in accounting, law, medicine, engineering, and business. Japanese Americans have no ghettos, little crime, and few instances of juvenile delinquency.

While they have embraced the American way, the Sansei and Yonsei cultivate their Japanese heritage. Cities on the

West Coast are enriched with Japanese art exhibits and gardens, Japanese Buddhist temples and Zen monasteries, Japanese martial arts and cookery classes, and Japanese grocery stores and restaurants.

Who are some prominent Japanese American political figures?

Probably the most recognized Japanese American politician is the Democratic senator from Hawaii, **Daniel K. Inouye**. Senator Inouye returned to the United States at the end of World War II as a decorated hero, who lost an arm defending his country. After the war, he took advantage of the GI Bill and attended the University of Hawaii. In 1952, Inouye received a law degree from George Washington University.

Soon after passing the bar exam in Hawaii, he was appointed assistant prosecutor for Honolulu, and in 1954, he successfully ran for a seat in the territorial House of Representatives and served as territorial majority leader. In 1958, he was again elected to public office, this time to the territorial Senate. When Hawaii achieved statehood in 1959, Hawaiian constituents elected Daniel Inouye to serve in the House of Representatives, where he served two terms. In 1962 Hawaii showed its confidence in Inouye again by electing him senator. During his tenure in the Senate, Daniel Inouye delivered the keynote address at the Democratic National Convention in 1968, served on the Senate committee conducting the Watergate hearings, and directed the Iran-contra Affair hearings in 1987. In 1962 *Life* magazine named Inouye "One of the 100 Most Important Men & Women in the United States."

After Inouye moved to the Senate, another Nisei Democrat from Hawaii and a fellow war veteran, **Masayuki "Spark" Matsunaga**, filled his seat in the House and went on to serve seven consecutive terms. Like Inouye, Matsunaga took advantage of the GI Bill; he obtained a law degree from Harvard University in 1951. Before his election to the United States

House of Representatives, Matsunaga served in the territorial legislature from 1954 to 1959. He joined Daniel Inouye in the Senate in 1976 and fought hard for the recognition of Asian Americans until his death in 1990. Among Matsunaga's greatest contributions was his sponsorship of the Civil Liberties Act of 1988.

In 1964, another Nisei, **Patsy Takemoto Mink**, became the first Asian American woman elected to Congress when Hawaii was awarded a second representative in the House. Mink received her law degree from the University of Chicago in 1951 and became the first woman of Asian descent to become a practicing lawyer in Hawaii. In 1956 she was elected to the territorial House, and from 1958 to 1959 and 1962 to 1964, Patsy Mink served in the Hawaiian Senate as Hawaii's first woman in the state legislature.

In 1976 California Republican **Samuel Ichiye Hayakawa**, known as S. I. Hayakawa, won a seat in the United States Senate. Born in Canada in 1906, Hayakawa went to the United States to study in the 1930s and soon decided to apply for U.S. citizenship. Although he was a Canadian citizen, U.S. immigration regarded him as Japanese, and due to the quota for Japanese Hayakawa was forced to wait until 1954 to obtain citizenship. After completing his education Hayakawa remained in academia and made valuable contributions to the field of general semantics with the publication of his book *Language in Action* in 1941. Hayakawa went on to be named president of San Francisco State University in 1968 and served in that post until 1973, when he decided to enter politics.

George Ryoichi Ariyoshi earned the distinction of being the nation's first lieutenant governor and governor. He was elected lieutenant governor of Hawaii in 1970 and went on to fill the post of governor in 1973, serving three full terms—the longest in Hawaiian history—before his retirement in 1986.

Japanese Americans have blazed new political trails on the

U.S. mainland as well. **Norman Yoshio Mineta** became the first Japanese American mayor of a large American city when he was elected mayor of San Jose, California, in 1971. In 1974 he won a seat in Congress, and has been reelected to the post nine times. **Robert Takeo Matsui** of Sacramento served two terms as a city councilman before his constituents elected him to Congress in 1978. Matsui has won reelection to Congress seven times and with his colleague Norman Yoshio Mineta played an instrumental role in the passage of the Civil Liberties Act of 1988.

Why was the passage of the Hart-Celler Act of 1965 important for Japanese Americans?

The Immigration Act of 1924 barred Asian immigrants from entering the United States, since they were ineligible for citizenship. However, the McCarran-Walter Act of 1952 changed the naturalization policy by allowing Asians to become citizens and granting them permission to immigrate. But the 1924 act also called for the establishment of the National Origins Quota System, which set an immigration quota for each nation corrolated to figures for each group given in the U.S. census of 1890. So even though the McCarran-Walter Act extended to Asians the right to immigrate to the United States, the quota assigned to Asian countries was very small, due to the relatively small Asian population in America at that time.

The Hart-Celler Act of 1965 eliminated the 1924 National Origins Quota System, and stipulated that 170,000 immigrants from the Eastern Hemisphere and 120,000 from the Western Hemisphere would be permitted to immigrate to the United States annually. Twenty thousand immigrants was the limit from any one country. The immigrants would be permitted to enter on a first-come, first-served basis, without regard to their nation of origin as long as the twenty-thousand-person limit had not been exceeded.

The liberalization of the immigration policy raised opposition from nativists, who feared that the changes would bring immigrants who did not resemble the white majority, and who, they believed, could not easily assimilate into the American mainstream. Such concerns were refuted by politicians and other groups, who predicted that immigration trends would not be altered dramatically, since the existing Asian population in America was small, and that white immigration would thus still dominate.

The passage of the Immigration Act of 1965 marked a new era in Asian immigration. The number of Asian immigrants entering the country soared; between 1961 and 1970, 445,300 Asians immigrated to the United States. This figure more than tripled, to 1.6 million, between 1971 and 1980, and from 1981 to 1990 an all-time high of 2.8 million Asian immigrants reached American shores.

Japanese immigration has represented a small portion of the total immigration from Asia. Between 1965 and 1984, the Japanese constituted only 3 percent of all Asians immigrating to the United States. Approximately 4,000 Japanese immigrate to the United States annually. The small size of Japanese immigration can perhaps be attributed to Japan's post-war economic expansion, which provided both jobs and financial security for its citizens.

Did the U.S. government provide redress to those Japanese Americans interned during World War II?

For many years, Japanese Americans interned during World War II silently suffered what they considered an act of gross injustice and betrayal by the U.S. government. Many hoped that in due time America would acknowledge its mistake and apologize.

In the 1970s, many former internees broke their silence and sought reparations for their suffering. On February 19, 1976, the thirty-fourth anniversary of Roosevelt's signing of Executive Order 9066, President **Gerald R. Ford** apologized on behalf of the United States of America for the internment. He revoked the executive order, proclaiming that "not only was the evacuation wrong, but Japanese Americans were and are loyal Americans."

In 1978 the JACL and its National Committee for Redress passed a resolution seeking $25,000 in reparation payments for each surviving internee. They were met with opposition not only from people outside the Japanese American community, but from JACL members who feared that such demands from a "model minority" would only drum up resentment of Japanese Americans. Other members who opposed monetary redress insisted that no sum would be adequate compensation for their suffering, and that monetary restitution simply put a price tag on freedom. Some viewed redress as another form of welfare; others as a reminder of a past best forgotten.

Opposition from within the Japanese American community motivated the JACL redress committee to support a bill introduced on August 2, 1979, calling for the appointment of a commission "to determine whether a wrong was committed against those American citizens and permanent residents relocated and/or interned as a result of Executive Order Number 9066 . . . and to recommend appropriate remedies."

S. I. Hayakawa, the Republican senator from California, was partly responsible for the JACL's change in tactics, because he refused to support any bill calling for cash payment. During the last days of the Carter administration in 1980, Congress established the Commission of Wartime Relocation and Internment of Civilians (CWRIC) to conduct an investigation and make appropriate recommendations. Nine members, one a Japanese American, sat on the CWRIC, which conducted countless interviews, examined wartime documents, held public hearings and listened to testimony from internees and officials involved in the relocation program.

Opinions were varied. **Abe Fortas**, who, as undersecretary of the interior, had supervised the War Relocation Authority, testified that the mass evacuation "was a tragic error" and "racial prejudice was its basic ingredient." Others, however, defended the internment. **John J. McCoy**, in defense of his immediate superior, **Henry L. Stimson**, urged the CWRIC to conclude that "the action of the President of the United States and the United States Government in regard to our then Japanese population was reasonably undertaken and thoughtfully and humanely conducted."

In 1983, the CWRIC concluded in its report, *Personal Justice Denied*, that the government had committed a "grave injustice" when it interned loyal Japanese Americans and resident aliens of Japanese ancestry. It determined that Executive Order 9066 was "not justified by military necessity," and that it was based on "race prejudice, war hysteria, and a failure of political leadership."

The committee recommended to Congress that each surviving internee be compensated with $20,000 for financial losses suffered due to the internment. In 1988, after much haggling, Congress passed the redress bill. Although President **Ronald Reagan** signed the bill into law before leaving office, it was not until November 1989 that President **George Bush** put his signature on a reparation payment program that extended from 1990 to 1993. Finally, the sixty thousand surviving Japanese Americans received what was long overdue.

What is "economic Pearl Harbor"?

Although Japanese Americans have experienced tremendous social and economic gains during the post-war years, their welfare still hinges, albeit to a small degree, on America's relationship with Japan.

Anti–Japanese American hate crimes, such as physical attacks, harassment, and murders, in recent decades appear linked to American resentment over "economic Pearl Harbor," Japan's economic dominance and perceived unfair trade practices. Instances of this abound. When members of the United Auto Workers once printed bumper stickers proclaiming "Toyota—Datsun—Honda = Pearl Harbor" and "Unemployment—Made in Japan," some Japanese Americans were bombarded with racial slurs. When **Bennett E. Bidwell**, Chrysler's executive vice president for sales and marketing, once suggested that the best way to stem the flow of car imports to America would be to charter the *Enola Gay*, the B29 that dropped the first atomic bomb on Hiroshima, Japanese Americans felt the impact of those remarks in terms of harassment. All Americans, innocent bystanders included, suffer when hatred rages in society. For instance, **Vincent Chin**, a Chinese American, was beaten to death on the night of June 19, 1982, by two men, one an unemployed autoworker, who had mistaken him for a Japanese man.

In recent times Japanese Americans have organized with other Asian Americans into coalitions geared toward bringing an end to anti–Asian American bias crimes and hatred. No longer are they willing to suffer hateful acts in silence.

What is Rafu Shimpo?

Founded in 1903 by **Rippo Iijima**, **Masharu Yamaguchi**, and **Seijiro Shibuya**, *Rafu Shimpo* is the oldest existing Japanese American newspaper in the United States. The founders of *Rafu Shimpo* launched the Japanese-language newspaper with the idea that it would fold once English became the language of choice of the Nisei and their children. As it turned out, Japanese Americans came to rely on the paper for its Japanese-interest stories, so *Rafu Shimpo* kept in step with its readers' language proficiency by adding an English section.

During the war years the printing presses at *Rafu Shimpo* were idle because the FBI arrested the newspaper's publisher, **H. T. Komai**, after the raid on Pearl Harbor. But on January 1, 1946, *Rafu Shimpo* resumed publication.

Besides politicians, who are some prominent Japanese Americans?

Japanese Americans have made valuable contributions in all fields of endeavor, including athletics, law, science, medicine, and the arts.

Dr. **Newton Wesley** played a key role in the development and perfection of the popular plastic contact lenses. Teaming up with Dr. **George Jessen**, Dr. Wesley helped to transform the bulky contact lenses manufactured in 1943 into smaller, more comfortable contact lenses.

Also in the field of medicine, Dr. **Paul Terasaki**, a professor of surgery at the University of California at Los Angeles, developed a test to determine the compatibility of a donated organ and a recipient. This test was critical to the success of the first heart transplant operation.

Physicist **Leo Esaki**, who emigrated from Japan to the United States in 1960, was lauded for his scientific achievements with the Nobel prize for physics in 1973.

Ellison Shoji Onizuka, the grandson of Issei sugar plantation workers, was a pioneer in space travel. On January 24, 1985, Onizuka became the first Asian American in space as a member of the crew of the space shuttle *Discovery*. He was later chosen to be a mission specialist for the space shuttle *Challenger* session 51L. On January 28, 1986, when the *Challenger* lifted off at 11:38 A.M., things went tragically wrong. Just after lift-off, the *Challenger* exploded. Onizuka and the six other crew members were killed instantly in what turned out to be the worst accident in NASA's history.

Conductor **Seiji Ozawa** enjoys an international following. In 1960 **Leonard Bernstein** of the New York Philharmonic Orchestra was so impressed by the rising star that he made Ozawa an assistant conductor. Ozawa went on to conduct the Toronto Symphony beginning in 1966, and then in 1973 he assumed the music directorship of the Boston Symphony Orchestra, where he conducts to this day. The young violinist

Midori has enjoyed international success since her surprise debut as a ten-year-old prodigy at a New York Philharmonic gala. At age fourteen she made headlines around the world for finishing a performance with the Boston Symphony at Tanglewood despite being hampered by two broken strings. At age twenty-one, Midori established Midori and Friends, a foundation aimed at helping to introduce children in public schools and hospitals to classical music.

In the art world, internationally acclaimed painter **Yasuo Kuniyoshi** was born in Japan in 1893 and came to the United States in 1906 at age sixteen to study industrial production. Kuniyoshi was so fond of America he decided to stay and went off to New York to study art. By the 1920s Kuniyoshi was an integral part of the New York art scene. Beginning in 1922 he regularly exhibited his works at the renowned Daniel Gallery in Manhattan. Among his other accomplishments, Kuniyoshi was awarded the Temple Gold Medal of the Pennsylvania Academy of Fine Arts in 1934 and first prize in the annual exhibition of American painting at the Carnegie Institute of Art in 1944. In 1948 the Whitney Museum of Art held a major retrospective exhibition of Kuniyoshi's art, a groundbreaking event since the museum had never before mounted a solo exhibit of works by a living artist. When he died in 1953 Yasuo Kuniyoshi still occupied center stage in the art world.

Isamu Noguchi, one of the greatest sculptors of the twentieth century, earned an international reputation for his stainless steel and stone sculptures, furniture, gardens, and akari lamps. (See "*What is an akari lamp?*" below.) Like most other Japanese and Japanese Americans of his generation, Noguchi spent time in a relocation center during World War II. Among the artist's most notable works are a 72-foot mural in Mexico City portraying major events in Mexico's history, the gardens at the UNESCO building in Paris, the Sunken Garden at Yale University's Beinicke Rare Book and Manuscript Library, and a 102-foot stainless steel sculpture entitled "Bolt of Lightning" in homage of Benjamin Franklin. For his artistic contributions Isamu Noguchi was awarded the Edward MacDowell Medal in 1982 and the National Medal of Arts in 1987. During most of his artistic life, Noguchi was also committed to American dance. He designed stage sets for Martha Graham's productions and also collaborated with George Balanchine and Merce Cunningham.

One of the most prominent modern architects, **Minoru Yamasaki**, has made invaluable contributions to the American cityscape. Yamasaki is perhaps best known for his role as the chief designer of the World Trade Center in New York City, whose twin towers were the world's tallest structures until the Sears Tower was erected in Chicago. Among Minoru Yamasaki's other major architectural contributions are the St. Louis Airport Terminal, completed in 1956, and Princeton University's Woodrow Wilson School of Public and International Affairs, built in 1965.

Sessue Hayakawa was one of the greatest actors in Hollywood during the silent film era. He rose to international stardom in 1915 with the release of *The Cheat*, in which he plays an Asian villain. When the "talkies" came along in the mid-1920s, Hollywood lost interest in Hayakawa, and the actor resorted to making movies in Europe. Then in 1949 Columbia Pictures cast Hayakawa opposite Humphrey Bogart in the melodrama *Tokyo Joe*. Sessue Hayakawa starred in several more films before winning an Academy Award nomination for his performance as Colonel Saito in the 1957 epic *The Bridge on the River Kwai*.

The only Japanese American actor to win an Academy Award is **Miyoshi Umeki**. She came to the United States in the 1950s, when she was in her twenties. Before long she was discovered by Warner Brothers, and the studio cast her in the 1957 romantic drama *Sayonara*. Among Umeki's other film credits are roles in *Cry for Happy* (1961), *Flower Drum Song* (1961), and *A Girl Named Tamiko* (1963). Baby boomers might also remember Miyoshi Umeki for her role as the housekeeper Mrs. Livingston in the ABC situation comedy *The Courtship of Eddie's Father*, which ran from 1969 to 1972.

Noriyuki "Pat" Morita is another of Hollywood's finest Japanese American actors. Morita endured spinal tuberculosis in childhood as well as internment in an American concentration camp during World War II. Beginning in the 1960s, he landed numerous supporting roles on television and the big screen, appearing in such films as *Thoroughly Modern Millie* (1967), *The Shakiest Gun in the West* (1968), *Midway* (1976), and *Savannah Smiles* (1983). High points in Morita's career include his nomination for an Academy Award for Best Supporting Actor for his role as the karate instructor in the 1984 hit film *The Karate Kid* and for his principal role in the 1987–1988 television series *Ohara*.

Actress **Nobu McCarthy** starred in Hollywood films over four decades. In the 1950s she was typecast as the geisha girl in screen productions such as *The Geisha Boy* (1958), *Tokyo After Dark* (1959), *Wake Me When It's Over* (1960), and *Walk Like a Dragon* (1960). In the 1970s and 1980s McCarthy landed unbiased roles in such films as *Farewell to Manzanar* (1976), *The Karate Kid, Part II* (1986), and *The Wash* (1988).

George Hosako Takei captured the hearts and imaginations of Americans, particularly "Trekkies," for his portrayal of Mr. Sulu on the TV science-fiction series *Star Trek*. Like Pat Morita, Takei spent part of his childhood interned in an American concentration camp during World War II. In the 1960s, 1970s, and 1980s Takei landed numerous big screen parts and also made appearances on television series such as *Perry Mason* and *The Twilight Zone*. George Takei earned the distinction of being the first Japanese American immortalized on Hollywood's Walk of Fame. In 1988 he was the recipient of a Grammy Award for Best Spoken Word performance for his reading of *Star Trek IV*.

Since the early 1970s, Takei has actively participated in the political arena, running for a seat in the Los Angeles City Council and in the state assembly. In 1981 he showed his support for Asian Americans by founding the Golden Security

Thrift and Loan Association, an institution devoted to serving mainly Southeast Asian immigrants.

The actor **Mako** won plaudits from critics and fans for his roles in such films as *Conan, The Destroyer* (1984), *Pacific Heights* (1990), and *Rising Sun* (1993). In 1984 he was immortalized on the Hollywood Walk of Fame.

On the culinary scene, **Hiroaki "Rocky" Aoki** has pleased many discriminating palates throughout the years in his restaurant chain Benihana. Aoki came to America in 1960 and sold ice cream in Harlem before he got his big break.

Who are some great Japanese American athletes?

Perhaps the greatest Japanese American athlete of all time, **Tamio "Tommy" Kono**, won gold medals in weight lifting at the 1952 Olympics in Helsinki and the 1956 Olympics in Melbourne. In 1960 he captured silver in Rome. Kono won his three medals in different weight classes, a first in Olympic history. In 1988 the International Weightlifting Federation ranked Tamio Kono first on its list of the thirty greatest weightlifters of all time. Two years later he was inducted into the U.S. Olympic Hall of Fame.

Two other Japanese American athletes captured gold medals at the 1952 Olympic games. **Yoshinobu Oyakawa** won gold in the 100–meter backstroke, breaking the Olympic record, while fellow swimmer **Ford Konno** took the gold medal in the 1,500–meter freestyle swimming and the 800–meter freestyle relay.

Kristi Yamaguchi, a fourth-generation Japanese American (a Yonsei) from California whose mother was born in an internment camp, won the gold medal in the ladies singles figure skating competition at the 1992 Olympic Games in Albertville, France. Born on June 12, 1971, with club feet, Yamaguchi began to skate at the age of six, after her condition was corrected with special shoes.

Which religions do Japanese Americans follow?

Up until the 1920s, the vast majority of Japanese immigrants were adherents of Shintoism and Buddhism. They erected temples in their communities and raised their children to be Buddhists and Shintoists.

In the years before World War II, an increasing number of Japanese Americans began to embrace Christianity. Early attempts by Christian missionaries to win converts in Japan were largely unsuccessful: the ruling party feared the political consequences of adopting Christianity and expelled all Europeans, except the Dutch, from Japan. By providing employment opportunities and helping the Japanese to assimilate into the mainstream, Christians found many converts among the Issei. Some Japanese American Christians even proclaimed that acculturation to American society could only be achieved through acceptance of the Christian faith. However, as time went on, the Christian church began to serve a completely different need, one of teaching and preserving the Japanese traditions that were fading among the Nisei and Sansei intent on assimilation.

Increasingly, Japanese American Buddhists came to be identified as a group who were less acculturated, and therefore less "American," than their Christian counterparts. Buddhists were viewed as pro-Japanese, with an intense desire to preserve Japanese ways. Some Christians chose not to associate openly with Buddhists, fearing they would be more vulnerable to attack for following a foreign religion. Their fears were substantiated after Pearl Harbor, when Buddhist priests were rounded up by the FBI for interrogation about their suspect ties to Japan.

Nowadays Japanese Americans are free to worship in whatever ways they choose. Since traditional Japanese spiritual practice embraces harmoniously disparate religious doctrines, many Japanese Americans adhere at once to different aspects of Buddhism, Shintoism, and Christianity.

What is Zen?

Zen, a word derived from Sanskrit meaning "meditation," is a Buddhist mystical sect that came to Japan from China. According to popular belief, Zen Buddhism was founded by an Indian monk named Bodhidharma, whose enlightenment came after a period of extreme and grueling asceticism, sitting and staring at a blank wall for nine years.

Central to the practice of Zen are the notions of sudden enlightenment, the connectedness of all to the universe, and the illusory nature of material existence. While other sects of Buddhism maintain that enlightenment can be achieved only by study, prayer, and right living after many cycles of reincarnation, Zen Buddhists believe that enlightenment may come in one pure moment, often in the midst of intense meditation.

Zen meditation centers on the contemplation of riddles or problems called *koans,* which on the surface appear absurd, illogical, and irrational. Some of the more popular koans include "What is the sound of one hand clapping?" and "What did your face look like before you were born?" Zen meditation is designed to bring the mind to the brink of enlightenment by freeing it of all attachments and judgments.

Thanks to the spread of Zen Buddhism from Japan to the United States, Zen monasteries are accessible to all. The Zen Mountain Center near Carmel, California, which boasts luxuriant hot springs conducive to a sense of well-being, and the Dai Bosatsu Zendo on Beecher Lake in upstate New York are just two of America's numerous Zen monasteries frequented by Japanese Americans, other Americans, and foreign visitors alike.

How did tea drinking become so popular with the Japanese?

Although Buddhist monks had originally introduced tea into Japan, it was not until Zen became a popular sect of Buddhism in Japan that tea drinking began to take root. The ritual of tea drinking began when a few monks gathered together before an image of Buddha in a Zen monastery to drink plain green tea out of a common bowl. The simple elegance of quietly sipping tea was conducive to Zen meditation and quickly developed into an exquisite ritual as stylized as a classical ballet.

Over the years, the Japanese populace as a whole began to develop an appreciation for the taste and aroma of green tea, so much so that they even relish green tea ice cream (ginger ice cream and red bean ice cream are also favorites). Japanese Americans have continued the tradition, and have even found a few converts for green tea among New Age non–Asian Americans, who tout its medicinal properties.

How has Zen influenced the Japanese sense of aesthetics?

The Japanese sense of aesthetics is derived from the Zen notion that beauty is found in simplicity. The Zen life is the uncluttered life; hence Japanese homes and artifacts, often made of common raw materials such as wood, straw, or paper, tend to be simple and functional.

Shoji screens, constructed of translucent paper pasted against a wooden, latticed frame, function both as doors and walls in the Japanese home. Unadorned, except perhaps for a simple design, the shoji, like other things Japanese, is a blend of both object and art.

Similarly, the woven straw matting that has covered the floors of Japanese homes for centuries is considered beautiful precisely for its stark simplicity. Called *tatami,* which means "to fold" in Japanese, it is made of matted rice straw about two inches thick, bound together by cloth tape and covered with woven reeds to give the surface a smooth veneer.

The folding fan, or *sensu,* was invented by a Japanese craftsperson in the seventh century. The wooden ribs, supposedly modeled after the attenuated bones in the wings of a bat, are partially covered with paper that is often ornamented with a poem or family crest.

Japanese immigrants brought the Japanese sense of aesthetics with them in their cultural baggage. Japanese American (and non–Asian American) architects and interior designers have embraced Japanese design to such an extent in recent decades that it has permeated the American mainstream as witnessed by the proliferation of futons and shoji screens.

What's an akari lamp?

Akari lamps have their origin in the ancient craft of paper lanterns. The internationally renowned Japanese American sculptor **Isamu Noguchi**, a comprehensive collection of whose works can be seen at the Noguchi Garden Museum in Queens, New York, began to popularize akari lamps in 1951. Unpainted, asymmetrical, of mulberry bark paper on a bamboo spiral frame, and lit by bulbs instead of candles, Noguchi's akari lamps radically depart from tradition. They exhibit a variety of forms incorporating both ancient and modern images, from samurai helmets to corner-deli paper bags.

Isamu Noguchi was born in Los Angeles on November 17, 1904, to an Issei father and a European American mother, but spent most of his childhood in Japan. At age fourteen he returned to the United States. By age twenty-one, he was a fixture in the New York art scene, having made a reputation as a sculptor in the modernist European vein. But Noguchi would not forget his Japanese roots, and beginning in 1949 he visited Japan frequently. Soon his art reflected a fusion of East and West, as epitomized in his akari lamps. Critics agree that the element of timelessness lies at the core of Noguchi's design. As Herbert Muschamp of *The New York Times* once noted, timelessness, for Noguchi, is an antidote to the alienation and isolation he felt most of his life. Noguchi himself once commented, "To start a home all that is needed is a room, a pad, and akari."

What is Nisei Week?

Nisei Week is a week-long celebration of Japanese American culture held annually in Los Angeles's Little Tokyo, one of the oldest and most vibrant Japanese American communities in the continental United States. The first festivities in Los Angeles were held in 1934, in the midst of the Depression years, to help Little Tokyo's struggling economy by encouraging Japanese Americans to patronize shops in their own community. Since then, Nisei Week has been held each summer, except during the period of internment and the five years following the end of World War II. Similar celebrations also take place in the Japanese American communities in Honolulu and San Francisco.

Cultural festivities during Nisei Week include flower and bonsai arrangement demonstrations, classes in Japanese cooking and brush painting, tea ceremonies, traditional Japanese dance performances, athletic events, and a parade.

Where's the beef in Japanese cooking?

Beef made a relatively recent entrance into the Japanese culinary scene, due in part to the Buddhist tradition of vegetarianism and the scarcity of land for grazing in Japan. The Japanese depended on traditional sources of protein—fish, whale meat, and soy products, such as tofu, made from curdled soy milk, and miso, a fermented soybean paste—until 1872, when the Meiji emperor first tasted beef and declared it appropriate for the Japanese. While the Japanese slowly incorporated beef into their diet over the next century, they did not abandon traditional sources of protein, and thus beef plays a relatively minor role in the Japanese kitchen. Japanese

American restaurateurs and chefs on the cutting edge of Japanese nouvelle cuisine derive inspiration not from Old World cuisines in which beef plays a prominent role, but from the bounty of the Pacific and the rich harvests on shore, as well as California's lively blend of cultures.

What is sukiyaki?

Called the "friendship dish" in Japan because of its popularity with foreigners, *sukiyaki* is a delicious blend of bite-sized pieces of beef, onions, mushrooms, other vegetables, and occasionally tofu, simmered in a broth of soy sauce, sugar, and sake. In America and Japan, sukiyaki is often prepared right at the table.

What is sake?

Sake, a yellowish, slightly sweet rice wine, made by fermenting rice and then distilling it, is the national alcoholic drink of Japan. In ancient times, the rice for sake was fermented by a rather strange process. Shrine virgins chewed the grain and then spit it into casks, where an enzyme in their saliva set the fermenting process in motion. Nowadays, sake is made under more sanitary conditions.

Sake is often served hot or warm, especially in winter, and is a critical ingredient in Japanese cooking in Japan and America.

What is fugu and why has it been called Japanese roulette?

A *fugu* is a puffer fish (also called swellfish or blowfish) and is considered by the Japanese as the tastiest of all fish. Translated literally, the Japanese character for *fugu* means "river pig." Fugu is usually eaten sashimi style, that is, served raw in thin slices, and dipped in soy sauce flavored with wasabi, a green-colored, sharp and fiery Japanese horseradish.

Fugu is edible only for a few months of year. What further adds to its allure is that the fugu's liver and ovaries contain a poison so lethal that even a small amount could kill a person instantaneously. A slight trace of the poison produces a numbing effect in the diner's mouth that appeals to some Japanese. Nowadays fugu chefs have to be licensed, and although deaths from eating fugu are rare, sampling the fish is still a risky sport—a kind of Japanese roulette. Some Japanese and Japanese Americans lament that the strict requirements regarding fugu preparation have taken away some of the thrill of victory.

What are some of the more popular Japanese systems of martial arts practiced by Japanese Americans?

Karate, judo, and aikido are some of the most popular Japanese martial arts practiced by Japanese Americans as well as Americans of other ethnicities.

It is believed that the Buddhist monk Bhodidharma, credited with founding Zen Buddhism, also developed its parallel school of martial-arts-type training, which he brought to China in the sixth century A.D.

Bhodidharma founded the legendary Shaolin monastery in Hunan province, where Shaolin monks developed a skillful style of fighting, which combined acupuncture's knowledge of bodily nerve centers as vulnerable points with a system of unarmed physical combat. As this style spread, the Chinese modified it to suit their needs. Workers in the rice paddies of the south, with strong upper torsos, refined techniques emphasizing the arms, while the runners and horsemen of the northern plains accentuated kicking.

The styles of fighting that emerged in southern China were brought to the island of Okinawa, where they were further adapted. When Okinawa came under Japanese domination, and weapons possession was made illegal, the unarmed style of fighting became even more popular among Okinawans. The Japanese occupiers wore wooden armor, and so the Okinawans emphasized foot and hand conditioning so that they could destroy the armor.

In 1917, the Ministry of Education in Japan invited **Funakoshi Gichin**, a proponent of the Okinawan style of fighting, to give demonstrations. The Okinawan style soon caught on throughout Japan. Originally called *tang,* which is Chinese for "hand," the style was renamed *karate,* meaning "empty hand." The change in terminology was not only motivated by the increasingly anti-China sentiment in 1930s but also by the desire to introduce the Zen concept of "emptiness" to the style.

Karate was brought to the United States by American servicemen stationed in Japan after World War II, as well as by Japanese instructors who moved overseas in the late 1960s and early 1970s. Karate now enjoys great popularity in the United States.

Why is there so much yelling in karate?

The yell, called a *kiai,* is supposed to help the muscles contract, so that the individual's physical and mental energies completely converge when punching or kicking an opponent.

How do judo and aikido differ from karate?

All three are Japanese styles of fighting. However, while karate emphasizes punches and kicks, judo entails throws and grappling holds, and aikido wrist and hand locks.

Judo was founded in Japan in the nineteenth century by **Dr. Jigoro Kano**. Called the "way of gentleness," judo is based on the principle of least resistance. When faced with an opponent, the objective of a judo practitioner is to break the opponent's balance, move in under his or her center of gravity, located below the navel, and either throw the opponent or sweep the opponent off balance and immobilize him or her with a grappling hold.

Aikido was founded by **Morihei Uyeshiba** as a style of fighting based on the principle of non-resistance. The *ai* in *aikido* means "harmony," *ki* denotes "spirit" or "energy," and *do*, "the way." Aikido practitioners neutralize their opponent's attacks by coordinating their movements with the opponent's. Thus, if you are pushed, you go along with the push; if you are pulled, you go along with the pull. By "going with the flow," you channel your opponent's force so that he or she is knocked off balance. At that point, the attacker can be neutralized with maneuvers aimed at the attacker's weak points, for example, wrist twists or elbow locks. With the correct techniques, the gentle can subdue the strong.

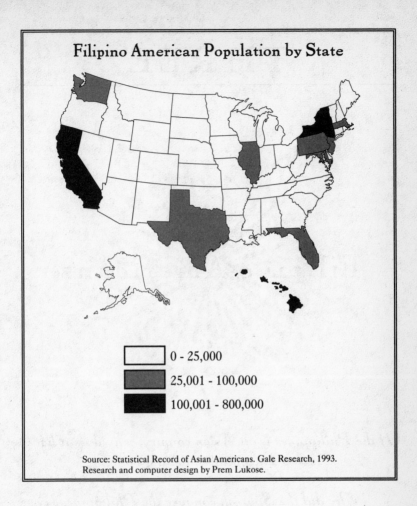

Filipino American Population by State

0 - 25,000

25,001 - 100,000

100,001 - 800,000

Source: Statistical Record of Asian Americans. Gale Research, 1993.
Research and computer design by Prem Lukose.

THREE

Filipino Americans

If the Philippines is an Asian country, why does it have such a European-sounding name?

Why did the Spanish conquer the Philippines?

Who were the Manilamen?

How did Roman Catholicism make its way to the Philippines?

Why do many Filipinos have Spanish names?

How did the Filipino rebellion against the Spanish
lead to United States domination
of the Philippines?

What legacy did the United States leave for the
Philippines and its people?

How did early Filipino immigration to the United
States differ from that of other Asian groups?

Who were the pensionados?

Why did Filipinos catch "Hawaiian fever"?

Did all the Filipino agricultural workers
head for Hawaii?

Why did Filipinas immigrate to America as part of the
second wave?

What was work like for the Filipinos in America?

What is the significance of America Is in the Heart?

Why did Filipinos get in a jam when they dated white
American women?

Could Filipinos and whites marry?

How did Filipinos fare in America during the
Great Depression?

What was the Tydings-McDuffie Act of 1934 and why was it bad news for Filipinos?

If Filipinos were legal aliens, why were they ineligible for U.S. citizenship?

Did Filipinos serve in the U.S. armed forces during World War II?

When did Filipinos resume immigrating to the United States in significant numbers?

What was the Immigration Act of 1965 and how did it affect Filipino immigration?

How is the third wave distinct from the second wave of Filipino immigrants?

How has the most recent group of Filipinos adjusted to American life?

Why are there no "Filipinotowns" in America and what impact does this have on Filipinos?

Are Filipino Americans becoming more visible?

Have Filipino Americans become politically empowered?

Who are some other prominent Filipino Americans?

What are some Filipino American holidays?

What foods do Filipino Americans like?

What is salabat?

How many ingredients are in halo-halo*?*

While Americans are somewhat versed in the culture and history of Japanese and Chinese Americans, most know relatively little about Filipino Americans. The reason is that they have long been a quiet and inconspicuous minority in the United States, though their number is actually quite sizable.

In fact, the 1990 census found that 1,406,770 Americans of Filipino ancestry reside in the United States, making them the second largest Asian American group. Many live in California, where the Filipino American population is larger than any other Asian group.

Filipino Americans have a unique place among Asian Americans because their history and destiny have been shaped largely by the United States—dating all the way back to the Spanish-American War.

If the Philippines is an Asian country, why does it have such a European-sounding name?

If you guessed "Spain," you're familiar with the mighty Spanish empire, which extended its sphere of influence to Latin America and Asia beginning in the early sixteenth century. The most striking evidence of Spanish domination in the Philippines is the country's name, taken from King Philip II of Spain.

Why did the Spanish conquer the Philippines?

While Japan and China contributed to shaping the history of the Philippines, the nation was most impacted by the rise of two empires many times zones away: Spain and later the United States.

Spanish involvement in the Philippines all began in 1521, when the explorer **Ferdinand Magellan** anchored off one of the pristine islands of this archipelago in the South China Sea during his voyage around the world, and claimed the lush land for Spain. The Filipinos were not as excited about Magellan as he was about their land. Six weeks later a native Filipino chief, Lapu-Lapu, killed the explorer in an act of resistance to Spanish rule. Spain refrained from retaliating full force and did not flex its muscles much in the Philippines until Philip II ascended the Spanish throne in 1556, vowing to increase the might of his empire and the Roman Catholic Church. Still, it took Spain until 1571 to subdue the Philippine natives completely. The Spanish domination thereafter proved mighty, lasting until the Spanish American War of 1898.

Who were the Manilamen?

During Philip II's reign, ambitious Spanish merchants swarmed the Philippines, intent on reaping megabucks. The merchants claimed exclusive trading rights in the Philippines, and transformed Manila into a major commercial port and trading center. The Spanish, who didn't want to give anyone else a piece of the pie, treated the Filipinos unjustly, stripping them of all privileges. Only the *illustrados*—natives with mostly Spanish blood—were given access to education, land, and high positions in the government.

The Spanish forced many Filipinos to labor as slaves or to join the Spanish armada and work along the trade routes linking the Philippines and Mexico. Many discontented Filipinos in the Spanish armada jumped ship at Acapulco, then a major port, and made their way north and east in the mid-1700s to the Louisiana Territory to settle in the bayous around New Orleans. There they established shrimping and fishing villages with names like Bayou Cholas, Manila Village, and St. Malo. They and their descendants, the first Filipinos on American soil, became known as Manilamen.

How did Roman Catholicism make its way to the Philippines?

With the merchants also came Spanish missionaries, who had the longest-lasting effect on the Filipinos. The missionaries were tremendously successful in their conversion efforts in the archipelago, managing to lure a large percentage of the indigenous population to Roman Catholicism. In 1946, approximately 80 percent of Filipinos followed Roman Catholicism, while only 6 percent belonged to the Philippine Independent Church, 4 percent adhered to Islam, and 2 percent to Protestantism. Even today, the vast majority of Filipinos and Filipino Americans are Roman Catholics.

Why do many Filipinos have Spanish names?

A colony is a colony. The Spanish not only impacted on the political, economic, and spiritual life in the Philippines, but also on the social structure. As the Filipino natives intermarried and interbred with their conquerors, they gradually assumed Spanish names. Thus their descendants bear distinctly Spanish names, such as Corazon Aquino, and converse in Spanish, almost as frequently as in the native languages of the Philippines. Due to the heavy Spanish presence, all Filipinos, regardless of their ethnic heritage, became more Westernized than their counterparts from other Asian countries.

How did the Filipino rebellion against the Spanish lead to United States domination of the Philippines?

The Filipinos never ceased in their efforts to rid the Philippines of Spanish rule. At the end of the nineteenth century, Filipino nationalists, under the command of Filipino revolutionary **Emilio Aguinaldo**, waged war against the Spanish to regain control of their nation. Aguinaldo allied himself and the independence movement with the United States, whose military might he was sure would bring Spain to its knees. In 1898 tensions between the United States and Spain mounted when the Americans promised to aid the Spanish colony of Cuba in its push for independence. Although the discord centered on Cuba, U.S. warships attacked the Spanish fleet in Manila Bay, signaling the start of the Spanish-American War. The Filipinos fought alongside the Americans, who promised them their independence in the event of a U.S. victory.

As Aguinaldo had predicted, the U.S. emerged victorious in the Spanish-American War in 1898 and ousted the Spanish from power in the Philippines. But the United States did not restore sovereignty to the Philippines as Aguinaldo had hoped. Instead, when the Treaty of Paris was signed, formally ending the war, control of the island nation passed from Spanish hands to American hands. The Philippines was declared a United States protectorate, not a sovereign nation free from foreign domination.

As the "protector," the United States would retain control of the Philippines until it judged the island nation fit to govern itself, that is, until it no longer was in the interest of American imperialists to control the country. Many Filipino nationalists were outraged by their new colonizers and rebelled against the American regime. Guerrilla fighting broke out between Filipino nationalists and the 100,000 American soldiers stationed in the Philippines to ensure a smooth transfer of power from Spain to the United States.

Guerrilla fighters intensified attacks in what became known as the Philippine-American War, although to downplay the bloodshed the United States dubbed the war an "insurrection." The little-publicized war was fierce and lasted until 1902, more than a year after the United States had captured the Filipino rebel leader Aguinaldo. Just as the Vietnam War stirred controversy in America, the war with the Philippines infuriated some Americans, including Mark Twain and

Andrew Carnegie, who protested the atrocities committed against Filipinos.

Though the "insurrection" was crushed, Filipino Muslim guerrilla fighters continued to rebel against American domination for many more years, until they too were finally subdued in 1913.

What legacy did the United States leave for the Philippines and its people?

Despite the rebels' resistance to foreign domination, the United States went to work "uplifting" a people whom it considered little more than savages and often referred to as "our little brown brothers." For one, the U.S. government instituted democracy based on the American model to set the stage for an eventual transition to independence for the Philippines. Americans also built roads, bridges, and railroads on the islands, and introduced a health program to eradicate tropical diseases.

In addition, the U.S. government set up a free public school system fashioned after the American one, including having English, not Tagalog or Spanish, as the language of instruction. The classrooms were open to all Filipino children, not just the *illustrados*. American teachers, called "Thomasites" because the first ones arrived on board the vessel the *St. Thomas*, came to the Philippines to instruct and "civilize" the native population, which further contributed to Westernizing the Filipinos. The Americans taught their Filipino students not about the history of their homeland, but rather about America's history, heroes, and values. Fully indoctrinated, Filipino children recited the "Pledge of Allegiance" to the American flag each morning and sang "The Star-Spangled Banner."

These lessons about American democracy and history had enormous ramifications on the future of the Philippines, for they inspired the first wave of Filipino immigration to America.

How did early Filipino immigration to the United States differ from that of other Asian groups?

With their long exposure at home to Western culture and the English language, those Filipinos who ventured to American shores before World War II experienced less culture shock and a smoother transition than other early Asian immigrants such as the Chinese and the Japanese, who knew little of the New World. Since they traveled as U.S. nationals with American passports, Filipinos, unlike other Asians, were not hampered by restrictions on entry into the United States—at least for the first few years. Even if they arrived with infectious diseases, as nationals they could not be turned away.

Although Filipinos were exempt from the discriminatory immigration legislation which virtually halted all Asian immigration to America from 1924 to 1941, they did not enjoy the privileges afforded American citizens. Like Chinese and Japanese aliens in America, Filipinos did not have the right to vote, own land, or attain U.S. citizenship.

Furthermore, they fell victim to the severe harassment and institutionalized racial discrimination that all Asians in the late 1800s and early 1900s suffered in America. Even worse, the white majority in America considered Filipinos the lowliest of all Asians, and so they suffered particularly brutal attacks. Their fellow Asians were just as unkind. Many Asians considered the Filipinos savage and filthy, and their habits strange, particularly their taste for wild weeds and grass, and their penchant for smoking and cockfights, the latter often ending in a brawl among the spectators. Asians generally believed rumors that all Filipinos wielded switchblades and were a threat to public safety.

Such negative stereotypes greatly hindered Filipinos in America. Still, their relative ease of movement to the United States, coupled with labor shortages in Hawaii, led thousands of Filipinos to set sail for America, especially in the 1920s, when the country was enjoying an economic boom. Before these economic migrants, though, came the *pensionados*, beginning in 1903.

Who were the pensionados?

The *pensionados* were Filipino students who traveled to America to pursue an education and to experience American life firsthand. They are generally considered the first significant wave of Filipino migration to the United States. From 1903 to 1910, in accordance with the Pensionado Act of 1903, the U.S. government handpicked the *pensionados* from among the Filipino best and brightest, arranged free secondary and post-secondary schooling for them in America, and put most up with host families. After completing their American studies, the majority of *pensionados* returned home, as the U.S. government had banked on, and secured positions of high status. They made valuable contributions to their island nation in fields such as agriculture, business, education, medicine, and government.

The U.S. government lent financial backing to the *pensionado* program only until 1910, but Filipino students, wishing to replicate the successes of the *pensionados* back in the Philippines, continued to come to America to expand their horizons. After 1910 Filipino students had to finance their education themselves. Some students' families mortgaged their houses to raise funds for college, hoping that their investment would pay off in the end. Often, this family support still fell short, and students were forced to drop out of school and take jobs as unskilled laborers to get by, a far cry from the elite posts they had envisioned themselves in back home.

Other students beat the odds and completed their studies at various colleges and universities, including Ivy League schools. Most successful students returned to the Philippines to assume high-ranking positions alongside the *pensionados*.

Why did Filipinos catch "Hawaiian fever"?

After the United States and Japan signed the Gentlemen's Agreement in 1908, which limited the importation of Japanese laborers to America, desperate Hawaiian sugar plantation owners began to eye the Filipinos as a source of cheap and efficient labor.

As soon as it could, the Hawaiian Sugar Planters' Association (HSPA) deployed recruiters to the Philippines to round up Filipino laborers for the sugar plantations. And so the second wave of Filipino immigration was unleashed, comprised of agricultural workers hungry for work.

Due to tough economic times and overpopulation in their territory, Filipinos of the Ilocano community were eager to take jobs as laborers in the Kingdom of Hawaii, particularly when recruiters offered them good pay. Enchanted by the stories of great riches to be made in Hawaii, many Filipinos soon came down with "Hawaiian fever."

The rags-to-riches stories were greatly exaggerated, of course, and many Filipinos were disappointed when they arrived in Hawaii. The "big" paychecks they earned on the Hawaiian sugar plantations hardly altered their standard of living, since higher prices in Hawaii rapidly depleted their income. The working conditions and living quarters, however, were good compared to what Filipinos would find in America.

Despite all the hardships on Hawaiian plantations, the HSPA's efforts to lure Filipino laborers to Hawaii were a huge success. From 1909 to 1934, some 119,470 Filipinos ventured to Hawaii to toil on sugar and pineapple plantations, hoping one day they would make their fortune and return home. Fully 86 percent of the recruits were men, since most Filipinas thought it unsavory to travel to Hawaii to work the land.

Did all the Filipino agricultural workers head for Hawaii?

No. Around the same time Filipino immigrant laborers set their sights on America but in much smaller numbers. In

1910, only 406 Filipinos lived in America, mostly in California. Soon the trickle became a flow, and by the 1920s, the number of Filipinos residing in California had jumped 91 percent. Over half of the Filipinos who migrated to California came via Hawaii.

The Filipinos in California worked in agriculture, often with Japanese Americans as their employers. They also provided cheap labor as domestic servants and hotel and restaurant workers. In Alaska they worked in the salmon canneries.

Why did Filipinas immigrate to America as part of the second wave?

The few women who were part of the second wave of immigration from the Philippines were driven to America for various reasons. Some immigrated to the United States to join their husbands or fiancés, who had already secured jobs as laborers. Other Filipinas came to pursue educational opportunities or professional training. Some women simply needed work to support their families and thought they would find suitable jobs in the United States.

Many Filipinas were able to obtain employment outside of agricultural and manual labor. Those with the qualifications managed to obtain the very semiprofessional and professional jobs in medicine, education, and business that Filipinos had been barred from in the United States.

What was work like for the Filipinos in America?

In America Filipinos found the same low-paying, back-breaking, sweaty jobs as in Hawaii. Filipinos working in agriculture had an even tougher time: conditions were cruel and wages were dreadful. These farmworkers, who called themselves *pinoys*, migrated from place to place with the crops, season after season. They endured "stoop labor," bending their weary backs under the scorching sun to tend the crops such as asparagus, tomatoes, berries, melons, apricots, peaches, grapes, and lettuce. The Filipinos usually did this physically draining labor six days a week from dawn to dusk. Sometimes the temperature in the fields was insufferable, reaching well above 100 degrees. If that was not bad enough, the dust from the fields mixed with the workers' sweat causing them to itch unbearably.

After work, the crowded makeshift shelters and inedible food provided little relief. As one *pinoy* recalled, "The bunkhouse was . . . crowded with men. There was no sewage disposal. When I ate swarms of flies fought over my plate. . . . I slept on a dirty cot: the blanket was never washed."

Filipinos who found work unloading, cleaning, cutting, and packing salmon in the canneries of Alaska were also victimized by ruthless employers. Hours in the dank, dark, and dismal canneries were long and tiring, and the work was fraught with health hazards. **Carlos Bulosan**, a Filipino immigrant, recounted a harrowing experience he had in an Alaskan salmon cannery in the 1930s: "I was working in a section called the 'wash lye.' Actually a certain amount of lye was diluted in the water where I washed the beheaded fish that came down on a small escalator. One afternoon a cutter above me, working in the poor light, slashed off his right arm with the cutting machine. It happened so swiftly he did not cry out. I saw his arm floating down the water among the fish heads."

Not only did Filipinos in the salmon canneries face extraordinary perils on the job, but they were paid less for their hardship than non-Asian employees. To make matters worse, the cannery owners withheld wages from the Filipinos' paychecks to cover "room and board." The Filipino immigrants were appalled that after months of grueling labor they pocketed virtually no money. When they tried to spend the little they earned at stores or restaurants, they often encountered inflammatory signs like "No Dogs or Filipinos Allowed."

What is the significance of America Is in the Heart?

America Is in the Heart is the touching "personal history" of **Carlos Bulosan**, a Filipino immigrant who came to the United States in search of the American dream. Published in 1946, *America Is in the Heart* became the voice for thousands of silent Filipinos who fought to survive in the harsh New World.

Born in the town of Binalonan on November 24, 1913, Carlos Bulosan spent the first seventeen years of his life in the Philippines. The archipelago nation was by then a U.S. colony and the American presence was clearly evident in Binalonan. American entrepreneurs pursuing business ventures in the region took up residence in the large white houses around town, and American tourists hungrily snapped photos of the Filipinos, a people they considered savage and primitive. Bulosan recalled, "One day an American lady tourist asked me to undress before her camera, and gave me ten centavos for doing it. I had found a simple way to make a living. Whenever I saw a white person in the market with a camera, I made myself conspicuously ugly, hoping to earn ten centavos."

Inspired by the example of Abraham Lincoln, who rose from abject poverty to the presidency, Bulosan sailed with high hopes to America in 1930. Hope soon turned to anguish, when with empty pockets, he unwittingly signed up to work in an Alaskan salmon cannery. After enduring a season with little pay to show for his labor, he became a migrant farmer, harvesting produce wherever he could. As he crisscrossed America, Bulosan experienced firsthand the blatant racism and violence aimed at Filipinos, and his American dream swiftly became a nightmare.

In the Philippines, American teachers had not taught Bulosan about the volatile racial climate in America that made minorities with a darker shade of skin vulnerable to physical attacks and harassment. He had not expected the brutality of America's racists and felt immensely betrayed. He wrote earlier of how his education in the Philippines conflicted with the reality of life in the United States: "Western people are brought up to regard Orientals or colored peoples as inferior, but the mockery of it all is that Filipinos are taught to regard Americans as our equals. Adhering to American ideals, living American life, these are contributory to our feeling of equality. The terrible truth in America shatters the Filipinos' dream of fraternity."

Carlos Bulosan died on American soil on September 13, 1956. His legacy lives on through *America Is in the Heart*, a poignant and vivid portrayal of the early Filipino experience in America.

Why did Filipinos get in a jam when they dated white American women?

The great majority of Filipino immigrants of the first and second waves were single men. The absence of Filipinas led many Filipinos to seek female companions outside of their enclaves. This caused the Filipinos no angst since they had long been exposed to Western ways in their homeland as a result of colonialism. They were generally relaxed about mingling with other ethnic groups, and had witnessed a number of Spanish-Filipino marriages.

This was dramatically different from the practices of Japanese male immigrants, who seldom socialized with non-Japanese women and placed their hopes on "picture brides," who were essentially wives they imported from Japan. While discriminatory laws on the American books forbidding interracial marriage contributed to the Japanese men's behavior, they were mainly governed by an intense desire to preserve ethnic purity. This was true for the early waves of Chinese and Korean immigrants as well.

The Filipinos' interest in white women scandalized American nativists and exclusionists. They clamored for Filipino exclusion from the United States, claiming that Filipinos posed a threat to white women's welfare. One racist judge expressed his views on the matter thus: "It is a dreadful thing when the Filipinos, scarcely more than savages, come to San Francisco, work for practically nothing, and obtain the society of these [white] girls. . . . Some of these [Filipino] boys . . . have told me bluntly and boastfully that they practice the art of love with more perfection than white boys, and occasionally one of the [white] girls has supplied me information to the same effect."

Despite such widespread condemnation of their social lives, Filipino men continued to seek the companionship of white women. Many Filipino laborers frequented dance halls to break the monotony of their workaday existence, and relax and socialize with women. Filipino men showed off their dancing skills in an attempt to woo the women. They would buy tickets to dance for about ten cents, and their lady partners would tear one off every minute or so. In this way, the Filipinos easily danced the day's pay away, but a few minutes of sheer pleasure outweighed the cost. Some found love, but others found heartbreak.

Those who found love stepped on a hornet's nest. Interracial couples often endured society's scorn, gossip, and cruel remarks, an immense strain on already fragile relationships. Restaurants and other establishments sometimes refused to serve interracial couples. Cruelty was not reserved just for Filipino men; their white wives were sometimes called "nigger lovers." Wishing to avoid such confrontations, many couples tried to stay out of public view.

Could Filipinos and whites marry?

These interracial couples also faced legal barriers in the form of anti-miscegenation laws. Initially, Filipinos were able to marry white women, since the anti-miscegenation laws only barred marriages between whites and persons with African or Mongolian blood. Since Filipinos are largely descendants of the Malay, they were able to bypass this law and legally marry white women.

However, racism ruled the day, and state legislators quickly revised their statutes to ban marriages between whites and those of the Malay race. Thus, Filipinos who wanted to marry white women had to travel to states where such marriages had legal sanction. Even after obtaining a marriage certificate, these couples were often harassed by legislators who often sought to suspend the women's rights to citizenship as punishment for breaking social strictures.

Due to the difficulties courtship with white women posed, Filipinos fraternized and intermarried with Mexican women quite frequently. Filipino men often found they had an affinity with Mexican women, as a result of the Spanish domination in the Philippines. Furthermore, the laws regarding intermarriage generally did not prohibit Filipinos and Mexicans from exchanging vows, and laws that did were not rigorously enforced. Even nativists and exclusionists refrained for the most part from harassing these interracial couples, and society as a whole was generally more accepting.

How did Filipinos fare in America during the Great Depression?

The Great Depression was a trying time for all Americans, and not surprisingly, people of color endured tremendous suffering.

In terms of racism, the Great Depression changed an already delicate situation into a fiasco for Filipinos in the United States. Desperate from the shortage of jobs across the country, racists often blamed their misfortunes on immigrants. They accused the Filipinos of stealing their jobs and scorned them for working for such low wages. In their eyes, Filipinos were unfair competition. Mob violence at Filipino workplaces became a frequent occurrence in the Depression years.

What was the Tydings-McDuffie Act of 1934 and why was it bad news for Filipinos?

The plight of Filipinos during the Depression worsened after the passage of the Tydings-McDuffie Act of 1934, also called the Philippine Independence Act, which altered their status from nationals to aliens.

The Tydings-McDuffie Act of 1934 was the triumph of years of effort by exclusionists and nativists in Congress who wanted to put an end to Filipino immigration. Previously, Filipino nationals were exempt from legislation that excluded the immigration of Chinese, Japanese, and eventually all person of the Mongoloid race. As wards of the United States, Filipinos were in a unique situation. As long as the American flag flew over the Philippines, Filipinos could not be barred from entering the United States.

Thus, certain members of Congress ingeniously proposed a solution to the Filipino problem. They would grant the Philippines its independence so that its citizens, now residing in an independent country, could be excluded along with other "undesirable" immigrants.

The Tydings-McDuffie Act, enacted on March 24, 1934, gave the Philippines commonwealth status and promised the islands independence in ten years. However, such promises merely masked the true intent of the legislation— Filipino exclusion. The Tydings-McDuffie Act limited Filipino immigration to the United States to just fifty persons per year. Furthermore, Filipinos in Hawaii were restricted from moving from Hawaii to the United States, and they were all reclassified as "aliens" rather than nationals. After successful lobbying, the Hawaiian Sugar Planters' Association also convinced Congress to allot additional spaces for Filipino immigrants to Hawaii, where cheap labor was needed.

Thus, the Tydings-McDuffie Act brought a screeching halt to Filipino immigration to the United States. Senator **Millard**

Tydings defended the Tydings-McDuffie Act by declaring that "It is absolutely illogical to have an immigration policy to exclude Japanese and Chinese and permit Filipinos en masse to come into the country. . . . If they continue to settle in certain areas they will come in conflict with white labor . . . and increase the opportunity for more racial prejudice and bad feelings of all kinds."

Some Americans wanted to go a few steps beyond prohibiting Filipino immigration, and clamored for the deportation of those Filipinos already established in the United States. In response, Congress passed yet another piece of anti-Filipino legislation, the Repatriation Act of 1935, which allowed for the allotment of funds for transportation to all Filipinos who wished to return to their homeland. Some Filipinos accepted the offer, but the vast majority declined, believing that though the racial and economic climate in the United States was almost unbearable, conditions in the Philippines were not much better. The Repatriation Act of 1935 succeeded in relocating only 2,190 Filipinos from the United States to the Philippines, a major disappointment for American exclusionists and nativists.

During the Great Depression, Filipinos without jobs or financial resources managed to survive on public assistance. However, Congress jeopardized the survival of Filipinos with the passage of the Relief Appropriation Act of 1937, which gave preference for relief assistance first to citizens, then to aliens with the right to become citizens. Filipinos were by now considered aliens ineligible for citizenship, and so they were cut off from public assistance. Since they could not find work and were ineligible for assistance, many returned home. In the 1930s the immigration of Filipinos to California cooled down considerably. Hawaii's Filipino population dwindled between 1930 and 1940. In 1931 4,768 Filipino immigrants went to Hawaii, while the very next year only 232 arrived there. From 1932 to 1936 only 402 Filipinos went to Hawaii.

If Filipinos were legal aliens, why were they ineligible for U.S. citizenship?

Although they were first categorized as U.S. nationals and then legal aliens, Filipinos were by and large ineligible for citizenship before 1946. The laws governing citizenship in effect at that time extended naturalization rights only to white and black immigrants. Legislation passed in 1925 made an exception for those Filipinos who had served in the United States armed forces for at least three years. Though most Filipinos were little more than mess attendants in the military, they were granted the right to apply for citizenship. With naturalization papers in hand, these Filipinos could no longer be legally excluded from the benefits U.S. citizens enjoyed. They had access to professions and licenses previously denied them as nationals and aliens. Still, though, they were not protected from racial harassment.

Did Filipinos serve in the U.S. armed forces during World War II?

During World War II, many Filipinos entered the U.S. armed forces and fought bravely to defend American interests. The War Department drafted Filipinos and organized them into a segregated regiment. Filipino contributions in the military were badly needed during World War II because the so-called "enemy" West Coast Japanese had been evacuated to internment camps for the duration of the war. The incarceration of the Japanese also left a huge void in West Coast agriculture that needed to be filled quickly to feed the nation as well as American GIs overseas.

World War II delayed the independence of the Philippines until 1946. Before the war had ended the public warmed to the Filipinos as a result of their valiant efforts to defeat the enemy, Imperial Japan. Thus, just before granting the Philippines sovereignty on July 2, 1946, Congress enacted legislation that extended naturalization rights to those Filipinos who had come to America before 1934. Some Filipinos wondered what purpose naturalization served, since many Americans still considered them "brown-skinned inferiors."

When did Filipinos resume immigrating to the United States in significant numbers?

Immigration from the Philippines began to pick up after World War II. The end of the Great Depression and the advent of a post-war economic boom provided abundant employment opportunities for Filipinos. However, the strict quota on Filipino immigration dictated by the Tydings-McDuffie Act of 1934 was still in place. Nonetheless, following World War II, many Filipinas circumvented the quotas by becoming the war brides of Filipino and white soldiers who had served in the United States armed forces. Consequently, the Filipino population in America exploded despite the quota. In just two decades, from 1940 to 1960, the Filipino population in the United States jumped by 78,000.

What was the Immigration Act of 1965 and how did it affect Filipino immigration?

The Immigration Act of 1965 liberalized immigration from Asia and unleashed the third wave of Filipino immigration. Overnight Filipinos became one of the largest immigrant groups in the United States. Many third-wave Filipino immigrants settled in California.

How is the third wave distinct from the second wave of Filipino immigrants?

While Filipinos of the second wave of immigration were primarily laborers, the majority of third-wave Filipinos were white-collar professionals. Once in America, many experienced difficulty securing positions in their field because they had to meet stringent U.S. certification requirements. Those who failed had to settle for jobs below their capabilities. For example, dentists from the Philippines were forced to work as dental aides in the United States unless they underwent more training. Even so, these immigrants were the first Filipinos to bypass the exhausting, low-paying jobs in domestic service and agricultural labor for positions in respected professions.

The post-1965 immigration era also brought many Filipinas to American shores. In 1960, women constituted 37.1 percent of immigrants from the Philippines. A decade later that figure rose to 45.6 percent. By 1980 the ratio of male and female immigrants from the Philippines balanced out even more, with women constituting 51.7 percent of the total Filipino immigrant population in America.

Filipino women played a critical role in the assimilation process. They married and started families that slowly sank roots into the American soil. At the same time, they worked to preserve Filipino heritage in America. They also tended to be financial providers in the family. Many were employed outside of the home, especially as nurses. Generations of Filipino women have been very successful in America and have participated in the labor force more than the women of other Asian American groups.

How has the most recent group of Filipinos adjusted to American life?

The most recent Filipino immigrants are on the whole well educated. Nonetheless, studies show that Filipinos in America continue to suffer from underemployment. Unlike other Asian immigrant groups, such as the Koreans, Filipinos own few businesses and have not flexed their entrepreneurial muscles. This may be attributed in part to their fine command of the English language, which allows them greater flexibility in the job market.

Why are there no "Filipinotowns" in America and what impact does this have on Filipinos?

In general, Filipinos in America exhibit less allegiance to their compatriots than do other Asians. Historically Filipinos have had difficulty preserving their cultural heritage and values due to the forces of colonialism that ravaged their homeland for centuries on end. Filipino culture was diluted by the Spanish and Americans, and thus Filipinos are not bound together by cultural pride. Nor do they have a single language.

The Chinese, Japanese, and Koreans in America all have their ethnic enclaves, their Chinatowns, Little Tokyos, and Koreatowns. Even more recent groups of immigrants like the Vietnamese have preserved their strong ethnic ties, as evidenced by the Little Saigons in Westminster, California, and Arlington, Virginia. Although Filipinos are the second-largest Asian group in the United States, they tend not to establish close-knit ethnic communities that serve as centers of social activity and bind the generations together. This is not to say that Filipino Americans never stick together. After all, California cities such as Los Angeles boast large Filipino communities. However, compared to other Asian Americans, Filipino Americans have dropped the clan mentality and embraced Western individualism.

This lack of cohesion and community has resulted in a collective identity crisis, as this second-generation Filipino described: "I'm still trying to find myself ethnically. . . . We have no model. . . . We have no recognition in terms of celebrated people. We have no political power. We have no Sony Corporation. We don't have anything to grab onto because the first generation never gave us anything. I have no sense of oral tradition. . . . There's no art. We don't have the dandy restaurants the majority can identify with. We have nothing. If you look at all the Asian groups . . . they're part of the successful American dream. I can't say that."

Chances are that this situation will not change. Filipino

youth, with no community to turn to, learn little about their ancestral heritage and thus inherit precious little to pass on to the next generation. American schools do not hold the answer, since most fail to include even survey courses on Asian history in their curriculums. To compound the felony, the media pay little attention to Filipino Americans in comparison to Americans of Chinese, Japanese, and Vietnamese ancestry.

Are Filipino Americans becoming more visible?

To combat the collective Filipino identity crisis, some Filipino Americans are fighting for visibility by promoting cultural awareness and ethnic pride. For example, the mostly Filipino Kababayan Club of the University of California at Irvine (UCI) recently staged a play that showcased Filipino cuisine, music, dance, and customs, and portrayed a Filipina American discovering her cultural heritage. Due to the Kababayan Club's efforts to increase awareness about Filipino culture on campus, a course on Filipino Americans is now offered regularly at UCI.

Similarly, other Filipino activists are working to provide a voice for America's invisible minority, urging Filipino Americans to unite and fight prejudice and discrimination in their midst.

Have Filipino Americans become politically empowered?

Not yet. Considering the size of the Filipino population in certain states like Hawaii and California, Filipino Americans have long been underrepresented in government at the local, state, and national levels. While Filipinos have been quiet in the political arena, they have not been silent. A handful of Filipino Americans have held elected office, and current trends indicate that the Filipino community is becoming more politically active.

In the past Filipinos tended to ignore politics and concentrate on establishing themselves and their families. Their financial survival was their primary concern. However, as Filipino Americans have found financial stability, they have begun to look toward empowerment in the political arena.

The first Filipino Americans elected to public office were in Hawaii, where the Asian majority provided support to Filipinos seeking public office. As early as 1955, a Filipino by the name of **Peter Aduja** held a seat in Hawaii's territorial legislature. Aduja was born in the Philippines and immigrated to America at age eight. His schooling in the United States led to a law degree from the Boston University School of Law. Aduja served a single term in Hawaii's territorial legislature before Hawaii governor Samuel B. King appointed him deputy attorney general. After Hawaii achieved statehood in 1959, Aduja served in Hawaii's House of Representatives for three terms.

Another Filipino American, **Bernaldo D. Bicoy**, was elected to Hawaii's House of Representatives in 1958. That same year, **Pedro de la Cruz**, a Philippines-born immigrant, was elected to the state's lower house. He continued to serve in Hawaii's legislature for many years. Other notable Filipinos who have held public office in Hawaii include **Eduardo E. Malapit**, the first Filipino mayor in the island chain. He earned this distinction in 1975, when his constituents elected him mayor of Kauai. In 1962, Hawaiian-born **Alfred Lareta** became the first Filipino American appointed to a seat in Hawaii's state cabinet, where he served as the director of the Department of Labor and Industrial Relations. In 1974, Filipina American **Thelma Garcia Buchholdt** achieved a political first when she was elected in a predominantly white district to serve in the House of Representatives in Alaska, a position she held until 1983.

In California, during the 1970s and 1980s, only a few Filipino Americans were elected to public office, usually on the local level. However, between 1980 and 1990 the Filipino American community in California more than doubled in size, and in some cities the growth rate was even higher. For example, Los Angeles County saw its Filipino American population swell by 122 percent, from 99,043 to 219,653. Along with this growth, though not yet commensurate with it, more and more Filipinos are taking action. Carson, California, which boasted a Filipino American community of 14,100 in 1990, elected its first Filipino American to the city council in 1992. And in June of 1993, Daly City, where Filipino Americans constitute a third of the population, followed suit by electing its first Filipino American, **Michael Guingona**, to the city council.

In the near future, Filipino Americans will undoubtedly seek office in greater numbers, putting to rest their reputation as America's silent minority.

Who are some other prominent Filipino Americans?

José Espiritu Aruego, a Filipino American book illustrator who draws upon his childhood experiences in the Philippines for his artwork, has illustrated over sixty books, of which he wrote at least ten. Born in the Philippines in 1932, Aruego came to the United States to study graphic art and advertising at the Parsons School of Design in New York City. His cartoons have appeared in such magazines as the *Saturday Evening Post, Look*, and *The New Yorker*. In 1969 he published his first children's book, *The King and His Friends*, and in 1970 he published *Whose Mouse Are You?* which was selected as an American Library Association Notable Book. In 1970 he also published *Juan and the Asuangs*, which captured the Outstanding Picture Book of the Year Award from *The New York Times*. In 1976 the illustrator visited the Philippines after being named the Outstanding Filipino Abroad in Arts.

The Filipina American writer **Jessica Taraheta Hagedorn** made her debut as a novelist in 1990 with the publication of her highly acclaimed *Dogeaters*, which was nominated for the National Book Award that year. The title of the novel makes reference to the racial epithet Americans used to hurl at Filipinos in their midst. In 1993 Hagedorn published her much talked-about work *Danger and Beauty*. That year also saw the publication of *Charlie Chan Is Dead: An Anthology of Contemporary Asian American Fiction*, a groundbreaking collection edited by Hagedorn.

In art, Filipino American **Orlando S. Lagman**, who once served as a U.S. seaman, became one of the leading portrait painters of his day. Lagman was given the honor of painting the official portrait of presidents Dwight D. Eisenhower, John F. Kennedy, Lyndon B. Johnson, and Richard M. Nixon.

Filipina American opera singer **Dalisay Aldaba** is known throughout the world. Highlights of her career include the leading role in the New York City Opera's 1948 production of *Madame Butterfly*. In ballet, Filipina American **Maniya Barreda** captivates audiences as prima ballerina with the Atlanta Ballet, one of America's most prestigious dance companies. She has worked with Mikhail Baryshnikov, Alicia Alonso, Maya Plisetskaya, and Burton Taylor, and has received the Philippines Award for Best Classical Performer Abroad.

The many Filipino American world-class athletes include **Vicki Manalo Draves**, who in 1948 made Olympic history as the first woman to win gold in both the platform and springboard diving events. In 1969 she was inducted into the International Swimming Hall of Fame. **Roman Gabriel** was an all-American quarterback for North Carolina State University who went on to achieve fame in professional football. He played with the Los Angeles Rams and the Philadelphia Eagles for a total of eleven years. Among his many distinctions, Roman Gabriel was named the National Football League's Most Valuable Player and Player of the Year in 1969.

TWENTY-EIGHT IMPORTANT BOOKS WRITTEN BY ASIAN AMERICANS

1. Carlos Bulosan, *America Is in the Heart* (1946)

2. Yutang Lin, *Chinatown Family* (1948)

3. Hisaya Yamamoto, *The Legend of Miss Sasagawara* (1950)

4. Jade Snow Wong, *Fifth Chinese Daughter* (1950)

5. Monica Sone, *Nisei Daughter* (1953)

6. Chin Yang Lee, *Flower Drum Song* (1957)

7. John Okada, *No-No Boy* (1957)

8. Louis Chu, *Eat a Bowl of Tea* (1961)

9. Richard Kim, *Lost Names* (1970)

10. Frank Chin, *The Year of the Dragon* (1974)

11. Maxine Hong Kingston, *The Woman Warrior* (1976)

12. Shawn Hsu Wong, *Homebase* (1979)

13. Joy Kogawa, *Obasan* (1981)

14. Yoshiko Uchida, *A Jar of Dreams* (1981)

15. Yoshiko Uchida, *Desert Exile* (1982)

16. Yoshiko Uchida, *The Best Bad Thing* (1983)

17. Kim Ronyoung, *Clay Walls* (1986)

18. Yoshiko Uchida, *Picture Bride* (1987)

19. Cynthia Kadohata, *The Floating World* (1989)

20. Amy Tan, *The Joy Luck Club* (1989)

21. Amy Tan, *The Kitchen God's Wife* (1991)

22. Gish Jen, *Typical American* (1991)

23. Gus Lee, *China Boy* (1991)

24. David Wong Louie, *Pangs of Love* (1991)

25. Lydia Yuri Minatoya, *Talking to the High Monks in the Snow* (1992)

26. Garrett Hongo, *The Open Boat* (1993)

27. Nina Vida, *Goodbye, Saigon* (1994)

28. Julie Shigekuni, *A Bridge Between Us* (1995)

What are some Filipino American holidays?

Since most Filipino Americans are Roman Catholic, church celebrations such as baptisms, confirmations, weddings, and anniversaries figure prominently in their lives. On such occasions Filipino Americans are apt to throw big parties, just as they do in the Philippines.

No holidays are celebrated with as much joy, however, as Holy Week, Easter, and Christmas. Christmas celebrations traditionally begin a week before the holy day, and Filipino Americans celebrate an early mass each day leading up to Christmas. The highlight of the week is the *Misa de Gallo*, the midnight Christmas Eve mass. In the days before the *Misa de Gallo* Filipinos hold competitions to see who can build the largest *parol*, or lantern, for the occasion. The *parol* is a symbol of the Christmas tree. Christmas Eve celebrations continue with a *panunulayan*, a traditional procession through the streets: a woman dressed as Mary and a man as Joseph lead the procession and reenact the story of Christ's birth. The procession ends at the church with mass and the celebration of the birth. The rites surrounding the birth of Christ continue during fiesta season in January, ten days of daily Mass in honor of Christ meant to focus the community's attention on the values of charity and understanding. The holiday ends with the Feast of El Niño, climaxing with a procession in which the Christ child is brought to the church.

Many Filipino American organizations see to it that cultural traditions are not lost by promoting Filipino secular holidays. Filipino Americans celebrate secular holidays with traditional Filipino music provided by a *rondalla*, or string band. Couples also perform traditional folk dances, such as the *fandango saw ila*, which demands dexterity since each dancer must balance an oil lamp on top of the head and in each hand. *Tinikling* dancers also perform intricate dances over and around bamboo poles.

Another enduring Filipino custom, kept alive in America, is the beauty pageant, held during every festival. Yet another is cockfighting, known to Filipinos as *sabong*, in which prize roosters fight to the death. While cockfighting has been illegal in the United States for quite some time, Filipino Americans have kept the tradition going—and the gambling that accompanies it.

What foods do Filipino Americans like?

Filipino Americans are fans of both American cooking and the distinctive cuisine of the Philippines. In Los Angeles, Filipinos might eat Mexican tacos, pizza, or other popular

"American" grub, or frequent Manila-based chains like Mami King, Max's Chicken, and Goldilocks, and shop at Asian Ranch Supermarket, the biggest Filipino market in California.

East meets West in the Filipino kitchen, as in the culture, and Malayan, Chinese, Japanese, Spanish, and American influences are readily apparent. Spanish cooking methods such as *adobado* (marinading) and *guisado* (sautéing) are popular in Filipino cooking. And Old World dishes on the Filipino menu, such as *arroz valenciana* (a chicken and rice dish), *menudo* (pork stew), and *empanadas* (flaky beef or chicken turnovers), reflect centuries of Spanish dominance. Like the Spanish, Filipinos enjoy an afternoon snack called a *merienda*.

Asian flavors also assert themselves in Philippine cuisine: no main dish is complete without steamed rice, the staple of Asian cooking. And Filipinos feast on dishes popular in Asian countries such as *pancit Canton*, fried noodles (which are Chinese in origin), and *lumpia*, Filipino fried egg rolls, filled with pork and vegetables and served with a distinctive vinegar and garlic sauce.

Reflecting Western influences, Philippine cuisine is characterized by mild seasoning, with garlic, palm vinegar, green tamarind, coconut milk, and the *calamansi*, a tiny lime, figuring prominently. Filipinos also flavor their food with native sauces like *patis* and *bagoong*, both with a fermented fish base.

Filipinos are particularly fond of barbecued and fried meats and fish. In fact, *sinangag* (fried rice) is often served for breakfast with a side of *longanisa* (pan-fried marinated pork patties), *tapa* (thinly sliced pan-fried marinated beef), or *tocino* (thinly sliced pan-fried marinated pork).

Favorite desserts include the Spanish-inspired *leche flan* and *bibingkang Malagkit*, a traditional sticky rice cake.

What is salabat?

A popular drink among Filipino Americans is *salabat*, a sweet and fragrant hot tea made with fresh ginger root and sugar.

Filipino Americans drink *salabat* when they need an energy boost. *Salabat* might be served at *merienda*.

How many ingredients are in halo-halo?

First of all, *halo-halo* is a wild 'n' crazy Filipino milkshake. It is usually concocted from about ten ingredients, including jackfruit, sweet red beans, coconut, egg custard, red gelatin, and milk. *Halo-halo* is sometimes served with a scoop of ice cream.

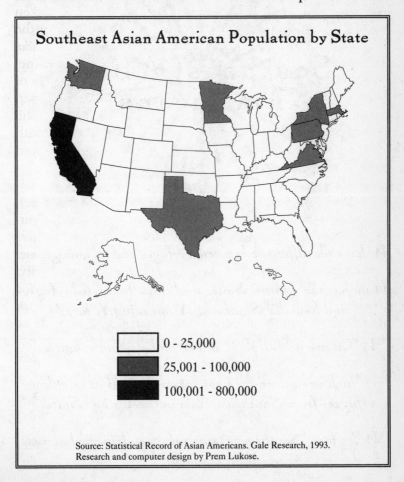

Southeast Asian American Population by State

0 - 25,000

25,001 - 100,000

100,001 - 800,000

Source: Statistical Record of Asian Americans. Gale Research, 1993.
Research and computer design by Prem Lukose.

FOUR

Southeast Asian
Americans

What's the difference between a refugee and an immigrant?

How has the United States traditionally treated refugees and how did Southeast Asian refugees fare?

What are first-asylum and second-asylum countries?

Which organizations have taken the lead in resettling refugees from Southeast Asia in the United States?

Why were Southeast Asian refugees dispersed across the country?

What is the 1.5 generation?

VIETNAMESE AMERICANS

What events in Vietnamese history led up to the mass exodus of Vietnamese to the United States in the twentieth century?

Did the Vietnamese rebel against French rule and who was Ho Chi Minh?

But wasn't Ho Chi Minh an American ally?

Why was the United States after World War II seen by some Vietnamese as yet another foreign interloper?

How was Vietnam divided into North Vietnam and South Vietnam?

How did the United States get involved in Vietnam?

How did the South Vietnamese feel about their American allies?

What was the Tet Offensive of 1968?

Besides Hippies, Jane Fonda, Bill Clinton, and Eastern Establishment intellectuals, who else opposed the war in Vietnam?

When did the Vietnam War finally end?

Why do many South Vietnamese blame the "leopard spot" arrangement of the Paris Peace Agreement for the loss of the South?

Why then did the South Vietnamese sign the Paris Peace Agreement?

By what means would the United States be able to "react vigorously" to a North Vietnamese violation of the peace agreement?

Is the term Vietnam War inaccurate?

Did the Vietnamese first come to America after the fall of Saigon in 1975?

Where were the refugees housed in 1975?

Who were the Vietnamese boat people?

Who are the Amerasians?

How have the Vietnamese adjusted to life in the United States?

How has the Vietnamese family structure been affected by life in America?

How have Vietnamese youth adjusted to the American school system?

How serious is the Vietnamese gang problem?

What does "throw out the anchor" mean?

How did the Vietnamese American community react to President Clinton's decision in 1994 to lift the trade embargo against Vietnam?

What is Little Saigon?

Who are Kieu Chinh and Le Ly Hayslip?

How have the Vietnamese had a head start over most other Asians in learning English?

What religions do Vietnamese Americans follow?

What is Cao Dai and do its followers really worship the French writer Victor Hugo, author of Les Misérables?

Who is Supreme Master Ching Hai?

What is the significance of Tet for Vietnamese Americans?

What foods do Vietnamese Americans enjoy?

What are cha gio?

What are the dos and don'ts of using chopsticks at a Vietnamese table?

What is a pho restaurant?

LAOTIAN AMERICANS

Who are the Laotians?

What historical events contributed to Laotian emigration to the United States?

Who are the Hmong and why was the CIA interested in them?

Why did the Laotians flee in such great numbers after the Pathet Lao gained control of the country in 1975?

How difficult has it been for refugees from Laos to adjust to American life?

Which Hmong customs are illegal in America?

Why do Hmong women have such a high birthrate?

What is sudden unexplained death syndrome?

What is phi?

CAMBODIAN AMERICANS

What is the story behind the arrival of Cambodians in the United States?

What were "the killing fields"?

How did Pol Pot's killing fields end?

How many Cambodians made their way to America?

What special problems have the Cambodians dealt with in the United States?

Why have so many Cambodian women in the United States gone blind?

Why are there so many single-parent Cambodian households in America?

Where have the Cambodian refugees settled in the United States?

Why did Lowell, Massachusetts, draw so many Cambodians?

How difficult has it been for Cambodians to acculturate to the American way of life?

What kinds of jobs have Cambodian Americans found?

Who is Dith Pran?

Who was Haing Ngor?

How did the 1993 elections in Cambodia affect Cambodian refugees in America?

Do Cambodians celebrate the New Year in the same way as the Vietnamese?

Do Cambodian Americans have their own restaurants?

Southeast Asian refugees began coming to America in significant numbers relatively recently, beginning in the 1970s for the most part.

Southeast Asians are a diverse group ethnically, culturally, and geographically, and include the Vietnamese; the ethnic Lao, Mien, and Hmong of Laos; the Khmer of Cambodia; the Thai (whose population in the United States doubled to 91,275 between 1980 and 1990); and the various ethnic groups of Indonesia, Myanmar, Brunei, Singapore, and Malaysia. Refugees from Vietnam, Laos, and Cambodia constitute the majority of Southeast Asians in America. The 1990 U.S. census counted 593,213 Vietnamese Americans, 147,375 Laotian Americans, and 149,047 Cambodian Americans. Discussion will be limited to those three groups.

What's the difference between a refugee and an immigrant?

The fundamental difference between refugees and immigrants lies in the circumstances surrounding their departure from their homeland. Refugees are forced to leave their native land due to fear of or experiences of persecution based on race, religion, nationality, social class, or political ideology. Refugees usually have little time or means to prepare for their journey. Most flee without any certainty as to how they will make the trip or where they will end up. Thus, many refugees who come to America are, in all likelihood, unprepared psychologically, financially, and emotionally for resettlement.

Immigrants, by contrast, usually leave their homeland voluntarily in search of better economic opportunities abroad and a promising future for themselves and their families and are thus better prepared. Asian immigration in the 1800s was on the whole economic in nature. For instance, the promise of jobs lured many Chinese to America during the Gold Rush, and many Japanese to sugar plantations in Hawaii beginning in the 1880s.

While immigrants have had no access to welfare programs in America and must pull themselves up by their own bootstraps, refugees have been eligible, at least in recent times, for various forms of public assistance, such as Aid to Families with Dependent Children, Supplemental Security Income, Medicaid, and food stamps.

How has the United States traditionally treated refugees and how did Southeast Asian refugees fare?

Throughout history the United States has provided refuge to persons displaced by war and persecuted by governments. In 1783 President George Washington proclaimed the nation's commitment to the downtrodden: "[T]he bosom of America is open to receive not only the opulent and respectable stranger, but the oppressed and persecuted of all nations and religions."

In keeping with Washington's promise, Congress on numerous occasions has set aside national quotas and permitted hundreds of thousands of refugees to enter the United States on an ad hoc basis. For example, the 1948 Displaced Persons Act allowed 400,000 refugees, primarily from Europe, to settle in the United States. Similarly, the 1953 Refugee Relief Act swung open America's doors to 2,800 Chinese refugees fleeing Mao Tse-tung's revolution.

Nonetheless, the U.S. commitment to refugees has occasionally been undermined by flare-ups of anti-immigration or restrictionist sentiment. For instance, the United States tragically turned away from its shores thousands of Jews who had escaped Nazi Germany in the 1930s.

The United States formalized its commitment to refugees with the passage of the Immigration and Nationality Act of 1952 also called the McCarran-Walter Act. The act not only permitted the immigration and naturalization of Asians, but vested in the U.S. attorney general the power to "parole" into the United States any alien for "emergency reasons or for reasons deemed strictly in the public interest." "Parolees" were refugees unqualified to immigrate to the United States and who thus had to wait two years to apply for permanent residency, a waiting period later reduced to one year.

The Refugee Relief Act of 1953 permitted those seeking asylum as a result of the spread of communism to enter the United States. The attorney general's authority to parole refugees has been used extensively for those fleeing Communist persecution, such as the Hungarians who left Soviet-occupied Hungary in 1956, the Chinese terrorized in the aftermath of the 1949 Communist takeover of mainland China, and the more than 145,000 Cubans in imminent danger after Castro's coup in 1959.

The 1965 Immigration Act afforded entry into the United States to refugees fleeing Communist-dominated regions of the Middle East, and also reasserted the attorney general's power to grant asylum to parolees in emergency situations.

In 1975, the attorney general granted parole status to thousands of refugees from Vietnam and Cambodia, and between April and December 1975, 130,400 refugees were admitted to the United States as parolees.

In 1976, the attorney general granted parole to even more refugees from Southeast Asia, and in the following years extended the parole to Vietnamese boat people. The United States had originally intended to evacuate only the approximately 17,600 Americans in Vietnam, but when it realized that the lives of many Vietnamese were in peril, it granted asylum to 4,000 Vietnamese orphans, 75,000 relatives of American citizens or residents, and 50,000 Vietnamese government employees.

In March of 1980, Congress, dissatisfied with its prior policy of ad hoc admission, passed the Refugee Act, hailed by many as the first comprehensive refugee legislation in United States history. The Refugee Act was passed largely in response to the refugee crisis that developed in Southeast Asia after the Communist takeover of the Indochinese countries in 1975. The new legislation eliminated the parole program and established a refugee quota of 50,000 per year through 1983. The president was given the power to admit more refugees into the United States if need be after consulting with Congress.

The 1980 Refugee Act redefined a refugee as "any person who . . . is unable or unwilling to return to, and is unable or unwilling to avail himself or herself of the protection of [a] . . . country because of persecution or a well-founded fear of persecution on account of race, religion, nationality, membership in a particular social group, or political opinion." In theory, the 1980 Refugee Act removed the ideological preference for refugees from Communist countries and expanded the scope of the legislation to include all persons with a "well-founded fear of persecution."

What are first-asylum and second-asylum countries?

First-asylum countries are nations declared safe havens for refugees fleeing persecution. Countries are generally given this title if they are located in the same region as the refugees' homeland. With regard to the Southeast Asian refugee crisis that erupted in 1975, Thailand, Malaysia, Hong Kong, the Philippines, and Singapore were named first-asylum countries for refugees fleeing Vietnam, Laos, and Cambodia en masse.

These first-asylum countries, especially Thailand, have been overwhelmed by the sheer numbers of refugees, all in need of housing, food, clothing, and medical attention. Despite assistance from international organizations, such as the Red Cross and the United Nations, these countries have been unable to meet all the refugees' needs. As a result, Malaysia announced in 1979 that its doors were shut to refugees. Similarly, other countries have refused admission to Vietnamese boat people arriving on unseaworthy boats. These countries have limited their hospitality to fueling the refugees' boats and providing enough food and supplies so they could return to sea in search of another safe haven.

Second-asylum countries permanently resettle refugees in their territory strictly on a voluntary basis. For the Southeast Asians, the United States has been the most prominent second-asylum country, although Canada, China, Australia, and France have all shared the burden. Due to its failed foreign policy in Indochina, the United States, perhaps more than any other nation, felt a moral obligation to alleviate the refugee crisis it had helped create.

Which organizations have taken the lead in resettling refugees from Southeast Asia in the United States?

Various international, national, and private organizations have been involved in helping refugees resettle in the United States. The most visible is the Office of the United Nations High Commissioners for Refugees (UNHCR), an international organization created by the United Nations in 1951. The UNHCR coordinates the efforts of various volunteer agencies and nations around the world working to provide relief to refugees in camps. The UNHCR has been involved extensively in resettling Southeast Asian refugees in the United States, and in 1981 it was recognized for its efforts with the Nobel Peace Prize.

On the national level, the Office of Refugee Resettlement has been largely responsible for providing information, social services, and cash assistance to new arrivals. VOLAGs—*vol*unteer *ag*encies under government contract to help resettle refugees through sponsors—have also played a part in the process. The long list of VOLAGs includes the United States Catholic Conference, the Lutheran

Immigration and Refugee Service, the International Rescue Committee, the United Hebrew Immigrant Aid Society, the World Church Service, the Tolstoy Foundation, the American Fund for Czechoslovak Refugees, the American Council for Nationalities Services, and Travelers' Aid International Social Services.

To help cover the cost of sponsorship, VOLAGs receive a $500 grant for each refugee they resettle. Sponsors tend to be families or church groups, rather than individuals, because of the tremendous effort involved in resettling refugees, a task that involves providing housing, clothing, and other necessities until the refugees get on their feet. Sponsors also assist refugees in securing employment and in enrolling their children in schools. They even offer lessons on new concepts like driving cars, performing transactions at banks and post offices, and shopping at supermarkets.

Mutual Aid Associations (MAAs) have also played a significant role in helping Southeast Asian refugees adjust to American life. MAAs were created in 1975, funded in part by the government and by private donations from corporations and individuals. MAAs are run by refugees who have assimilated into the American mainstream and are able to volunteer their time to help new arrivals. They show refugees the ropes, offer translation services and English-language classes, and keep new arrivals abreast of services available to them in the community, such as counseling. Many new refugees are more comfortable seeking help from MAAs because the volunteers have the same background and language.

In addition to giving lessons about America, MAAs also encourage Southeast Asian refugees to keep their native traditions alive. They sponsor festivities during holidays that refugees traditionally observed in their homeland. Over time, MAAs have developed political clout, and under MAA auspices, refugees lobby their congressmen and congresswomen on issues regarding Southeast Asia, refugees, and other matters of concern.

Why were Southeast Asian refugees dispersed across the country?

The rationale behind dispersing refugees over the whole country was to minimize the economic threat that a concentration of refugees might pose to a local community. Twenty-one percent of the first wave of Southeast Asian refugees were settled in California, and the rest were scattered across America, with at least one hundred in every state except Alaska. In the process, some families were even split apart because individuals had to go wherever sponsors could be found.

Cultural isolation and separation from family and friends swiftly bred discontentment among the refugees, leading many to relocate after their initial settlement. By 1980, about 45 percent of the first wave of Southeast Asian refugees had moved to ethnic enclaves, mostly in California, Texas, and Louisiana.

As they clustered together in neighborhoods, the refugees revitalized many of America's communities. For instance, Vietnamese Americans have transformed the red-light district near Union Square in San Francisco into a thriving enclave of Vietnamese hotels, homes, and businesses. Vietnamese Americans have also turned the downtown areas of San Jose and Santa Ana, and a skid-row district in Los Angeles, into bustling neighborhoods. A section of the Washington, D.C., suburb of Arlington, Virginia, has also been largely revitalized thanks to Vietnamese Americans.

What is the 1.5 generation?

No, it's not Generation X. Immigrants and refugees born abroad but educated and socialized in the United States belong to the 1.5 generation, a generation straddling two countries and two cultures. The term was first used to refer to Korean American youth who accompanied their parents to the United States and later helped bridge the gap between the older generation and American-born Koreans. The 1.5ers from Southeast Asia fled their homelands as children, adolescents, or young adults, and later developed strong ties and deep roots in the New World. Most of the Southeast Asian 1.5 generation has been eager to adopt the American lifestyle, but rapid assimilation has alienated them from their parents and grandparents.

VIETNAMESE AMERICANS

What events in Vietnamese history led up to the mass exodus of Vietnamese to the United States in the twentieth century?

Ever since its inception in 207 B.C., the year the Kingdom of Nam viet was formed, Vietnam has suffered long periods of foreign conquest and internal instability. For over one thousand years, China's Han dynasty occupied much of the northern and central region of present-day Vietnam. In 939 A.D., after staging numerous unsuccessful rebellions against Chinese rule, the Vietnamese wrested their country from China. Vietnam remained independent, for the most part, until French forces under the command of Napoleon III invaded in 1862 in an effort to end the persecution of Western missionaries and Roman Catholic converts in Vietnam.

The French easily defeated Vietnamese imperial forces in 1883, and the Vietnamese court assigned France as a protectorate over the north and central regions of Vietnam. Vietnam thus was divided into the protectorate of Tonkin (northern Vietnam), the protectorate of Annam (central Vietnam), and the colony of Cochin China (southern Vietnam).

After conquering Vietnam along with Kampuchea and Laos, France consolidated its power in the region, which it renamed *Indochine,* or Indochina, to reflect the dual influences of China and India.

Did the Vietnamese rebel against French rule and who was Ho Chi Minh?

Although the Vietnamese rebelled against French rule, as they did against Chinese rule, it was not until 1941 that Vietnam, under the leadership of Ho Chi Minh, the founder of the Indochinese Communist Party, posed a threat to the French. Ho Chi Minh appealed to Vietnamese nationalists to form a national front of "patriots of all ages and all types, peasants, workers, merchants and soldiers" to oust both the French and the Japanese who were occupying Vietnam at the time. The Communist-led national front was called the Vietnam Independence League, or the Viet Minh.

At first, the Viet Minh enjoyed widespread support among all the Vietnamese, who were bent on putting an end to French colonialism. In 1945, as Imperial Japan began to succumb to Allied forces in World War II, Ho Chi Minh seized the opportunity and declared Vietnam's independence in a document modeled on the Declaration of Independence of the United States.

Ho Chi Minh wrote several letters to President Harry S Truman asking for recognition and support from the United States. The letters went unanswered. Presumably Washington refused to recognize Ho Chi Minh because it mistrusted the career Communist and his friends the Soviets and Communist Chinese.

But wasn't Ho Chi Minh an American ally?

Sort of. The U.S. Office of Strategic Services (OSS), the CIA's wartime predecessor, was headquartered in the southwestern Chinese province of Yunnan. During World War II, the OSS trained Ho Chi Minh's forces in the jungles of Vietnam. An American pilot downed on a mission was in fact saved by Ho Chi Minh's guerrilla forces. And an American OSS officer, Major **Archimedes L. A. Patti**, gave Ho Chi Minh a helping hand in formulating the Vietnamese Declaration of Independence.

Why was the United States after World War II seen by some Vietnamese as yet another foreign interloper?

Because the United States was allied with France during World War II, and then sanctioned France's attempts to recolonize Vietnam. President Roosevelt had in fact promised the French that they would get their overseas colonies back after the war. Roosevelt later tried to discourage France's colonialist quests and proposed that postwar Indochina be placed under an international trusteeship, since the French had "milked it for some hundred years." Then in 1945, in yet another switch, the president suggested that Indochina be turned over to General **Chiang Kai-shek**, the non-Communist nationalist Chinese leader. Chiang Kai-shek refused the offer, insisting that the Indochinese "would not assimilate into the Chinese people."

In the end, Roosevelt accepted France's repossession of its colonies in exchange for a promise that they would eventually be declared independent, despite the fact that Ho Chi Minh sent many letters to Roosevelt in 1945 and 1946, requesting that the United States prevent France from trying to recolonize Vietnam.

The French ignored Ho Chi Minh's declaration of national independence and returned to Vietnam after 1945 to claim what they thought was rightfully theirs. The United States backed France and even ended up financing 80 percent of the French war effort to recolonize Vietnam. In fact, by 1954, fearful that Indochina would fall to the Communists, the United States had spent $2.5 billion on French efforts to regain Vietnam, an amount that made the financial support France received under the Marshall Plan seem like a pittance.

The French-Indochina War between France and the Viet

Minh began in late 1946 and lasted until 1954, when the Vietnamese defeated the French at Dien Bien Phu, a city in northeastern Vietnam. Soon after the defeat, the French and the Viet Minh signed the Geneva Accords, which granted Vietnam its independence from France.

How was Vietnam divided into North Vietnam and South Vietnam?

Under the terms of the Geneva Accords, Vietnam was to be partitioned at the 17th parallel until 1956, when national elections would be held to reunite the country. From 1954 until 1956, the region north of the 17th parallel would be under the control of the Viet Minh with Ho Chi Minh as leader, and would be called the Democratic Republic of Viet Nam. The region south of the 17th parallel would be under the control of an anti-Communist government, led by Ngo Dinh Diem, and would be called the Republic of Viet Nam.

Civilians were allowed a certain amount of time to resettle either in the north or in the south if they wished. About 850,000 Vietnamese moved south during this period.

How did the United States get involved in Vietnam?

In 1947, **George F. Kennan**, then an American diplomat in Moscow, recommended a policy of containment to prevent countries around the world, in a domino effect, from falling to communism the way Eastern Europe succumbed to Soviet domination after World War II. The domino theory dominated United States foreign policy for the next two decades.

The United States became involved in Vietnam when it lent a hand to the French battling the Communist-led Viet Minh and, in the process, aligned itself with, rather than against, colonialism. Following the Geneva Conference of 1954, the United States strengthened its position in Vietnam in order to halt what it foresaw as imminent Communist expansion into South Vietnam, a territory designated non-Communist under the Geneva Accords.

Because South Vietnam played no role in the Geneva Accords, South Vietnamese president **Ngo Dinh Diem** refused to hold elections as specified by the accords. North Vietnam responded by initiating acts of insurgency in the South in the early 1960s, by installing a Communist organization, the National Liberation Front (NLF), in the region, and by strengthening North Vietnamese military installations to the south.

An alarmed United States, under President **John F. Kennedy**, began to send not only military supplies but also military advisers to support the South. By 1962, as many as 8,000 American soldiers were stationed in Vietnam, and by late 1963, the number had increased to 16,000. Under President **Lyndon B. Johnson**, American involvement escalated to a much greater degree as the United States committed hundreds of thousands of ground troops to Vietnam.

How did the South Vietnamese feel about their American allies?

Many South Vietnamese who were anti-Communist supported American involvement in the war. Many believed that communism was a greater evil than even a foreign presence, and so were willing to ally themselves with another power to defeat the Communist Vietcong. South Vietnamese optimism soured, however, as the Americans began to make critical mistakes. It was plain to the South Vietnamese why the Americans botched up: they wouldn't listen. The opinion expressed by a South Vietnamese chaplain is one commonly held by other South Vietnamese: "The Americans . . . refused to pay attention to the advice of the Vietnamese officers. . . . Rather, they forced the Vietnamese military to fight Communists the 'American way' . . . and many Vietnamese Nationalists were ambushed and killed conducting operations according to the will of the Americans after the Americans had been told their way was wrong. . . . In many operations it was not the Communists who defeated us, but American advisors. . . . The Americans were naive. If a Vietnamese person spoke English well, the Americans trusted him, so the Communists sent infiltrators who spoke excellent English; the Americans believed these people more than the loyal Vietnamese who worked for them but whose English wasn't so good."

What was the Tet Offensive of 1968?

Tet means "New Year" in Vietnamese. The Tet Offensive was launched by 70,000 Communist soldiers on the evening of January 31, 1968, in violation of a New Year's truce they had pledged to observe. The offensive was targeted not against fortifications in the countryside but specifically against towns and cities in the South. Saigon was hit hard during the Tet Offensive, and one of its main targets was the United States embassy.

Nineteen Vietcong commandos were assigned to attack the U.S. embassy. In preparation for their mission, they smuggled arms into Saigon and stored the matériel in an auto repair shop owned by their agent. At three o'clock in the morning of January 31, 1968, the commandos pulled in front of the embassy in a taxicab and in five minutes had killed four American soldiers guarding the compound. Television coverage beamed the maneuver right into America's living rooms, with images of U.S. soldiers scrambling to secure the embassy as Vietcong lay dead in the courtyard.

Although the Tet Offensive did not cause Saigon's population to turn on the Americans or the South Vietnamese government, as the Vietcong leaders had hoped and predicted, it did cast doubt on the rosy, reassuring reports American officials had been broadcasting from Vietnam.

The Tet Offensive is also why Americans are apt to associate Tet, the Vietnamese New Year, with chaos and mayhem.

Besides Hippies, Jane Fonda, Bill Clinton, and Eastern Establishment intellectuals, who else opposed the war in Vietnam?

Vietnamese students and religious leaders, among them Catholics, Buddhists, and members of the Hoa Hao sect, led the anti-war movement in South Vietnam. These people opposed the war for a variety of reasons. Some believed that U.S. involvement in the war constituted interference in the domestic affairs of Vietnam and domination over a Third World country; others opposed the war because they felt that American tactics, such as the use of napalm and agent orange, and the resettlement of villagers from their homes into "strategic hamlets," showed a callous and racist disregard for Vietnamese lives; and still others opposed to war because they preferred the Communists, since the Americans had supported French colonialism.

When did the Vietnam War finally end?

In early 1968, President Johnson put a halt to the massive buildup of American troops in Vietnam even as the war waged on. Under President Nixon, the United States and North Vietnam began negotiations that culminated in the signing of the Paris Peace Agreement on January 27, 1973. Under the terms of the agreement, a cease-fire between the United States and North Vietnam was declared, and U.S. troops were withdrawn from Vietnam in 1973, an act President Nixon officially called "peace with honor." In other words, since the United States could not declare that it had won the war, the phrase "peace with honor" allowed the country to save face.

While the United States declared the war had ended with the signing of the Paris Peace Agreement, the negotiations essentially proved ineffectual, as fighting continued within Vietnam and then spread to the neighboring countries of Laos and Cambodia. In the spring of 1975, South Vietnam's capital, Saigon (later renamed Ho Chi Minh City), fell to the Vietcong, unleashing a mass exodus of Vietnamese from their homeland.

Why do many South Vietnamese blame the "leopard spot" arrangement of the Paris Peace Agreement for the loss of the South?

The Paris Peace Agreement, which officially ended the war as far as the United States was concerned, called for a cease-fire between the United States and North Vietnam, U.S. troop withdrawal, and an exchange of prisoners. The remaining political issues were to be resolved later by an interim body with representatives from South Vietnam and North Vietnam, as well as neutral parties to supervise the process of reconciliation.

Pending the final political settlement, both sides existed as separate entities and remained in control of the areas they had seized prior to the cease-fire, thus leaving many Communist strongholds—leopard spots—in South Vietnam. Unlike the Geneva Accords of 1954, which had required Communist forces to be regrouped to the north, the Paris Peace Agreement thus allowed 150,000 Vietcong to remain in the South, in control of the territories they had seized earlier, even though U.S. troops had been withdrawn.

Why then did the South Vietnamese sign the Paris Peace Agreement?

The South Vietnamese government had no choice but to sign the agreement. President Nixon warned South Vietnam that if it rejected the agreement, the United States would enter into a separate agreement with North Vietnam and cut off all aid to South Vietnam. President Nixon also threw the South Vietnamese a bone, promising that if they signed the agreement, he would petition Congress energetically for aid to

South Vietnam and, more importantly, would pledge to "react vigorously" to any serious violation of the cease-fire by North Vietnam.

By what means would the United States be able to "react vigorously" to a North Vietnamese violation of the peace agreement?

In the words of President Nixon, the United States would use its air force bases in Thailand, with huge fleets of fighter-bombers and B52s, as a deterrent to North Vietnamese attacks. A direct chain of secure radio communications was set up between the Nakhon Phanon U.S. air base in Thailand and South Vietnamese I Corps and II Corps in Danang and Pleiku. In an emergency, the South Vietnamese corp commanders could send direct requests to Nakhon Phanom for immediate American aid.

Is the term Vietnam War inaccurate?

Well, it's inaccurate as far as the Vietnamese are concerned. Vietnam has had many wars, against the Chinese, for example, and the French. The "Vietnam War" is but a single war in Vietnam's long history, and thus the term is nondescript and misleading. Of course, from the American perspective, the term *Vietnam War* is specific and accurate.

Did the Vietnamese first come to America after the fall of Saigon in 1975?

Actually, the Vietnamese were present in very small numbers in the United States before the exodus of 1975. In 1964, there were reportedly 603 Vietnamese in America, most of whom were students, teachers, and diplomats, whose stay overseas was temporary. By 1985, however, 643,200 Vietnamese had taken refuge in the United States.

The first wave of Vietnamese refugees headed for the United States shortly before the fall of Saigon on April 30, 1975, as a Communist victory appeared imminent. In the last days of April, the streets of Saigon turned to total chaos, as people jammed the American embassy trying to prove they had some connection, however tenuous, to the United States or to the South Vietnamese regime, so as to be included in the American evacuation program. The U.S. government initially planned to evacuate only about 17,000 American employees and their dependents, but it quickly expanded the evacuation to include Vietnamese employees and those whose lives were in imminent danger. About 86,000 people fled Vietnam at the end of April, some cramming into helicopters that lifted off the roof of the American embassy and others on the few remaining planes departing from Saigon's Tan Son Nhut Airport.

Between April and December of 1975, the U.S. government granted entry to 125,000 Vietnamese refugees. This first wave of refugees consisted mainly of well-educated urbanites, who fled out of fear that their religious beliefs or social class made them targets of the new Communist regime. Many had also worked in some capacity with the South Vietnamese government and the United States, and feared that the Vietcong would brand them traitors.

Although only 10 percent of the population of Vietnam had embraced Christianity, 50 percent of the refugees who left in the first wave were Christians, primarily Catholics, many of whom had already fled communism once before in 1954, when they resettled in South Vietnam after the Geneva Accords designated North Vietnam as a region under the jurisdiction of the Viet Minh.

Where were the refugees housed in 1975?

The Vietnamese refugees of 1975 were placed in camps set up in the United States, such as Camp Pendleton in southern

California, which opened on April 29, 1975, and later at Fort Chaffee in Arkansas, Eglin Air Force Base in Florida, and Fort Indiantown Gap in Pennsylvania. At these camps, which were under the direction of the Interagency Task Force and the U.S. military, the refugees underwent interviews and physical examinations, received identification numbers, and registered with an agency in charge of resettlement. The refugees also received housing, food, and lessons on American culture and the English language. Most of the refugees left the camps when they found sponsors to support them until they got on their feet.

Who were the Vietnamese boat people?

Many Vietnamese who were desperate to leave their country in the wake of the Communist victory were unable to do so through official channels. Either they had no government or American connection that would entitle them to a spot on an American plane, or there was no space for them on the planes, or they had no money to buy a seat when one became available. For most, the only other means of escape, and a perilous one at that, was by boat. And so a second wave of refugees fled Vietnam on rickety, overcrowded boats vulnerable to attacks by pirates on the South China Sea.

In the first weeks after the Communists seized Saigon, between forty thousand and sixty thousand Vietnamese fled by boat. Many of these first Vietnamese boat people were rescued by U.S. naval ships, which transported them to Guam and the Philippines, where they would wait for resettlement.

Other Vietnamese resolved to stay in their homeland, believing that peace would prevail in Vietnam after the Communist victory. However, in 1979 the new government instituted oppressive measures such as the collectivization of the South's agriculture, the expropriation of private businesses in the South, the "re-education" of those associated with the Saigon regime, restrictions on the press, and the relocation of urban populations to "New Economic Zones." This sent a third wave of refugees out of Vietnam, again surreptitiously, by boat.

In the late 1970s to early 1980s, the profile of the Vietnamese boat people changed, as more Vietnamese of Chinese ancestry fled persecution in Vietnam. Although the ethnic Chinese constituted only 7 percent of the population in Vietnam, they owned or controlled 80 percent of the retail trade, which was devastated by the Communists. When border disputes between Vietnam and China flared up in 1979, even more ethnic-Chinese Vietnamese left to avoid mistreatment by the Vietnamese government. In fact, 40 percent of the third wave of refugees were Vietnamese of Chinese ethnicity.

Boat people often prepared for their escape over many months, slowly gathering such supplies as food, water, and gasoline. Once they left the shore, they had to face the peril of an ocean voyage and outwit government officials, ubiquitous Thai pirates, and starvation. They also had to find a country that would grant them asylum, which itself was not an easy task. Not surprisingly, untold numbers of boat people died at sea.

Many of those who survived made landfall in Thailand and other first-asylum countries, where they were given shelter in crowded and squalid refugee camps. Some lived in these camps for years before they were resettled elsewhere.

Who are the Amerasians?

The Amerasians are children born of Asian mothers (mostly Vietnamese) and U.S. servicemen stationed in Southeast Asia. When their fathers were transferred out of Vietnam in 1975, most Amerasian children were left behind. They were often badly treated and discriminated against by the Vietnamese people and the government, who saw them as reminders of the American presence in Vietnam.

In a sympathetic and morally correct response, the United States passed the Amerasian Homecoming Act of 1987 to facilitate the transfer to American soil of Vietnamese Amerasians born between January 1, 1962, and January 1, 1977. By 1994 more than 75,000 Amerasians and accompanying family members, mostly from Vietnam, had begun new lives in the United States. They are part of a fourth wave of Vietnamese immigrants that also includes detainees and former prisoners of re-education camps.

How have the Vietnamese adjusted to life in the United States?

The Vietnamese have adapted to life in America with various degrees of success. The first wave of Vietnamese refugees, from the educated upper and middle classes, has assimilated more easily than subsequent waves. These refugees had long been exposed to Western culture and values and had some knowledge of English, thus they were more prepared for the United States than were later arrivals. They have built careers in their fields, and many have set up prospering small businesses.

Despite their skills and education, many in the first wave accepted jobs that were lower in status in comparison to those they had held in Vietnam. For example, a study in 1978 showed that 30 percent of the refugees had been professionals in Vietnam, but after twenty-seven months in America, only 7 percent had managed to regain their status. Of the 15 percent who had been managers in Vietnam, only 2 percent had found equivalent employment.

The post-1975 refugees tended to be much less educated and less skilled, and thus less employable, than the earlier arrivals. Most did not speak any English, a major obstacle to success in America. As a result, this pool of refugees has suffered from a high rate of unemployment and has remained on welfare well beyond the average period of adjustment to the

United States. Many post-1975 refugees remain trapped in low-paying jobs, and isolated from the mainstream by language and cultural barriers, and from the more established Vietnamese community by economic and regional differences. They have been forced to rely primarily on their children, who most often are the only family members with any knowledge of the English language.

Nonetheless, a good number of post-1975 refugees have managed to overcome the obstacles and have started small businesses. Between 1982 and 1987, the number of Vietnamese-owned businesses increased 415 percent, from 4,989 to 25,671.

How has the Vietnamese family structure been affected by life in America?

The family is of utmost importance for the Vietnamese, who characteristically place their family's needs before those of individuals. In Vietnam, large groups of relatives lived close together, and "family" included extended family: grandparents, uncles, aunts, and cousins. However, during and after the Vietnam War, families were torn apart either by migrations from the dangerous countryside to cities or by the evacuation process.

Those who managed to escape Vietnam with their families intact had difficulty remaining together, since sponsors generally could not afford to finance large groups. Thus, different branches of the same family often went their separate ways. Those families who managed to stay together had to contend with American zoning regulations, which typically prohibit large groups of persons considered unrelated from living under one roof.

How have Vietnamese youth adjusted to the American school system?

Vietnamese kids have adapted to the American school system with good results. Many earn high grade-point averages, and go on to college. In 1988, a study was taken on Southeast Asian refugee youth in San Diego County in southern California, an area with a high concentration of Indochinese refugees. Data showed that Vietnamese American students were among the highest achievers and were in the best position to succeed of all Southeast Asian youth, perhaps because they have been in the United States longer. The report pointed out that 25 percent of valedictorians and salutatorians in San Diego high schools were Vietnamese, although the Vietnamese constituted only 7 percent of the graduating classes. Vietnamese American students also have received above-average math scores on national American standardized tests.

The Vietnamese, as well as other Southeast Asian students, do better in school than most other groups of students. The San Diego County study showed that only Chinese, Japanese, and Korean American students outperformed Southeast Asian students.

Several factors contribute to the success of the Vietnamese students in America, among them, the enormous emphasis parents place on education and the culture's traditional reverence for scholarship.

How serious is the Vietnamese gang problem?

Known as the "lost generation," the Vietnamese who have found their way into gangs by and large came to America as unaccompanied minors with no knowledge of English. Gang members are usually boys, although all-girl Vietnamese gangs occasionally surface, such as the Wally Girls.

These gangs have become a source of both pain and fear for Vietnamese American communities across the nation. Vietnamese gang members, known as *bui doi*, the "dust of life," are less preoccupied with defending their "turf" than other ethnic gangs, and tend instead to wander around Vietnamese neighborhoods looking for other Vietnamese to rob.

Post-1975 refugee families, who prefer to hoard their money at home rather than deposit it in banks, are particularly vulnerable to gang violence since some gangs even cruise around the country in search of Vietnamese houses to ransack. They either depend on the "Nguyen" page in the local telephone book to track down Vietnamese or consult other undesirables in town about the best houses to hit.

What does "throw out the anchor" mean?

"Throwing out the anchor" is a strategy Vietnamese parents have devised to gain access to the United States. They send their children abroad, preferably to the United States, to avoid the draft, or obtain a better education. Once the "anchor is thrown out," the children become naturalized citizens and send for their parents.

How did the Vietnamese American community react to President Clinton's decision in 1994 to lift the trade embargo against Vietnam?

In February of 1994, President **Bill Clinton** announced that the United States would rescind the trade embargo against Vietnam, which since 1975 had prohibited American citizens from conducting business with that country. Vietnamese Americans have had heated arguments over this issue.

Those in favor of lifting the embargo feel that normal relations, not isolation, will encourage Vietnam to continue in the direction of greater liberalization. They also believe that the restoration of human rights should be a precondition for normalization of relations between the United States and Vietnam. Others view lifting the embargo as a declaration of Vietnam's victory in the war, since the United States would be left with no effective bargaining chip to resolve the remaining POW-MIA issue.

Even before President Clinton's announcement, a growing number of Vietnamese entrepreneurs had been returning to their homeland to set up businesses. Known as the *viet kieu,* or "overseas Vietnamese," they have opened restaurants and hotels, have constructed office buildings, and have participated in other joint-venture projects.

What is Little Saigon?

As the Vietnamese reached America after the fall of Saigon, the U.S. government tried to resettle them around the nation. A few stayed put, but many found their way to California, where 400,000 Vietnamese Americans reside today.

By 1988, so many Vietnamese American businesses had cropped up along a two-mile stretch of Bolsa Avenue in Westminster, California, that the area was officially named "Little Saigon." In "Little Saigon" one is more likely to hear Vietnamese than English in the over fifteen hundred restaurants, cafes, grocery stores, and shops catering to the Vietnamese American community.

Westminster's "Little Saigon" enjoys political as well as economic clout. Westminster became home to the first Vietnamese American—**Tony Lam**—to serve in elected office, when the city chose him as councilman. Since then, "Little Saigon" has frequently been a stop on the campaign trail for all kinds of candidates.

Who are Kieu Chinh and Le Ly Hayslip?

Kieu Chinh is a Vietnamese American actress who captivated American audiences with her outstanding performance in a supporting role in the 1993 box office hit *The Joy Luck Club,* based on the novel with the same name by Chinese American writer Amy Tan. Kieu Chinh was born in Hanoi in the 1930s. After Vietnam was partitioned at the 17th parallel into North and South in 1954 as dictated by the Geneva Accords, Kieu Chinh and other members of her family fled Ho Chi Minh's

North Vietnam and the Viet Minh. Kieu Chinh managed to reach Saigon by plane, but she left family members behind and would never lay eyes on them again.

In Saigon, Chinh landed a part in one of the Vietnamese film industry's first efforts. She went on to act in films all over Asia, and even starred in the Hollywood productions *A Yank in Vietnam* (1964) and *Operation C.I.A.* (1965). By the end of the 1960s, Kieu Chinh was a household name throughout Southeast Asia. Her career on the Asian big screen came to an abrupt end with the Communist takeover of Saigon in the summer of 1975. Chinh found her way to southern California in hopes of making a splash in Hollywood. In 1989 her big break came when she landed parts in *Welcome Home* and *Vietnam, Texas.*

Vietnamese American writer and humanitarian Le Ly Hayslip captured the attention of the media and the public in 1993 with the release of *Heaven and Earth,* a motion picture based on her autobiographical accounts of life in Vietnam and America. Her first autobiographical account (written with Jay Wurts) is entitled *When Heaven and Earth Changed Places: A Vietnamese Woman's Journey from War to Peace* (1989) and chronicles the harrowing experiences of a young peasant girl who finds herself trapped in the violence of the Vietnam War. In 1993 Le Ly Hayslip published her second autobiographical work, *Child of War, Woman of Peace,* a rumination on the author's experiences as a refugee in the United States.

Le Ly Hayslip was born in Ky La, a village in central Vietnam, on December 19, 1949. As a young girl she was tortured and raped by South Vietnamese soldiers, and filled with shame, she fled to Saigon with her mother, where she worked as a servant in a wealthy household. She was made pregnant by the master of the house and was subsequently let go. Le Ly Hayslip went next to Da Nang, where she sold American goods on the black market to survive. In 1970 she married an American and came to the United States, settling in southern California. In 1986 Le Ly Hayslip journeyed back to Vietnam to visit her family, and the hardship she saw there inspired her in 1988 to launch the East Meets West Foundation, an organization devoted to repairing the devastation wrought in Vietnam and promoting peace between the United States and Vietnam.

How have the Vietnamese had a head start over most other Asians in learning English?

They already know the Roman alphabet. Originally, the Vietnamese used the Chinese writing system, which they later modified into an arcane form of Chinese ideographs. In the seventeenth century, though, Alexandre de Rhodes, a French Jesuit, developed an alphabetical writing system based on the Roman alphabet, and this system has been used for Vietnamese ever since.

What religions do Vietnamese Americans follow?

Since Buddhism is the predominant religion in Vietnam, introduced by the Chinese and the Indians early on in the country's history, most Vietnamese Americans are Buddhist. Those from northern Vietnam practice primarily Mahayana Buddhism, and those from the South practice Theravada Buddhism. The Vietnamese also follow Christian religions, primarily Catholicism.

Most Americans believe that the Vietnamese and Vietnamese Americans are either Catholic or Buddhist. But the truth is that many Vietnamese follow two or more religions at the same time, usually some combination of Buddhism, Confucianism, Taoism, Catholicism, Protestantism, Hoa Hao, Cao Dai, or Lao Tsu. They harmonize their beliefs in such a way that conflicts rarely emerge, and when they do, they rarely pose a moral dilemma. Thus a Vietnamese Buddhist may also be a Taoist and a Catholic. In fact, Confucianism and Taoism are essential facets of Vietnamese culture, and most Vietnamese adopt some aspects of Confucian and Taoist ethics.

THIRTEEN ASIAN AMERICAN WOMEN WHO HAVE MADE A DIFFERENCE

1. Anna Chennault

A Chinese American activist in the political arena, Anna Chennault first joined the Republican party in 1960 and emerged during President Nixon's term in office as one of Washington's leading lobbyists and hostesses. On numerous occasions she has used her political clout to aid Chinese Nationalists in Taiwan. Chennault is vice-chair of the president's Export Council and an avid supporter of Asian American participation in the political system.

2. Connie Chung

A highly successful and sought-after Chinese American broadcast journalist, Connie Chung has anchored the news for both CBS and NBC. Chung has also hosted her own weekly show, *Face to Face with Connie Chung*, which combines investigative pieces, features, and interviews with people in the news. In 1987 she visited China for the first time as part of an NBC news team, and had the opportunity to meet with some of her relatives and even interview several of them on the air about their experiences during the Cultural Revolution.

3. Shamita Das Dasgupta

Indian American Shamita Das Dasgupta, a psychologist and professor of women's studies at Rutgers University, helped found Manavi, a self-help organization run by volunteer feminists that addresses the experiences and concerns of South Asian immigrant women. Manavi offers its clients legal aid, therapeutic referrals and advice, and access to translators, among other services.

4. March Kong Fong Eu

A noteworthy political figure, March Kong Fong Eu was a

member of the California state legislature from 1966 to 1974. In 1975 she became the first Asian American woman elected secretary of state in California. In that capacity she supported over four hundred bills dealing with women's rights and human rights. In 1994 she resigned as secretary of state to assume the post of U.S. ambassador to Micronesia. March Kong Fong Eu is a role model for Americans of Chinese ancestry and all women.

5. Carol Kawanami

Carol Kawanami became the first American woman of Japanese ancestry to serve as mayor, when the people of Villa Park, California, elected her to the post in 1980.

6. Maxine Hong Kingston

Maxine Hong Kingston is one of the first Asian American writers to enjoy an international as well as national following. She has authored the books *The Woman Warrior* (1976) and *China Men* (1980), vivid accounts of the Chinese American experience, as well as short stories, poems, and articles. Her first novel, *Tripmaster Monkey*, was published in 1989. An advocate of world peace, Kingston took part in protest marches condemning the massacre in Beijing's Tiananmen Square. In 1980 she became the first Chinese American named a "Living Treasure of Hawaii." In celebration of her contributions, PBS has created and aired a documentary chronicling Kingston's life.

7. June Kuramoto

June Kuramoto plays the *koto*, a harp-like Japanese classical instrument, as a member of the group Hiroshima. Hiroshima has gained recognition and commendations for weaving together the instruments and rhythms of Japan and America to create a unique jazz and rock sound. In 1980 *Performance* magazine named Kuramoto Breakout Artist of the Year and in 1988 Hiroshima's album *Go* was named Best Jazz Album at the

Soul Train Music Awards. In addition to performing with Hiroshima, Kuramoto has teamed up with other musicians in concert and in the studio, and has worked on musical scores for film and television.

8. Maya Ying Lin

In 1980, Chinese American Maya Ying Lin, then an architecture student at Yale University, designed the Vietnam Veterans Memorial, which was unveiled to high critical acclaim. The Wall, with its black granite panels into which the names of over 58,000 Americans are etched, is one the most visited sites in Washington, D.C. Lin earned a master's degree in Architecture from Yale in 1986 and a year later went to work designing the Civil Rights Memorial in Montgomery, Alabama, in honor of the struggle for African American civil rights. Among her other accomplishments, Maya Ying Lin has designed a topiary park in Charlotte, North Carolina, and a hanging sculpture for the Pennsylvania Railroad Station in New York City.

9. Midori

Internationally renowned Japanese American violin virtuoso Midori gave her first public recital at the tender age of six. In 1990 she debuted as a soloist at Carnegie Hall before a sell-out crowd. Midori performs about eighty concerts a year, appearing with many of the world's leading orchestras and most famous conductors.

10. Patsy Takemoto Mink

A U.S. congresswoman from Hawaii who has served in public office for three decades, Patsy Takemoto Mink won a seat in the U.S. House of Representatives in 1964 to become the first Asian American woman elected to Congress. Mink was reelected over and over again until 1976, when she decided not to run and instead took a government position as assistant secretary for oceans and international environmental and scientific affairs, working on numerous critical issues such as acid rain. From 1983 to 1988 she served as a member of the Honolulu City Council. In 1990 Mink was victorious in her bid for reelection to the U.S. House of Representatives.

11. Irene Natividad

In 1985, academician and political activist Irene Natividad became the first Asian American to chair the bipartisan National Women's Political Caucus. She remained at that post until 1988, and a year later *Ladies Home Journal* voted her one of a hundred most influential women. In the 1992 presidential race Natividad campaigned for the Clinton and Gore team. President Clinton appointed Natividad director of Sallie Mae, the government organization in charge of student loans.

12. Angela Oh

A criminal defense lawyer and the author of numerous articles on race relations, Angela Oh was the most visible spokesperson in the Korean American community during the Los Angeles riots in 1992. When ABC's *Nightline* needed a Korean perspective during the riots, Oh was there to provide valuable insights.

13. Amy Tan

Chinese American writer Amy Tan, whose Chinese name, An-mei, means "blessing from America," has won the hearts of millions of readers. Her first novel, *The Joy Luck Club* (1989), became the surprise best-seller of the year and was made into a movie in 1992. In 1991 Tan published her second novel, entitled *The Kitchen God's Wife* and based on her mother's life. The year 1995 saw the publication of her *A Hundred Secret Sense*, which became an instant best-seller. Before turning to fiction, Amy Tan wrote speeches for businesses under the alias "May Brown," and was a consultant for programs geared toward disabled children.

Thus Vietnamese family members might be baptized and go to church on Sundays with Buddhists and Confucianists, and later attend Buddhist services at a pagoda with other Catholics.

This tendency to adhere to the teachings of different religions has at times caused bewilderment among American sponsors of refugees. Refugees sometimes attend Christian churches with sponsors as a show of appreciation, and then cause them confusion by following an eclectic assortment of moral and religious beliefs.

What is Cao Dai and do its followers really worship the French writer Victor Hugo, author of Les Misérables?

The Cao Dai religion certainly appeals to Vietnamese eclecticism, since it is a mixture of religious and secular beliefs. Cao Dai was founded by a mystic named Ngo Van Chieu, who claimed to commune with the Cao Dai spirit. And, yes, among its saints are Victor Hugo, not to mention Jesus, Buddha, and Joan of Arc. The Cao Dai religion met with mass acceptance in Vietnam. By the end of World War II, nearly 1.5 million adhered to the religion, which later found its way to the United States with Vietnamese refugees.

Who is Supreme Master Ching Hai?

Born in Vietnam, and an honorary American citizen since 1993, Supreme Master **Ching Hai** is a symbol of spiritual wisdom and guidance for hundreds of thousands of seekers of enlightenment around the globe. She teaches, free of charge, a non-denominational form of meditation called the Quan Yin method in thirty-six centers worldwide. Supreme Master Ching Hai has achieved international fame for her humanitarian and disaster-relief efforts on four continents. In recognition of her contributions, she received the International

Peace Commendation and the World Spiritual Leadership Award in 1993. Master Ching Hai has been the honored guest of world leaders and has addressed the United Nations in New York and Geneva on numerous occasions.

According to Master Ching Hai's philosophy, all of the world's religions teach the same fundamental truth: universal brotherhood and sisterhood, moral courage, and purity of mind. Master Ching Hai's Quan Yin method of meditation is referred to in ancient scriptures as the "Key to Immediate Enlightenment." At the core of the Quan Yin method is silent contemplation of the "inner soundstream," by which the individual may experience higher levels of consciousness and uncover the path to enlightened understanding.

What is the significance of Tet for Vietnamese Americans?

For most Americans, "Tet" recalls the Tet Offensive of 1968, when the Vietcong attacked Saigon, storming the United States embassy. For Vietnamese, Tet, short for Tet Nguyen Dan, meaning "festivity on the first morning," is the celebration of the Vietnamese New Year and usually extends for one week sometime between January 19 and February 20. Tet is the most important secular holiday on the Vietnamese calendar.

Many Vietnamese families save all year long so that they may celebrate Tet as lavishly as possible. Tet demands months of preparation, during which houses are thoroughly cleaned, sometimes even repainted, in order to usher in a brand-new and hopefully lucky year.

Vietnamese Tet is similar to the Chinese New Year. Both occur at the same time of the year and feature dragon dances and firecrackers to repel evil spirits. Both Vietnamese and Chinese give children new money wrapped in bright red envelopes. Both cultures have adopted a twelve-year cycle, represented by a sequence of a dozen animals: rat, ox, tiger, hare, dragon, serpent, horse, ram, monkey, rooster, dog, and pig.

The year 1994, for example, was that of the dog, and it will not recur until the Gregorian calendar year 2006. The personality of the individual born in a certain year is thought to correspond with the traits attributed to that animal.

In the United States, Tet has been modified to fit the American work calendar. For example, if Tet falls in the middle of the week, festivities are scheduled for the weekend before and the weekend after Tet. Tet festivals in the United States include events such as concerts, ballroom dancing, beauty pageants, karaoke contests, martial arts competitions, table-tennis matches, chess matches, and community education. For Vietnamese Americans, the celebration of Tet is a way to strengthen cultural values and ties within the community.

What foods do Vietnamese Americans enjoy?

The eating habits of Vietnamese Americans are much like those of other Americans. Most Vietnamese Americans also enjoy Vietnamese cooking, sometimes called the nouvelle cuisine of Asia. Vietnamese cuisine is a blend of foreign influences and native ingredients and varies from region to region. In the north, the preponderance of stir-fried dishes and black pepper betrays Chinese influences, while in the south the influence of India is apparent in the use of curry, cocoa, and tamarind. The inclusion of potatoes, asparagus, pâté de foie gras, french breads, and croissants on the Vietnamese table throughout the country but particularly in the South point to the French influence.

Fresh herbs and spices, including mint, cilantro, basil, ginger, lemon grass, chile peppers, and garlic, lend a distinctive flavor to Vietnamese cooking. Fish and seafood are popular, as is pork. Unlike other Asians, the Vietnamese serve many uncooked or lightly steamed vegetables, and many dishes are accompanied by plates heaped with lettuce, carrots, cucumbers, and bean sprouts. Nuoc mam, an all-purpose condiment made of fermented fish sauce, red chile peppers, garlic, sugar, and lime juice, accompanies Vietnamese food. The Vietnamese often wrap cooked foods such as grilled meats with lettuce, fresh herbs, and vegetables in soft rice wrappers, which they dip in *nuoc mam*.

What are cha gio?

Cha gio are Vietnamese spring rolls, which are rolled in thin wrappers made from rice and traditionally stuffed with cellophane noodles, shredded carrot, pork, and scallions, and are dipped in *nuoc mam*. Vietnamese spring rolls are much lighter than their Chinese counterparts.

What are the dos and don'ts of using chopsticks at a Vietnamese table?

According to Vietnamese tradition, it is bad luck to lay chopsticks down so that they crisscross or to eat with a mismatched pair. In addition, every new beginning—such as weddings, Tet, and the cradle ceremony for babies—calls for a brand-new set of chopsticks.

Vietnamese Americans never ask for chopsticks if they are not provided, and they find the American habit of requesting them amusing. When the Vietnamese place chopsticks on the table for guests, they gently tap the table to level them as a show of respect.

What is a pho restaurant?

The Vietnamese so love *pho*, or noodle soup, that they even eat it for breakfast. In fact, pho is such an integral part of Vietnamese cuisine that it has been called the unofficial national dish of Vietnam. In Saigon, the chain of Pho 79 restaurants were as popular as McDonald's, and in Little Saigons across the United States, Vietnamese Americans have re-created a bit of home and opened pho restaurants of their own. Pho Hoa, a pho restaurant that got its start in California, even has franchises as far away as Toronto and Falls Church, Virginia.

Pho comes in many varieties, but *pho bo*—beef and noodle soup—is a traditional favorite among Vietnamese and Vietnamese Americans. Each steaming bowl of pho is accompanied by plates of garnishes such as bean sprouts, thin slices of hot peppers, green onions, lime or lemon wedges, mint, cilantro, and basil. Bottles of chile-garlic sauce, fish sauce, and sugar are also on hand. Typically the Vietnamese eat the noodles with chopsticks in one hand and sip the broth with a spoon in the other. They pause from time to time to add some bean sprouts or herbs to flavor the soup.

LAOTIAN AMERICANS

Who are the Laotians?

Laos, once known as the Kingdom of the Million Elephants, is the only landlocked country in Southeast Asia. About half of the inhabitants of Laos are the ethnic Lao, who trace their ancestry to the Tái, Hmong, and Mien, each with its own distinctive language, customs, and religion. The rest of the peoples of Laos are the Hmong, Mien, Khmu, and other smaller groups.

What historical events contributed to Laotian emigration to the United States?

Much like Vietnam, Laos has endured foreign domination and internal strife throughout its history. And like Vietnam, it is a small country that was suddenly thrust onto the world stage when the superpowers vied for dominance during the Cold War.

Early in its history, Laos was involved in continuous border struggles with Burma and Siam (Thailand). In the fourteenth century the mighty Kingdom of Lan Xuang was founded, but in 1893 France ensnared the kingdom, which by then had split in two, and established a protectorate. France governed the rest of Laos as a colony until World War II, when the Japanese wrested Indochina from the French occupiers. After the Japanese surrendered to the Allies, France sought to reassert rule over its former colonies. This time, Laos, like Vietnam, fought for independence. The Pathet Lao, which means "Lao Country," allied itself with the Viet Minh in Vietnam to free both countries from French domination.

When the Geneva Accords were struck in 1954, Laos officially gained its independence from France. Soon after, however, Laos was riddled by internal conflicts between the Royal Lao and the Pathet Lao, which vied for control of the country. The Viet Minh supported the Pathet Lao to ensure that the Ho Chi Minh Trail, a North Vietnamese military supply line that ran through Laos, remained intact. The United States, fearing the domino effect of communism, came to the defense of the non-Communist Royal Lao in its struggles against the Pathet Lao.

Who are the Hmong and why was the CIA interested in them?

The Hmong were originally from China, but in the mid-1800s they began migrating into neighboring Vietnam, Thailand, and Laos to escape Chinese persecution. The Laotian Hmong inhabited the high mountains, practiced slash-and-burn agriculture, and grew opium as a cash crop. Until 1953, when missionaries arrived in their villages, the Hmong had no written language, and relied instead on the oral tradition of folk tales to record their history.

When the Vietnam War spread into neighboring Laos in

the 1960s, the Central Intelligence Agency began to recruit Hmong mountain tribesmen to fight against the Pathet Lao and its ally, the Viet Cong. The Hmong's mission was to interrupt the Ho Chi Minh Trail, rescue American soldiers, and gather enemy intelligence. The Americans had no qualms about delegating high-risk operations to the Hmong, and as a result, Hmong fighters suffered one of the highest casualty rates of any group involved in the Vietnam War—five times higher than that of U.S. soldiers in combat.

Why did the Laotians flee in such great numbers after the Pathet Lao gained control of the country in 1975?

The Laotians fled when the Pathet Lao won in 1975 for much the same reasons that many Vietnamese fled after the Communists took control of Saigon. Those who had aided U.S. and Royal Lao forces during the war feared retaliation and persecution by the opposing Pathet Lao. Others fled because they feared religious persecution, repression of civil liberties, and forced work in communes, which they suspected the new Communist government would institute.

The mountain tribes, specifically the Hmong, who fought for the U.S. and the Royal Lao forces by waging guerrilla warfare against Pathet Lao soldiers were especially vulnerable to reprisals by the new regime and fled in large numbers. Entire villages, with as many as 16,000 inhabitants each, crossed the border to Thailand, where they remained in refugee camps until they could leave for the United States.

Approximately 70,000 ethnic Lao, 10,000 Mien, and 60,000 Hmong arrived in America after the Pathet Lao gained control of Laos in 1975. Although the Hmong represented a mere 10 percent of the population of Laos, they constitute nearly half of the Laotian refugee population in America. Approximately 33,000 Hmong reside in Fresno County in California alone. Nowadays more Laotians live in America than in the Laotian capital Vientiane.

How difficult has it been for refugees from Laos to adjust to American life?

U.S. government agencies have noted that of all Southeast Asian refugees, Laotians have had the most difficulty adjusting to life in the United States. Though the ethnic Lao and the Mien from Laos have had their share of problems, the Hmong have experienced terrible culture shock due to stark differences in customs, culture, and religion.

The Hmong have found it very difficult to meet the demands of a post-industrial and technological America. Previous to their coming to the United States, most of the men had spent their entire adult lives as fighters in the CIA's secret war in Laos and had acquired no skills they could apply in the West. They had to learn how to navigate the bureaucracy of welfare, set up a household, and acquaint themselves with the school system. For the Hmong who lived in the mountains of Laos, even simple modern-day tasks such as using an electric stove or a toilet seemed strange and daunting.

To further complicate matters, 70 percent of the Hmong who came to America were illiterate in their own language. Only in 1953 was a written form of the Hmong language devised, and the idea that written symbols could convey meaning was alien to many Hmong. Thus, the process of learning English has been doubly taxing for the Hmong, because they have had to attain literacy in their native language first before tackling English.

Unemployment among the Hmong hovers at a startling 90 percent. Those who find work make a meager living selling handicrafts, doing housecleaning, or laboring as seasonal migrant workers. According to a 1987 California study, three in ten Laotian refugee families have been on public assistance from four to ten years, with the Hmong remaining on welfare the longest.

Even though most Laotian refugees, including both Hmong and Mien, worked as independent farmers in their homeland, the American science of farming is as foreign to them as the English language. In Laos, farmers simply waited for rain. In the United States, they use irrigation to maximize their yield. Most Laotian farmers were unfamiliar not only with modern farm machinery and technique, but also with the realities of life on the American farm, for example, the use of pesticides, the marketing of produce, and the bewildering maze of federal regulations.

Which Hmong customs are illegal in America?

In keeping with Hmong tradition, Hmong men marry girls who are between the ages of twelve and fourteen. This custom of marrying young minors, especially girls, has no legal sanction in the United States. Many states not only have minimum-age requirements for marriage, but also have age-of-consent laws regarding sex with minors. Therefore, a man's marrying a girl less than a certain age may have no legal sanction and may also constitute statutory rape.

Despite the law, scores of Hmong refugee men wed underage girls, who fear that if they do not marry early they will not marry at all. As a result of early wedlock, Hmong women are burdened with the highest fertility rate in the world—an average of 9.5 births per woman.

In Hmong culture it is also common for a man to select the woman of his choice as his wife, and then to take her to his house to have sex with her without necessarily having her consent. Such a practice constitutes kidnapping and rape in the United States.

Why do Hmong women have such a high birthrate?

Not only do Hmong women marry early, but in Hmong culture, if they do not give birth to a boy, husbands are allowed to choose other wives. Young Hmong women with baby girls live in a state of anxiety over whether their husbands will leave them for women who can bear a male child. Thus, many get pregnant repeatedly in hopes of giving birth to a boy.

The practices of early marriage and multiple births may account for an estimated 62 percent of Hmong refugees in the United States being dependent on welfare.

What is sudden unexplained death syndrome?

For no apparent reason, a number of Hmong men in America who suffered from no apparent physical ailment have met sudden and mysterious deaths. Nerve gas, which was used in Laos, has been ruled out as a cause of mortality. Their deaths have been attributed to sudden unexplained death syndrome (SUDS) an affliction which strikes men in Asia and the United States between the ages of thirty and fifty who as young men between the ages of fifteen and twenty had gone into battle. SUDS is particularly prevalent among Hmong immigrants and refugees in the United States. Relatives of the deceased have described choking and breathlessness as two symptoms that signal the onslaught of death in these cases. Theories abound as to the cause of SUDS. Doctors have attributed it such things as severe stress caused during the process of aculturation, a thiamine deficiency, irregular potassium levels, and an abnormal heart. In the case of the Hmong others have pointed to the belief in evil spirits and their nocturnal visits as a possible cause of intense fear that could lead to heart failure and death.

What is phi?

Most Lao and Laotian Americans are adherents of Theravada Buddhism, a branch of Buddhism. At the same time that they practice Buddhism, most also follow the cult of *phi*, meaning "religious spirits." Rather than causing conflict, Theravada Buddhism and phi coexist harmoniously in the Laotian belief system, perhaps because they pertain to separate realms: Buddhism deals with the next realm, while *phi* concerns itself with progress on this plane of action.

CAMBODIAN AMERICANS

What is the story behind the arrival of Cambodians in the United States?

Cambodia, later known as the Khmer Republic and then as Democratic Kampuchea, has been shaped by a long history of border struggles and foreign occupation, similar to Vietnam and Laos. The Khmer empire flourished from the ninth century to the fifteenth century. The Khmer, the majority in present-day Cambodia, ruled over much of Thailand, Laos, and southern Vietnam during this period, and built magnificent temples at Angkor, temples which reflected both Buddhist and Hindu influences. In 1432, Angkor was abandoned as the Khmer empire went into decline. The ruins at Angkor include one of the largest religious buildings in the world, the Angkor Wat.

As the Khmer empire fell apart in the 1400s, the Annamese (Vietnamese) and Siamese took control of Cambodia. The next four hundred years brought internal and external strife. In 1863, France gained control of Cambodia, and under the terms of a treaty signed that year, the country became a French protectorate. In 1887 French Indochina was formed when Cambodia was joined with Cochin China, Annam, and Tonkin.

Like the Vietnamese and Laotians, the Khmer fought against French colonialism until World War II, when the Japanese briefly gained control of the region. During Japanese occupation, Khmer prince **Norodom Sihanouk** proclaimed Cambodian sovereignty, and in 1946, Cambodia was declared an autonomous state. However, after the Japanese surrendered to the Allies, the French came back to reclaim what they thought was theirs, but this time they were out of luck. In 1954, in accordance with the terms of the Geneva Accords, France withdrew from Indochina and finally recognized the independence of Cambodia. Cambodia's former prince Norodom Sihanouk was named the only legitimate authority for Cambodia in 1960.

During the Vietnam conflict, Sihanouk, mistrustful of the United States, allied his country with China and North Vietnam. In 1965, Prince Sihanouk allowed the North Vietnamese to transport supplies and troops across Cambodian territory in the continuing war effort against the South Vietnamese government. All the while, internal dissension grew in Cambodia, and in March 1970 a coup headed by General **Lon Nol** overthrew Sihanouk, a move which the United States endorsed.

Once General Lon Nol came to power, Cambodian ties with North Vietnam were cut. Lon Nol ordered the immediate departure of North Vietnamese forces from eastern Cambodia and allowed American and South Vietnamese troops to enter Cambodia to clear out all Communist sanctuaries. Cambodia became the Khmer Republic, and Lon Nol named himself the country's first president. The United States continued to support Lon Nol with money and supplies while the North Vietnamese gave support to a Communist guerrilla organization headed by the exiled Sihanouk and called the Khmer Rouge. The United States also extended the Vietnam War into Cambodia by bombing Vietnamese depots and supply lines hidden there.

Shortly before the fall of Saigon, in early 1975, the Khmer Rouge, led by **Pol Pot**, launched a major offensive. North Vietnamese troops entered Saigon, and the Khmer Rouge stormed the capital of Cambodia, Phnom Penh, on April 17, 1975, and assumed control of the country. Lon Nol fled and Prince Sihanouk became head of state. The regime instituted a new constitution in 1976, renaming the country Democratic Kampuchea. In April 1976, Sihanouk was ousted and **Dhien Sanipan** became the first president, with Pol Pot as prime minister.

What were "the killing fields"?

Pol Pot's rule of Cambodia is often referred to as the years of "the killing fields." Under his leadership, draconian and horrific measures were taken to institute socialist reforms in the country, and millions of Cambodians suffered and died as a result. Pol Pot closed schools and hospitals, and resettled millions of city dwellers to the labor camps in the countryside, where they were forced to work in the fields, mainly cultivating rice and building irrigation canals and dams. The laborers endured unbelievable hardship in the camps, working long hours with short breaks and little food to sustain them. Khmer Rouge soldiers were ordered to kill those who resisted migrating or working under the unbearable conditions. Those who remained quite often died from overwork, disease, and starvation.

Pol Pot wanted to purify his country and was bent on destroying all who had been tainted by Western influences. The regime zealously targeted intellectuals, students, elitists, anti-Communists, and people who had supported the U.S.-backed Lon Nol government. Even wearing eyeglasses became dangerous under the new government, since corrective eyewear was considered too intellectual.

In the face of such atrocities and certain death, hundreds of thousands of Cambodians attempted to flee to safety by trekking to Thailand. Doctors, lawyers, military personnel, students, and others in imminent peril who could not escape disguised their identities so they would not be executed.

Although exact figures are unknown, the death toll in Cambodia during this reign of terror rose to an estimated two million, or approximately one-third of the entire population.

How did Pol Pot's killing fields end?

Pol Pot's rule ended when Vietnam invaded Cambodia in 1978 and quickly took control of the country, renaming it the

People's Republic of Kampuchea. After the overthrow of Pol Pot, the Heng Smarin and Hun Sen governments, which were backed by the Vietnamese, came to power, bringing to an end the era of mass extermination of the Cambodian people.

The Vietnamese occupation unleashed a mass exodus of Cambodians to Thailand. During the Pol Pot years, few Cambodians managed to escape to Thailand, because the Pol Pot regime strictly controlled the movement of the population. In addition, many Cambodians in the labor camps were too weak from hunger and illness to escape. However, the newly installed Vietnamese government afforded the Cambodians more freedom of movement. Thus, those with the strength escaped.

These escapees subsisted in the squalor of Thai refugee camps, sometimes for years, until they could find sponsors to help them permanently resettle elsewhere. The Vietnamese continued to occupy Cambodia until late 1989, when civil war erupted and different factions attempted to overthrow the Hun Sen government. Civil war continued to plague Cambodia until 1991, when a peace accord was signed.

How many Cambodians made their way to America?

Over 100,000 Cambodian refugees came to American shores between 1975 and 1990 and attempted to make the United States their permanent homes. The total Cambodian population in the United States, including those born here, has risen to more than 200,000.

What special problems have the Cambodians dealt with in the United States?

A large number of Cambodians are plagued by the psychological scars that they carry with them from years of torture at the hands of Pol Pot and his soldiers. Many suffer from what has been termed post-traumatic stress disorder, a condition which has also afflicted survivors of World War II Nazi concentration camps and other individuals who have endured unspeakable horrors such as torture, starvation, disease, constant fear, and witnessing countless executions. Many Cambodian Americans exhibit the classic symptoms of post-traumatic stress disorder, such as emotional numbness, depression, withdrawal, recurring nightmares, and loss of appetite.

A report on Southeast Asian youth in the San Diego area revealed that Khmer parents, particularly women, were more likely to suffer from depression than other Southeast Asian refugees. Western-style counseling and therapy do not seem to help these people much.

Why have so many Cambodian women in the United States gone blind?

Between 1982 and 1989, over a hundred Cambodian women in California reported to doctors that they were blind. Curiously, when the doctors gave the women eye examinations, they could not detect any physical signs of impairment. Thus the condition was described as "psychosomatic blindness," also referred to as "hysterical blindness." The women had apparently lost their sight because their minds had been so overwhelmed by the horrors they witnessed and endured in Cambodia.

One woman reported that her vision had failed immediately after she bore witness to the execution of her family. Another Cambodian woman noted that her world had become dark after evidence was found confirming the execution of her brother and his family at the hands of soldiers. Yet another recalled that she lost her sight for a period of time after watching soldiers beat up a man and then throw him into a fire. One woman suffered from poor vision and painful headaches after witnessing her daughter being bludgeoned to death. A psychologist who interviewed these women concluded that "their minds simply closed down, they refused to see anymore."

Why are there so many single-parent Cambodian households in America?

In addition to psychological hardships, many Khmer families suffer from disruption and disorganization of the traditional social structure. A high percentage of Khmer refugees lost their spouses during Pol Pot's reign of terror. Many are single parents faced with the daunting task of raising their children in a brand-new culture. A report on Southeast Asian youth in the San Diego area found that only 49 percent of Khmer youths lived in families headed by both a mother and a father.

Where have the Cambodian refugees settled in the United States?

Initially, Khmer refugees settled all around the country, wherever they could find an American to sponsor them. However, many refugees found their new hometowns inhospitable, either due to the climate, few employment opportunities, or a lack of support groups and cultural networks. Thus, many Khmer relocated to places that suited their needs, and for the majority that meant California.

Today, as a result of this secondary migration, Long Beach, California, boasts the largest Khmer population in America, and the largest Cambodian ex-patriate community in the world for that matter. Cambodians gravitate to Little Phnom Penh, which has sprouted up on Anaheim Street in Long Beach. Besides Long Beach, a significant number of Cambodians also settled in Lowell, Massachusetts, during the 1980s. In a decade, the Cambodian population in Lowell swelled dramatically from less than a hundred people to 25,000, or 20 percent of Lowell's entire population. Lowell now boasts the second-largest Cambodian community in the United States.

Why did Lowell, Massachusetts, draw so many Cambodians?

Since it was founded in 1826, Lowell, Massachusetts, has had the reputation of being a town built by immigrants. During the 1800s, Lowell was a textile and industrial giant that first drew teenage girls from surrounding areas into its labor force, then European immigrants searching for work.

The economic downturn in the textile industry in the 1920s sent Lowell into a downward spiral. The city was revitalized only in the late 1970s when Wang Laboratories, Inc., moved into the area and provided jobs in its electronics assembly plants and construction projects. Wang soon became the largest employer in the city. The promise of jobs and economic opportunity in Lowell drew Cambodians, continuing the city's long tradition as an immigrant haven.

In 1984 a Buddhist temple was erected to serve the growing Cambodian population in Lowell, the majority of whom are Buddhist. The temple soon became a gathering place for the Cambodian residents. Many more Cambodians, attracted by the strong Cambodian presence, began arriving in Lowell. The great migration to Lowell wreaked havoc on a public school system unequipped to meet the special needs of the refugee children and caused unrest in the community. When Wang experienced financial setbacks in the late 1980s and workers were laid off, resentment against the Cambodians turned fierce. In the face of such economic difficulties and blatant hostility, the steady flow of Cambodians to Lowell ceased.

How difficult has it been for Cambodians to acculturate to the American way of life?

Assimilation has been especially difficult for the Cambodians, since the Khmer Rouge stripped them of everything. As **Haing Ngor** described in his biography,

In Cambodia a way of life had evolved over many hundreds of years. It was much simpler than America, and that was part of its beauty. In Cambodia we didn't have welfare or Social Security. We didn't need them. All we needed were our families and the monks. . . . The system was not perfect, but it worked. Everybody had enough to eat. Cambodian society was stable. For generation after generation we followed our customs, until in 1975 the communists put an end to our way of life. We lost everything—our families, our monks, our villages, our land, all our possessions. Everything. When we came to the United States we couldn't put our old lives back together. We didn't even have the pieces.

What kinds of jobs have Cambodian Americans found?

Like other refugee groups, Cambodians have had difficulty finding employment outside of dead-end, low-paying jobs. The majority of Khmer lack a formal education, and this has compounded their problems.

However, many Cambodians in California met with success during the 1980s in the doughnut industry. **Bun Tek Ngoy**, a Cambodian pioneer in doughnuts, became a millionaire. He set up his first doughnut shop in 1977, as the only Cambodian to own a doughnut shop back then, and then expanded his business to a chain of doughnut shops. Following suit, many other Cambodians entered the doughnut industry as family operations, hoping to reap a profit in the daily grind of doughnut-making by night and selling by day. Family members contributed either by watching the counter and helping customers or by baking doughnuts all night long.

Other Cambodians, such as **Bun H. Tao** (who is the nephew of Bun Tek Ngoy and who learned the tricks of the trade from his successful uncle), became distributors of doughnut shop supplies. Bun H. Tao runs a doughnut supply distribution company serving a mostly Cambodian clientele, to which he extends instant credit and loans of vital supplies and machines to operate doughnut shops. With such help many Cambodian refugees were able to make it in the doughnut business during the 1980s.

However, due to the explosion of doughnut shops in the state and a general decline in the doughnut business in the 1990s, distributors such as Bun H. Tao and Cambodian doughnut shop owners, who own about two-thirds of all such shops in California, have all been feeling the pinch. Bun H. Tao's customers cannot afford to pay him for their supplies because not enough customers are buying their product.

THE TEN RICHEST ASIAN AMERICAN BUSINESSMEN

1. Kanetaka Yamaguchi

CEO of Union Bank; net worth of over a billion dollars

2. An Wang

Late founder of Wang Laboratories; net worth of $790 million

3. Gerald Tsai, Jr.

Chairman of Primerica; net worth of $580 million

4. Tadaichi Ikagawa

CEO of Sumitomo Bank in California; net worth of $377 million

5. Jay S. Sidhu

CEO of Sovereign Bancorp; net worth of $271 million

6. Sirjang Lal Tandon

Founder of Tandon Corp.; net worth of $270 million

---

7. Winston Chen

Chairman and CEO of Solectron; net worth of $205 million

8. Gene Lu

Founder of Advanced Logic Research; net worth of $169 million

9. Chuck Thakkar

Founder of DCT Systems Group; net worth of $150 million

10. Roy Yamaguchi

Founder of Roy's Restaurant, originally in Honolulu but now franchised in Guam and in Tokyo; net worth of $13 million

Who is Dith Pran?

Dith Pran is a Cambodian refugee and a survivor of the Khmer Rouge holocaust who immigrated to the United States and now works as a photographer for *The New York Times*. Formerly, he worked as assistant to **Sydney Schanberg**, then a journalist for *The New York Times* covering the drama that unfolded in Cambodia between 1973 and 1975.

In 1975, when the Khmer Rouge ousted Cambodia's president Lon Nol and Pol Pot took power, Dith Pran became one of the millions of Cambodians targeted by the Communist regime. He was forced to evacuate Phnom Penh and was relocated to a labor camp in the countryside, where he miraculously survived four years of torture. As he has recounted, he lost his teeth because of the poor diet in the camps, and his feet and legs were badly infected from wading in animal manure used to fertilize the rice fields.

Typical of the Cambodian refugee experience, Dith Pran suffered tremendous personal losses as well. Four of his siblings died at the hands of Khmer Rouge soldiers. His father suffered a similar fate, but his death came much slower, from starvation. Fortunately, Dith Pran's wife and children had fled Cambodia for the United States in 1975 and managed to escape the Khmer Rouge ordeal. Dith Pran himself also made it through, when on October 3, 1979, he crossed the border into Thailand.

In 1984, the highly charged motion picture *The Killing Fields*, based on the life story of Dith Pran, was released. Prior to its release, the public was generally unaware of the atrocities that had occurred in Cambodia under Pol Pot. This critically acclaimed film brought the horrors of the Khmer Rouge to light and brought Dith Pran recognition and the opportunity to help his fellow Cambodians.

With an invitation from **Hun Sen**, the prime minister of Cambodia, Dith Pran returned to his homeland for the first time in 1989 as a delegate on the Cambodia Documentation Commission, a group seeking to put the Khmer Rouge on trial in the World Court for the crime of genocide. Upon his return to Cambodia, he was reunited with a sister and a few surviving relatives and friends. To this day, Dith Pran continues to travel and lecture widely, working with various organizations devoted to the plight of Cambodian refugees.

Who was Haing Ngor?

Haing Ngor was another survivor of the Khmer Rouge terror, who escaped to Thailand in 1979 and came to America in 1980 with the help of a cousin already established here. Though his own history of survival under the Khmer Rouge is quite remarkable (and has garnered widespread attention), Ngor initially gained recognition for his portrayal of Dith Pran in the film *The Killing Fields*, for which he won an Oscar for Best Supporting Actor in 1985.

Haing Ngor's life in Cambodia during Pol Pot's reign of terror closely parallels the troubled life of Dith Pran. Growing up in a village south of Phnom Penh, Ngor knew only political turmoil. Nonetheless, he aspired to be a doctor and attended medical school in Phnom Penh, earning his medical degree in 1975, a couple of months before the Khmer Rouge gained solid control of Cambodia.

Ngor chose to remain in his homeland, convinced that the new regime could be no worse than the corrupt government of Lon Nol. Despite warnings that he was in imminent danger and should flee the country, Ngor stayed behind, insisting that the Khmer Rouge needed him alive because of the shortage of doctors in Cambodia. He continued to practice medicine until one April day in 1975 when Khmer Rouge soldiers burst into his medical office as he was operating on a patient. A young Khmer Rouge soldier entered the operating room and demanded to know where the doctor was. Sensing his life was in danger, Ngor lied to the officer and convinced him that the doctor had already left.

Haing Ngor and his wife were forced to go to the countryside to labor in the fields. Realizing that the Khmer Rouge had specifically targeted doctors for extermination, Ngor took on a new identity as a cab driver. Even when he saw people suffering around him, he dared not help lest he reveal his medical expertise. Ngor's wife was a teacher, an occupation that also made her vulnerable, and she too concealed her identity.

The torturous conditions in the labor camps threatened Haing Ngor's life on several occasions, but miraculously he was spared. He and his wife suffered from severe hunger, and Ngor was reduced to stealing food to survive. Tragically, his wife succumbed to the brutal conditions under the Khmer Rouge. Weak and severely malnourished, she died in 1978 during childbirth, along with their unborn child. Haing Ngor escaped from Cambodia in 1979, when the Vietnamese occupied Cambodia. He worked as a doctor in the refugee camps before coming to the United States.

Unfortunately, his medical degree was not valid in the United States, and Ngor was barred from practicing medicine here. He had a difficult time mastering English, and this prevented him from regaining his practice. Locked out of his profession, Haing Ngor resorted to working as a security guard while he strove to develop competence in English. Later, he landed a job as a caseworker assigned to helping fellow Indochinese refugees.

After Haing Ngor was cast as Dith Pran in *The Killing Fields*, his life changed considerably. He began to give speeches calling for peace in Cambodia and for the improvement of conditions for refugees. After the film's release, Haing Ngor wrote several books about his experiences in Cambodia and lectured extensively about the atrocities he endured at the hands of the Khmer Rouge.

How did the 1993 elections in Cambodia affect Cambodian refugees in America?

In May of 1993, elections were held in Cambodia for the first time in two decades. Naturally, most Cambodian Americans were tuned in to these groundbreaking events in their homeland, but some went a step further by actually getting involved in the political process. During the elections, a number of Cambodian refugees ran for one of the 120 seats open in the Cambodian assembly. These 120 seats were of utmost importance, since the Cambodians elected to fill them would join an assembly in charge of drafting a brand-new constitution and forming a new government for Cambodia.

When Cambodian Americans declared their candidacy, this was cause for great consternation in the United States, since American citizens are not allowed to hold foreign public office. Still, they ran in the hopes of helping their home country. One candidate in the running explained, "It is a historic moment in the history of Cambodia, and we just felt an enormous desire to come back and help." Another who felt compelled to participate was Bun Tek Ngoy, the Cambodian doughnut pioneer, who stated, "I see this as an opportunity to set up the kind of freedom and democracy that makes America great here in Cambodia."

In addition to running for seats in the assembly, Cambodians in the United States also had the opportunity to vote in the elections. In order to do so, they first had to register to vote and then they had to travel to New York, the only polling place in America, to cast their ballots. Such obstacles prevented many Cambodians from voting, but did not curtail heated debates about the political parties vying for power in Cambodia.

The Royalist Party, known by its initials FUNCINPEC, won the election with 45.47 percent of the vote and garnered 58 seats in the assembly, while the Cambodian People's Party, the ruling party, received 38.22 percent of the vote and captured 51 seats. Smaller parties split the rest of the seats in the assembly.

Not surprisingly, the defeated ruling party claimed that the winners had rigged the elections and threatened to reject the results. In a compromise, FUNCINPEC and the Cambodian People's Party finally agreed to a power-sharing arrangement. All the ministries would have two ministers, one from each side. Thus, **Prince Norodom Ranariddh** of FUNCINPEC was named the first prime minister and **Hun Sen** of the Cambodian People's Party was designated the second prime minister.

Nevertheless, bloodshed still plagues Cambodia and its people as the Khmer Rouge continues to wage guerrilla warfare against the ruling parties in an attempt to seize power once again.

Do Cambodians celebrate the New Year in the same way as the Vietnamese?

While Vietnamese Tet takes place in January or February, the Cambodian New Year occurs at the end of harvest season, generally in April. Like the Vietnamese, Cambodians celebrate for many days, even up to a month. However, Cambodian Americans usually celebrate only on April weekends to accommodate working people.

The New Year's celebration is a time for Cambodian Americans to make a fresh start and to remember their homeland and worship their ancestors. Festivities include many cultural performances and an abundance of ethnic food. For many Cambodian Americans the New Year provides the opportunity to instruct the young about Cambodian culture and history. Whatever the case, New Year's festivities bring Cambodian Americans great happiness and a sense of nostalgia and pride, which draw the community together.

Do Cambodian Americans have their own restaurants?

When the Cambodian refugees first arrived in the United States, they prepared all their meals at home, as is the Cambodian custom. On the rare occasions that they dined out, they usually patronized Chinese restaurants. As survival in America necessitated that Cambodian women abandon household duties and join the workforce and as Cambodians saw a need to create communal places, Cambodian restaurants sprung up in Cambodian American enclaves. Little Phnom Penh in Long Beach, California, boasts numerous Cambodian restaurants, where all the traditional flavors of Cambodian cuisine—namely pickled and fermented fish, lime, lemon grass, tamarind, basil, mint, and coconut—come into play. The most opulent restaurant in Little Phnom Penh is New Paradise, praised by Cambodian Americans for its extensive traditional menu that includes such dishes as *amok*, fish wrapped in spinach and banana leaves and steamed in coconut cream and spices.

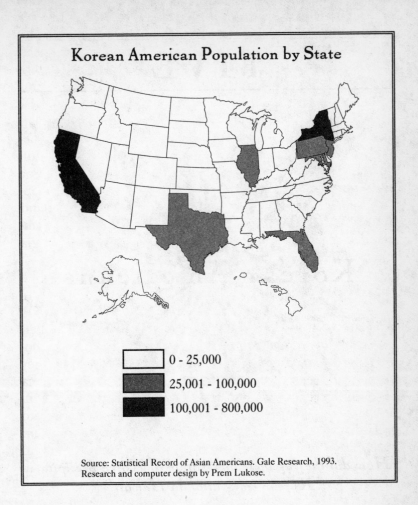

Korean American Population by State

0 - 25,000
25,001 - 100,000
100,001 - 800,000

Source: Statistical Record of Asian Americans. Gale Research, 1993.
Research and computer design by Prem Lukose.

FIVE

Korean Americans

How did the Japanese annexation of Korea precipitate Korean emigration to Hawaii?

How did the Chinese Exclusion Act encourage Korean immigration to Hawaii?

What role did Christian churches play in the immigration of Koreans to Hawaii?

Why was Korean emigration halted in 1905?

*How long did the Koreans stay
on the Hawaiian plantations?*

*How did Japan play a role in controlling Korean
emigration to the United States until the end of
World War II?*

*What kind of reception did Americans give the Korean
immigrants?*

Were Koreans allowed to own land in California?

*What united the Korean community
in America after 1910?*

*Why did the Korean nationalist Chang In-hwan
achieve hero status after assassinating the American
Japanophile Durham Stevens?*

*Whom did the Koreans support during World
War II, and what was the Declaration of the
All-Korean Convention?*

*What happened on December 7, 1941, and how did
this infamous act impact on Koreans in America?*

*Why were Koreans originally classified as "enemy
aliens" by the United States government?*

*Why did Koreans in the United States wear signs that
read "I'm no Jap"?*

How did some Korean nationalists agitate against Japanese Americans?

Did Korean Americans serve in the U.S. armed forces during World War II?

How did the Korean War unleash the second wave of Korean immigrants to the United States?

Where did the word gook come from and what does it mean anyway?

What triggered a third wave of Korean immigrants to America?

Why are there more North Koreans than South Koreans in the United States today?

What is a Korean kae?

How has the kae financial strategy helped Korean businesses flourish in the United States?

Why did so many Koreans in New York City choose to open greengroceries instead of becoming professionals?

How have Korean American greengrocers achieved such success?

What about the rumor that Korean American small-business owners get their money from the Reverend Sun Myung Moon's Unification Church?

How did Korean-bashing, combined with the 1980s recession, hurt the kae?

What were these riots that took such a toll on Korean American businesses?

What was the Korean American civil rights protest in New York City about?

How were other Asian Americans affected by the ethnic clashes between Korean Americans and African Americans in New York's inner city?

Are any Korean Americans active in U.S. politics?

Who are some great Korean American athletes?

What contributions have Korean Americans made to classical music?

What other contributions have Korean Americans made to the arts?

Who is Angela E. Oh?

What traditions from the old country do Korean Americans adhere to?

What Korean holidays do Korean Americans celebrate?

What is Hangul Day?

What is New York's Korean Day Parade?

"Have you eaten rice yet?"

Which five flavors and five colors are essential in Korean cuisine?

What are some other classic Korean dishes?

What is kimchee?

Are the Japanese the only Asians who drink sake?

Can you name the meat Koreans and Korean Americans eat to bolster their strength?

What is traditional Korean medicine?

What is acupuncture and what is acupressure?

What is ginseng?

According to the 1990 U.S. Census, approximately 800,000 Americans of Korean ancestry reside in the United States. The Korean population in America in 1960 stood at only 10,000, but with the passage of the Hart-Celler Act of 1965, that figure skyrocketed to 500,000 by 1985.

Koreans have excelled in all fields of endeavor, especially business. In fact, Koreans are some of America's most gifted entrepreneurs. Approximately 100,000 Korean Americans live in New York City, where they have set up thriving small businesses, such as the over 3,500 "Korean-on-the-corner" greengroceries that supply New Yorkers around the clock with everything from cucumbers and tofu to fresh squeezed orange juice and yellow calla lilies.

When New York Koreans do their own shopping, they often head to vibrant Koreatown, a strictly commercial area filled with restaurants and stores that stretches from Twenty-third Street to Thirty-second Street between Fifth and Sixth Avenues in Manhattan. Koreatown is also the center of operations for Korean corporations, wholesalers, and import-export companies, as well as three Korean newspapers.

While New York City has a thriving Korean community, the largest Korean enclave outside of Seoul is in Los Angeles, the metropolis that approximately 150,000 Koreans call home. Olympic Boulevard between Hoover and Western Avenues in L.A. is the site of a bustling Koreatown, which in 1992 boasted over 3,200 Korean American businesses.

How did the Japanese annexation of Korea precipitate Korean emigration to Hawaii?

After Japan defeated China in the Sino-Japanese War in 1895, and Russia in the Russo-Japanese War in 1905, it turned its full attention to Korea. Japan's Meiji government sent troops to Seoul, assassinated Korea's Queen **Min**, and forced Korea to sign treaty after treaty designed to increase Japanese dominance in Korea. In 1905, Japan made Korea its protectorate, and in 1910, it annexed the country outright.

From 1910 to 1945 Japan occupied Korea and instituted a campaign to wipe out Korean culture by ordering Koreans to worship at Shinto shrines, speak Japanese, and adopt Japanese names and by preventing them from publishing newspapers and organizing political groups. Koreans responded to the Japanese occupation with numerous acts of sabotage, ranging from guerrilla warfare to non-violent resistance. Over time, Japanese soldiers killed 7,000 Korean protesters, imprisoned 50,000, and razed entire villages. With their country in almost total ruin, many Koreans dreamed of escaping to a country free of Japanese control. Many got their chance, since Hawaii had already opened its doors to Korean immigration, and since America would soon follow suit.

How did the Chinese Exclusion Act encourage Korean immigration to Hawaii?

When the United States annexed Hawaii on August 12, 1898, U.S. federal laws were extended to the island chain. Thus the Chinese Exclusion Act signed in 1882 eventually brought a halt to the importation of Chinese labor to Hawaiian sugar and pineapple plantations. Plantation owners feared that the remaining Japanese laborers would band together into a volatile protest movement, so they explored the option of bringing in Puerto Rican, Italian, Portuguese, and African American laborers from the American South to keep the work force diverse and hence less cohesive.

In 1903, plantation owners targeted Koreans, for their animosity toward the Japanese, to undercut the growing Japanese power on Hawaiian plantations. Since Korea was a protectorate of Japan, Hawaiian labor contractors could recruit Koreans just as they did Japanese. Contractors lured the Koreans with promises of high wages, free transportation, and educational opportunities. With Korea crippled by rice shortages brought on by drought, many Koreans were eager to go to Hawaii. While only 93 Koreans made their way to Hawaii in 1902, this figure swelled to 11,000 by 1905.

What role did Christian churches play in the immigration of Koreans to Hawaii?

Many of the Koreans who sailed to Hawaii were Christians. Presbyterian and Methodist missionaries in Korea urged new converts to go to Hawaii, promising them that they would become better Christians in a Christian country and thus would be blessed with great riches.

In Hawaii these Koreans established their own chapels on the plantations. Plantation owners encouraged and financially supported the Korean churches because they believed religious observance made the laborers more stable and efficient.

Why was Korean emigration halted in 1905?

Like other laborers, the Koreans endured horrendous working conditions in Hawaii. They were made to work in the fields under the hot sun for ten hours a day, and to live in makeshift shelters. In an act of protest, Japan, whose responsibility it was to oversee the treatment of Korean citizens, brought Korean emigration to Hawaii to a halt in 1905.

How long did the Koreans stay on the Hawaiian plantations?

Out of all the immigrants who came to work in Hawaii, the Koreans were the first to leave the plantations. By 1907, approximately one thousand Koreans had migrated from Hawaii to the United States, mainly to California, but also to Utah, Colorado, and Wyoming, where they worked in the copper and coal mines. Others were drawn from Hawaii to America by the wages railroad companies offered for the construction of the transcontinental railroad. By the time the Great Depression hit, thousands of Koreans had abandoned the Hawaiian plantations for America.

Unlike the Chinese and the Japanese, the Korean immigrants had had some exposure to urban life back home. Some sought employment in the cities, where they were forced to take menial jobs as restaurant workers, gardeners, janitors, and domestic help. Little by little, Koreans became involved in the hotel business. In 1906 **Wu Kyong-sik** opened the first Korean hotel in Sacramento, and by 1920 more than twenty Korean-owned hotels had sprung up around the country. Most of the approximately seventy Koreans who lived in New York City in 1920 were Christian converts and academicians who took up residence around Columbia University on Manhattan's West Side. Thirty of them organized their own Korean church at 633 West 115th Street, and invited political refugees and students into their fold.

How did Japan play a role in controlling Korean emigration to the United States until the end of World War II?

Upon signing the Gentlemen's Agreement with the United States in 1908, Japan agreed to restrict Japanese emigration to America. The Japanese government stopped issuing passports not only to its own citizens, but also to Korean laborers wishing to go to the United States.

From 1910 to 1924, Japan allowed only Korean wives and "picture brides" (Korean women whose marriages had been arranged with Korean men who had emigrated to the United States; the couple met for the first time when the woman arrived in America) to emigrate to the United States to join their spouses. Approximately one thousand Korean picture brides came to America during this period.

With the Immigration Act of 1924, the influx of Koreans into America came to a halt, and did not resume until after World War II, when the second wave of Koreans entered the United States between 1951 and 1964.

What kind of reception did Americans give the Korean immigrants?

Like other Asians, Koreans experienced overt racial discrimination in America. White landlords often refused to rent houses to Koreans, movie theaters sometimes forced them to sit in a corner (with the Mexicans) away from white filmgoers, and recreational facilities and restaurants usually refused to serve Koreans. Many Koreans held fast to the notion that their ill treatment stemmed from the Chinese and Japanese immigrants, who had soured Americans' views of Asians by retaining the ways of the old country and not assimilating into the mainstream. To reverse the tide of discrimination, Koreans believed that they had to prove their willingness to conform to American ways.

Were Koreans allowed to own land in California?

The United States government categorized Koreans just as it did the Japanese, as aliens ineligible for citizenship. Thus the Alien Land Act of 1913 prohibited not only the Japanese but also the Koreans from owning and leasing land in California.

What united the Korean community in America after 1910?

Kwangbok, the future restoration of sovereignty for Korea, became the unifying force in the Korean community in America in 1910. When Koreans left Korea between 1903 and 1905, they were a people with a homeland. When Japan annexed Korea in 1910, Koreans in the United States suddenly became yumin, drifters without a country. Korean migrants who returned to their native country after the Japanese took control were appalled with what they found, and alerted Koreans in America to stay put.

Independence for Korea became the rallying cry for many Koreans in America grieving the loss of their homeland. The movement to free Korea of Japanese domination gave meaning to many immigrants' lives and heightened Korean nationalism. Koreans, particularly entrepreneurs, worked hard to turn a greater profit in order to contribute more dollars to the patriotic fund. Parents became more determined to instill Korean values in their children and ensure that they received a Korean education.

In 1909 the patriots founded the Tae-Hanin Kungmin-hoe (THK), or the Korean National Association of North America, in order to unite all the nationalist organizations that the independence movement had spawned around the country. This organization, headquartered in San Francisco, was devoted to *kwangbok* and the preservation of the Korean national identity. The THK essentially metamorphosed into a Korean government-in-exile, which represented Koreans in their relations with the U.S. government.

Many Korean nationalists advocated violent means to achieve their end. They organized quasi-military programs in the United States as a training ground for a possible armed struggle against the Japanese to regain control of their homeland.

Why did the Korean nationalist Chang In-hwan achieve hero status after assassinating the American Japanophile Durham Stevens?

Hatred of the Japanese was intense in the Korean community in America, and anyone who took Japan's side incurred the wrath of the Koreans. A white American by the name of **Durham Stevens** was just such an individual. He had been employed by the Japanese government to convince the U.S. government that the Koreans supported the Japanese takeover.

In March 1908 Stevens made a stopover in San Francisco en route from Korea to Washington, and his public statements justifying the Japanese occupation of Korea were printed in a local newspaper. On March 23, 1908, a group of Koreans confronted Stevens for his actions in front of the Ferry Building. Among them was an enraged **Chang In-hwan**, who shot Stevens, mortally wounding him.

Korean immigrants honored Chang as a national hero, and contributions for his legal defense poured in from around the world. Many Koreans in America donated as much as a week's salary to Chang's cause.

Whom did the Koreans support during World War II, and what was the Declaration of the All-Korean Convention?

On April 20, 1941, an all-Korean representative convention was held in Honolulu to pledge support for the Allied Powers. According to the Declaration of the All-Korean Convention, the Koreans made a pact to "unite together as one body and support the Allied Powers until they bring a final victory of the present war against the Axis powers."

A nine-point program was also adopted that was designed to unite all Korean organizations and support a common goal: the independence of Korea. The United Korean Committee handled all diplomatic and political affairs. **Syngman Rhee** was appointed chairman of the committee and was given sole authority to represent Koreans in America before the Korean provisional government-in-exile in China.

What happened on December 7, 1941, and how did this infamous act impact on Koreans in America?

On December 7, 1941, Imperial Japan bombed Pearl Harbor. The United States' declaration of war against Japan was welcomed by Koreans, who believed American involvement in the war would lead to the destruction of Japan and hence the restoration of Korean national independence. Korean support for the war effort was tremendous. Between 1942 and 1943, Koreans in America, who numbered only ten thousand, purchased $239,000 worth of U.S. defense bonds.

Why were Koreans originally classified as "enemy aliens" by the United States government?

The war years were also a time of painful disorientation for Koreans. Korea was officially a protectorate of Japan. Thus, in 1940, the Alien Registration Act gave Koreans the classification of subjects of Japan. When the United States declared war against Japan, Koreans as well as Japanese in America were designated "enemy aliens." Koreans were insulted by and took exception to this classification, since for so long they had fought for Korean independence from Japan.

In Hawaii Koreans employed in defense operations were horrified when they learned that they were classified not as subjects of Japan but as Japanese. They were ordered to wear badges with black borders to signify their restricted-category status. Infuriated over this case of mistaken identity, the Koreans in Hawaiian defense staged protest after protest until finally they were allowed to print on their badges the declaration "I am Korean."

Why did Koreans in the United States wear signs that read "I'm No Jap"?

Koreans in the Hawaiian defense were not the only ones to resort to wearing badges. Americans directed animosity toward Koreans in all walks of life, whom they mistook for Japanese. Koreans took to wearing their traditional dress to ward off incidents of mistaken identity. Some also attached signs to their clothing that read, "I'm no Jap!"

How did some Korean nationalists agitate against Japanese Americans?

While some in the Korean community sympathized with the plight of Japanese Americans during World War II, many Korean nationalists were just as suspicious of the Japanese in their midst as most Americans. As early as 1941, **Kilsoo Haan**, the leader of the Sino-Korean People's League, alleged that the 35,000 to 50,000 Japanese in Hawaii would come to Japan's assistance against the United States. In 1942, Kilsoo Haan went to California, where he called for the forced evacuation of West Coast Japanese.

Did Korean Americans serve in the U.S. armed forces during World War II?

Like the Filipinos in the United States, Koreans were chomping at the bit to join the American armed forces. The U.S. government took advantage of the Koreans' command of Japanese and employed them as language instructors and translators of classified documents. Many Koreans also worked on the propaganda front as radio broadcasters or became underground agents in parts of Asia occupied by Japan. One-fifth of the Korean population in Los Angeles signed on with the California National Guard, which organized them into a special unit called the Tiger Brigade. The Tiger Brigade drilled regularly for three to four hours every weekend to prepare for a possible enemy invasion of California.

Koreans in America contributed to the war effort in other ways as well. Elderly Korean men served as emergency fire wardens and elderly women volunteered in the Red Cross.

As a reward for Korean service in the U.S. armed forces during World War II, **Joseph R. Farrington**, a Hawaiian territorial delegate, introduced in Congress a bill that would extend naturalization rights to Koreans. The bill did not pass.

How did the Korean War unleash the second wave of Korean immigrants to the United States?

Of the five million Americans serving in Korea during the three-year Korean War that ended in an armistice signed on July 27, 1953, fewer than 1 percent were women. Thus many

American soldiers met and married Korean women, and when they were sent back home, they took their Korean wives with them. These "war brides" were the first Korean immigrants allowed legally into the United States after 1924. Since U.S. forces were stationed in South Korea after the war, marriages between American GIs and Korean women continued for many years. Between 1951 and 1964, over 28,000 Korean war brides found a new life in America.

For the most part, these war brides, influenced by their GI husbands, shied away from established Korean communities in America, and assimilated into the mainstream.

Where did the word gook come from and what does it mean anyway?

Gook, the American racial epithet for all Asian Americans, is actually the Korean word for "country." Koreans call the United States of America Mee Hap Joon Gook, which they shorten to the more familiar Mee Gook. Similarly, Koreans have shortened Dae Han Min Gook or the People's Republic of Korea to Han Gook.

During the Korean War, American soldiers gave the word gook a derogatory slant and used it to refer to Koreans. The term gook went through yet one more transformation when American servicemen in Vietnam used it to refer to the Vietnamese, particularly the Vietcong.

What triggered a third wave of Korean immigrants to America?

The Hart-Celler Act of 1965. Signed by President **Lyndon B. Johnson** on October 3, 1965, it was the primary factor contributing to the great third wave of Koreans immigrating to the United States.

From 1924 to 1965, American immigration policy was based on the National Origins Quota System, which favored immigrants of northwestern European origin. The Hart-Celler Act essentially eliminated the National Origins Quota System. It provided instead for the annual admission of 120,000 immigrants from the Western Hemisphere and 170,000 immigrants from the Eastern Hemisphere, with 20,000 slots per Eastern Hemisphere country. Immediate family members—specifically spouses, children, and parents of American citizens—were exempt from the quota system. Preferential treatment was also given to Eastern Hemisphere professionals, laborers whose skills were in demand, and refugees.

The Hart-Celler Act, combined with the difficult economic situation in Korea after the Korean War, led many Koreans to immigrate to America. In 1965, only 2,165 Koreans were admitted into the United States, while between 1965 and 1980, about 299,000 Koreans came to America's shores.

Since the Hart-Celler Act favored skilled laborers and professionals, many educated Koreans, particularly doctors, found their way to America. In fact, at one time more Korean doctors were practicing in the New York metropolitan area than in rural Korea. When other Korean professionals back home, such as chemists, accountants, engineers, and technicians, saw that doctors had done so well, they took the immigration leap, and many were quickly snapped up by American corporations. Since 1976, more than 30,000 Koreans have immigrated to the United States annually. The majority settle in either California, especially Los Angeles, or New York.

The new law was by no means designed to create a radical change in the complexion of future immigrants. As a matter of fact, one of the major selling points of the Hart-Celler Act was that it would discourage Asian immigration. In a statement designed to reassure his colleagues, Congressman **Emanuel Celler** of New York declared at the time: "Since the people of . . . Asia have very few relatives here, comparatively few could immigrate from those countries because they have no family ties in the U.S." History proved Emanuel Celler wrong.

Why are there more North Koreans than South Koreans in the United States today?

Many of the Koreans who emigrated to the United States after 1965 were North Koreans who had fled to South Korea between 1945 and 1951. In those years more than one million North Koreans, many of whom were Christians, migrated from the northern to the southern part of Korea.

A 1981 survey found that North Koreans constituted 22 percent of all Koreans in the Los Angeles area, although they constituted only about 2 percent of the South Korean population. Since so many of the North Koreans were Christians, Christianity is the backbone of the Korean American community today.

What is a Korean kae?

A Korean *kae* is a credit-rotating system similar to the Chinese *woi* and the Japanese *tanomoshi*. Koreans who belong to a *kae* contribute money to the fund and allow other members to borrow from it. *Kae* members are usually family members or very close friends who pool their money on the basis of trust. The borrower who draws from the *kae* must return the loan, plus interest. Then, a month later, members contribute to the *kae* once again, which is then drawn upon by another member until it has rotated to everyone.

Each time the fund rotates, interest rates decrease so that by the time the last member draws from the *kae*, the loan is interest-free. *Kae* members in America are often reluctant to talk about this financial strategy because they fear IRS scrutiny of reported interest income derived from the *kae*.

How has the kae financial strategy helped Korean businesses flourish in the United States?

By pooling money and investment capital in the *kae*, Koreans in the United States have started new businesses and supported other members of the community in financial need for nearly a century.

Koreans in America have exhibited perseverance and extraordinary business savvy. The first Korean entrepreneurs in New York City sold wigs, purses, and sweatsuits on street corners in dangerous neighborhoods Jewish and Italian retailers had abandoned, or drove taxis. Often they were robbed, but they never threw in the towel. By 1983, Koreans had become a vital force in the retail produce business, owning three-quarters of the thousands of greengroceries in New York City alone.

Why did so many Koreans in New York City choose to open greengroceries instead of becoming professionals?

While medical professionals met with success, Koreans in such fields as accounting, education, and administration were often thwarted by occupational downgrading, highly competitive job markets, and racial discrimination. With limited opportunities for advancement in their fields, many turned to self-employment. Koreans have the highest self-employment rate among Asians, twice as high as the American average, and second only to that of Greek Americans. Sixty-one percent of South Koreans who plan to immigrate to the United States expect to own their own business, even though most have not been self-employed in Korea. Many amass capital for launching their business while they are still in Korea.

European Jews and Italians traditionally dominated the fruits and vegetables business. Then in the 1960s and 1970s, middle-class whites began to flee America's inner cities for the suburbs, and older white merchants relocated or retired.

As third-generation Jews and Italians shunned family businesses for more prestigious professions, a greengrocery niche was created for the Koreans to fill. Koreans leapt at the opportunity to run greengroceries because the start-up costs were minimal and fluency in English was not a necessity. In the late 1960s, Koreans ran only ten or twenty greengroceries in New York City. By the late 1980s, Korean greengrocers dominated the approximately $500 million retail produce business.

Like other Korean owners of small businesses in New York City, such as the thousand dry cleaners and over 300 fish-mongers, the majority of Korean greengrocers have college degrees. They keep their businesses open around the clock and for employees, they rely either on family members or on the pool of Korean workers locked out of the mainstream labor market because of their limited knowledge of English.

How have Korean American greengrocers achieved such success?

It's partly a case of buying low and selling high. Korean business owners often set up shop in distressed locations where the rents are cheap and the returns high. In the 1960s, Koreatown in Los Angeles was an out-of-favor district. It has been estimated that by the 1980s property values in Koreatown had increased twentyfold. Today, Koreans dominate the inner-city grocery business in Atlanta and Washington, D.C. They have established operations on Chicago's South Side; in Newark, New Jersey; and in Harlem, the South Bronx, and Herald Square in New York City. When these areas bounce back from poverty, Korean Americans will be sitting on a gold mine.

Another decisive element in the Korean American small-business success story is that organizations have been set up to match Korean newcomers with established Korean suppliers and distributors and with other contractors that small businesses rely on in setting up and running their stores. In this way the Koreans keep profits and work opportunities in their communities.

Another key to the Koreans' success is that they bring with them to the United States capital to invest. South Korea has had a policy of encouraging emigration, and the Korean middle class, which has money to invest, sells its property or businesses and leaves the country with capital—a maximum of $200,000 is allowed by the government.

Korean Americans also heavily utilize traditional sources of loans—*kae* funds and banks. Many Korean American banks are affiliated with a parent bank in Korea, are able to check on the borrower's credit history, and thus may be more willing to lend to Koreans than are mainstream American banks.

Last, Korean Americans take the Protestant work ethic to heart, and stay on the job twenty-four hours a day, seven days a week, fifty-two weeks a year.

What about the rumor that Korean American small-business owners get their money from the Reverend Sun Myung Moon's Unification Church?

In addition to securing loans from banks and the *kae* rotating credit fund, Koreans have also turned to the church for financial help, but not the Reverend **Sun Myung Moon**'s Unification Church.

In recent years, Korean churches have provided a focal point not just for worship and socializing but also for networking. Although only 25 percent of Koreans in Korea are Christian, 75 percent of Americans of Korean ancestry belong to Christian churches, mostly Presbyterian. Some churches lend money on the condition that a portion of the profits be donated to the congregation, while others hold "fellowship hours" to brainstorm about new joint ventures.

How did Korean-bashing, combined with the 1980s recession, hurt the kae?

Due to the recession that America is just recovering from and recent riots against Korean American–owned businesses in California and New York, Korean Americans financed by *kae* funds have suffered losses and have been unable to repay their loans. A more serious problem is fraud. As the Korean American community grows larger, *kae* members are apt to be strangers, which increases the possibility of fraud. Although the *kae* originally operated on good faith and nothing more, distrustful members of *kae* have increasingly asked for written promissory notes.

In response to fraud, *kae* funds also sometimes name a general manager and creditor, who does not have to contribute to the fund but who must make up for losses if another member defaults before every *kae* member has had a turn.

What were these riots that took such a toll on Korean American businesses?

The Korean American success story has inspired both praise and resentment. In recent years, conflicts have arisen between African Americans and Korean American shopkeepers, with great frequency and intensity in Los Angeles and in Brooklyn. An outbreak of violence in 1992 in Los Angeles brought the destruction of about 2,300 Korean-owned businesses, with an estimated loss of more than $400 million.

Trouble in Flatbush, Brooklyn, began in January 1990 between Korean greengrocer **Bong Jae Jang** and a Haitian customer, **Ghislaine Felissaint**, who claimed that Jang insulted and physically assaulted her. The store employees tell a different story. They claim that Felissaint became furious when they helped another customer while she looked for money to pay for her purchases, and screamed racial slurs against the Koreans.

African Americans in the neighborhood launched a full-scale boycott of the store, and as tensions mounted, they demanded that the Koreans sell the store and leave the community. The fourteen-month boycott in Brooklyn was chronicled in the national media, and Koreans gained greater visibility in America.

Even though Bong Jae Jang was acquitted in a criminal case of any wrongdoing, he suffered severe financial setbacks. On one of his worst days, he sold only three onions for thirty-eight cents. Citing the financial catastrophe the store suffered due to the boycott, the owners applied for and were granted a court order limiting demonstrators' proximity to the store entrance to fifty feet. The court also demanded that police officers enforce the court order in spite of their fear that their presence would exacerbate community resentment toward the police.

What was the Korean American civil rights protest in New York City about?

Most Korean immigrants tend to confine themselves to a cultural and economic island; they read primarily local and imported Korean-language newspapers, dine at Korean-owned restaurants, shop at Korean-operated stores, and watch local Korean television. Key factors in their economic success—tight-knit communities, small businesses operated by family members, and self-reliance—have also kept them isolated from the mainstream.

The over 100,000 Korean Americans in the New York metropolitan area in 1990 fit this mold. However when racial tensions flared in Brooklyn, Korean New Yorkers left their enclaves to rally in support of Bong Jae Jang. In September 1990, 10,000 Korean Americans gathered to protest the Brooklyn boycott and call for racial harmony. **David Dinkins**, mayor of New York City at the time, appeared at the rally held in front of Bong Jae Jang's greengrocery and made a symbolic anti-boycott purchase.

How were other Asian Americans affected by the ethnic clashes between Korean Americans and African Americans in New York's inner city?

The yearlong boycott did not help race relations in Flatbush one bit. On May 13, 1990, a large group of African American youths attacked three Vietnamese American men with baseball bats, knives, bottles, and anti-Korean epithets, after mistaking them for Koreans.

Are any Korean Americans active in U.S. politics?

Republican congressman **Jay Kim** in Los Angeles, one of the few Korean Americans ever elected to a political post, is living testimony of the growth and strength of the Korean community in America. In 1992 he earned the distinction of being the first Korean American elected to the United States Congress.

The first Asian American appointed to a U.S. federal judgeship was Judge **Herbert Y. C. Choy**. Before coming onto the federal bench, Choy was a partner in the law firm of Fong and Miho in Honolulu. On May 16, 1975, President Nixon appointed him to the U.S. Court of Appeals for the Ninth Circuit.

Who are some great Korean American athletes?

Sammy Lee, a Korean American physician who was part of the U.S. Army Medical Corps in Korea from 1943 to 1955, was the first male diver to win gold medals in high diving two Olympics in a row—in 1948 and in 1952. At the 1952 Olympics in Helsinki, Lee also captured the bronze medal in three-meter springboard diving. In 1953 he earned the distinction of being the first non-white person to receive the James E. Sullivan Award, given each year to an outstanding American athlete, and in 1968 he was named to the International Swimming Hall of Fame. From 1971 to 1980, Sammy Lee served on the President's Council on Physical Fitness and Sports, and he was also

Greg Louganis's coach at the 1976 Olympics in Montreal, where Louganis captured a silver medal in platform diving.

Los Angeles Dodgers pitcher **Chan-ho Park**, the first Korean American starting pitcher for a major league team, has received much fanfare in the baseball world. Another great athlete is **Jim Paek**, one of few Korean American professional hockey players. Paek joined the Pittsburgh Penguins in the 1990–1991 season.

FAMOUS ASIAN AMERICAN ATHLETES

1. Michael Chang

Top-seeded tennis player Michael Chang, a Chinese American, made tennis history in 1987 when at age fifteen he became the youngest player to win a U.S. Open match. In 1989 Chang became the youngest male tennis player, and first U.S. male player since 1955, to capture the French Open. His victory at the French Open catapulted him to stardom.

2. Eugene Chung

One of the few Asians in professional football, Chinese American Eugene Chung plays offensive line guard for the New England Patriots.

3. Vicki Manalo Draves

In 1948 Filipina American Vicki Manalo Draves became the first woman in Olympic history to win gold medals in both platform diving and springboard diving, and the first woman of Asian ancestry ever awarded an Olympic gold medal. In 1969 she was inducted into the International Swimming Hall of Fame.

4. Roman Gabriel

A great Filipino American football player, Roman Gabriel was an all-American quarterback for North Carolina State Univer-

---

sity. He went on to achieve stardom during eleven years of play with the Los Angeles Rams and the Philadelphia Eagles. In 1969 Gabriel was named the NFL's Most Valuable Player and Player of the Year.

5. Tamio "Tommy" Kono

Japanese American Tamio Kono won gold medals in weight lifting at the 1952 Olympics and the 1956 Olympics, and a silver medal at the 1960 Olympics. Kono made history by winning the three medals in different weight classes. In 1988 the International Weightlifting Federation ranked him number one on its list of the thirty greatest weight lifters of all time. In 1990 Kono was inducted into the U.S. Olympic Hall of Fame.

6. Sammy Lee

Sammy Lee, a second-generation Korean American physician, was the first male diver to capture gold medals in high diving two Olympics in a row when he won in 1948 and in 1952. In 1953 Lee became the first non-white to receive the James E. Sullivan Award given annually to an outstanding American athlete. In 1968 he was named to the International Swimming Hall of Fame. Sammy Lee was Greg Louganis' coach for the 1976 Olympics in Montreal, where Louganis won a silver medal for America in platform diving.

7. Mike Nguyen

Mike Nguyen left Vietnam at the tender age of two. He was later awarded a sports scholarship to UCLA, where he became the first Vietnamese American to play college football.

8. Jim Paek

One of the few Korean American professional hockey players, Jim Paek joined the Pittsburgh Penguins in the 1990–91 season.

9. Chan-ho Park

The first Korean American named a starting pitcher for a major league baseball team, Chan-ho Park played for the Los Angeles Dodgers. He is currently working on his pitching in the minors.

10. Kristi Yamaguchi

In 1989 world-renowned figure skater Kristi Yamaguchi, a Japanese American, became the first skater in thirty-five years to qualify for the World Championships in two events. She won the National and World Championships in 1992 and later that year captured the gold medal in the women's singles championships at the Winter Olympics in Albertville, France. A month after the Olympics, Yamaguchi won her second consecutive world championship.

What contributions have Korean Americans made to classical music?

America boasts an extraordinary number of great classical musicians of Korean ancestry. Established in 1967, the **Chung** trio, with pianist **Myung-Whun** and his sisters, cellist **Myung-Wha** and violinist **Kyung-Wha**, has achieved popularity throughout the world. Myung-Whun Chung is also a world-renowned conductor who has worked with most of the major orchestras in Europe, including the Berlin Philharmonic and the London Symphony Orchestra. In 1984 he took a post as musical director and principal conductor for the Radio Symphony Chorus in Saarbrücken, Germany, and in 1989 he was named musical director of the Bastille Opera in Paris.

The Ahn trio, with pianist **Lucia Ahn** and her sisters, cellist **Maria Ahn** and violinist **Angela Ahn**, has captivated contemporary audiences. Another violinist, **Chouhei Min**, born in Seoul, began to study the violin at age five. After receiving professional training at the Boston Conservatory of Music and the Hart College of Music, she was named associate concertmaster of the Dallas Symphony Orchestra and in 1976 joined the Minnesota Orchestra. **Earl Kim** is a Korean American composer, best known for his musical scores to texts by Samuel Beckett and his *Where Cried Slumbers*, which sets the works of French poets Rimbaud and Apollinaire to music, and was performed by the American Composers Orchestra at Carnegie Hall in 1988.

What other contributions have Korean Americans made to the arts?

Video artist **Nam June Paik** has gained an international reputation for his electronic music and "action concerts." In the 1960s Paik's performances included such antics as musicians smashing a piano, while his more recent video productions are a little more tame and comment on the role of television in society. Paik's work has been exhibited at such cultural institutions as the Museum of Modern Art and the Whitney Museum in New York, the Metropolitan Art Museum in Tokyo, and the Museum of Contemporary Art in Chicago. One of his well-known installations is entitled *Video Fish* (1975): it displays tanks of tropical fish amid televisions playing videos of tropical fish.

Many Korean Americans have earned distinctions for their writing. **Younghill Kang**, a professor of literature at New York University in the 1930s and a language consultant for the American government during World War II, published an exceptional account of life in Korea, *The Grass Roof*, in 1931. In 1933 Kang became the first Asian American awarded the prestigious Guggenheim Fellowship. Four years later he published *East Goes West*, a gripping chronicle of his search for ethnic identity in America. Another distinguished American writer of Korean ancestry is **Richard E. Kim**, whose 1964 novel *The Martyred*, an examination of human suffering and God's relation to humankind during wartime, has been compared to the writings of Albert Camus. Another of Kim's noteworthy contributions is *Lost Names* (1970), an account of his first thirteen years of life in Japanese-occupied Korea.

More recently, the Korean American novelist and artist **Gloria Hahn** (born Kim Ronyoung in Los Angeles on March 28, 1926) caught the attention of the literary world with the publication in 1986 of *Clay Walls*, about a Korean American woman who ruins her eyesight doing embroidery work to support her family after her husband gambles away the family's savings and then dies. Tragically, Gloria Hahn passed away in 1987, but her memory has lived on in the United States, as well as in South Korea, where a Korean translation of *Clay Walls* has been published.

Writer and scholar **Elaine H. Kim**, who teaches Asian American studies at the University of California at Berkeley, has done much to advance Asian American scholarship. In 1982 she published *Asian American Literature: An Introduction to the Writings*, one of the first literary histories of Asian America. Kim later coedited two groundbreaking contributions to Asian American scholarship: *Making Waves: An Anthology of Writings by and about Asian American Women* (1989) and *Writing Self, Writing Nation: A Collection of Essays on Theresa Hak Kyung Cha's "Dictee"* (1993).

Filmmaker and scholar **Christine Choy**, who teaches film and television at New York University, has addressed on film and video the Asian American experience, as well as more general topics such as domestic violence and the American prison system. *Who Killed Vincent Chin?* is one of Choy's best-known works. The documentary, a collaboration with Renee Tajima, chronicles the murder of Vincent Chin, a Chinese American, at the hands of two auto workers in Detroit who mistook him for Japanese. *Who Killed Vincent Chin?* was so powerful and well wrought that it was nominated for an Academy Award. Christine Choy has also put together dramatic films and helped found media outlets for Asian Americans, namely Third World Newsreel, Asian CineVision, and the National Asian American Telecommunications Association.

On the silver screen, character actor **Philip Ahn**, whose career in Hollywood spanned three decades and three hundred films, was well-known to American audiences for his roles as Chinese and Japanese villains in such films as *Back to Bataan* (1945), *Halls of Montezuma* (1952), and *Battle Hymn* (1956). Ahn captured the spotlight again in the 1970s for his part as a kung fu master in the popular television series *Kung Fu*, with David Carradine. Philip Ahn is the first Asian American actor to be immortalized with a star on the Hollywood Walk of Fame.

On the stage, **Randall Duk Kim** is another great Korean American actor, who has gained a national reputation as one of the finest interpreters of Shakespeare. In 1980 he cofounded the American Players Theater, which explores classical dramatic literature, predominantly Shakespeare.

Comedian **Margaret Cho**, who starred in ABC's *All-American Girl*, TV's first prime-time sitcom about an Asian American family, has won the hearts of millions of Americans with her laughs.

Who is Angela E. Oh?

Another Korean American high achiever is **Angela E. Oh**, an attorney in private practice who specializes in criminal law. Oh served as the spokesperson for the Korean American community during the Los Angeles riots in the late 1980s and is active in helping to rebuild L.A.

What traditions from the old country do Korean Americans adhere to?

Strongly influenced by Confucian precepts, Korean Americans feel they must respect and honor their relatives, and many live in multigenerational homes rather than striking out on their own. Another tradition is the arranged marriage, which is still preferred in Korean culture. Some Korean Americans have adhered to this tradition, while others have broken with it, causing great distress in their families.

Korean women face their own set of cultural dilemmas as they attempt to reconcile their traditional roles as housewife and mother with American feminism, which has given millions of women access to the workforce. Two-thirds of Korean American women now work outside the home, but they are saddled with a double burden, for they must also care for the home and children.

What Korean holidays do Korean Americans celebrate?

While all Americans celebrate Mother's Day and Father's Day, Koreans and Korean Americans also celebrate Children's Day, which falls on the fifth of May each year. Throughout history, Korean tradition has dictated that younger generations must respect their elders. However, during hard times, when the country was economically crippled, a man named Bang led a children's movement, based on his belief that the children of Korea were the country's only hope. So on May 5, Koreans and Korean Americans pay homage to their children.

Other festive days on the Korean calendar include *chanchi'i*, celebrations of the first and sixty-first birthdays. Infant mortality rates in Korea were once quite high, so children who made it to their first birthday were honored. Similarly, because the natural lifespan was considered to be sixty years, which coincides with the cycle of years in the lunar calendar, a sixty-first birthday also received recognition. Despite the fact that Korean Americans live long healthy lives like the rest of Americans, these traditions continue today.

Hwan'gap, one of the most important events in a Korean's life, is predicated on the Chinese belief in twelve-year cycles—hence the twelve animal zodiacs—that symbolize human life. After five of these cycles, elder Koreans are relieved of the burdens of life and their children are expected to take over their care. At a *hwan'gap* ceremony, the elder is enthroned on a cushioned chair set against a background of fruit, rice cakes, cookies, and candies. Children and grandchildren then pay their respects to the family elder with kowtows.

What is Hangul Day?

Hangul Day is none other than a national holiday on which Koreans pay tribute to the Korean alphabet. While Americans don't commemorate their ABCs, Koreans and Korean Americans pay homage to hangul, their alphabet, because it represents freedom from Chinese and Japanese domination and the restoration of sovereignty in Korea.

Hangul, meaning "great writing," is the Korean indigenous script. Before hangul was invented, the Korean language had no writing system of its own and had to be written in Chinese characters. The Chinese language's ideographic system of writing (based on pictures) was unsuitable for the Korean language, which has its own unique tones and structure.

What is New York's Korean Day Parade?

On the third Saturday in October, Korean Americans in New York City flock to mid-Manhattan to celebrate the Korean Moon Festival, the Korean equivalent of Thanksgiving, with a parade down Broadway. The Korean Day Parade features Korean American beauty queens atop floats, marching bands, Korean American folkloric groups, official Korean delegations, marchers from Korean American Associations, and floats representing Buddhist temples and Korean churches. Korean American greengrocers march next to fishmongers and owners of dry cleaners.

"Have you eaten rice yet?"

Like the Chinese, Koreans and many Korean Americans

greet one another with the question "Have you eaten rice yet?" As the primary staple food, rice is eaten with almost every meal.

Which five flavors and five colors are essential in Korean cuisine?

Korean cooking is dominated by five flavors: salt, sweet, sour, hot, and bitter. Beet sugar, honey, and sweet potatoes sweeten Korean food; table salt, soy sauce, and bean paste add a salty taste; mustard and dried red chile peppers lend hotness; rice and citron vinegar, sourness; and ginger, bitterness. Koreans also try to put together foods that represent the five traditional colors of Korea: green, red, yellow, white, and black. The first four colors are easily found in a variety of foods. Koreans often rely on cloud ear mushrooms to add a touch of black.

What are some other classic Korean dishes?

The Korean table is famous not only for some delicious dishes, such as beef soup, braised short ribs, and meat and vegetable dumplings prepared in hundreds of ways, but for its extraordinary assortment of side dishes. Kimchee, pickled fish or crab, hot-and-salty fish intestines, whole garlic cloves in broth, whiting eggs, and hot sauces are common complements to Korean dining.

Bul koki, the famous Korean barbecue, is a favorite in Korea and in America. Thin strips of beef, chicken, squid, or octopus are first marinated in a mixture of soy sauce, sugar, garlic, ginger, and sesame seeds, and cooked to perfection at the table on a grill fueled by gas jets or the special hardwood that Koreans favor. The grilled meat is served with rice or wrapped in lettuce leaves. *Kalbi*, beef short ribs, is another popular Korean grilled dish.

What is kimchee?

The Korean national dish, kimchee, is a pungent and spicy pickled vegetable condiment that accompanies most Korean meals. Kimchee can be made with an array of vegetables, but the most common variety calls for fresh cabbage and white radish, which are washed, cut, salted, and placed in brine brimming with chili peppers and garlic. The mixture is pickled and then stored in huge sealed earthenware crocks either buried in the backyard or set on a rooftop. The kimchee is dug up as needed in the kitchen. More exotic vegetables, such as pumpkin and eggplant, also make for delicious kimchee. For those who don't have a yard or don't want to dig it up, commercial kimchee is available in most Korean and Chinese grocery stores in the United States.

Are the Japanese the only Asians who drink sake?

Makkolli, the national rice brew of Korea, is similar in taste and texture to sake, the national alcoholic drink of Japan. Students and working-class Koreans in America's Koreatowns pour into *suljips*, or pubs, to drink *makkolli* accompanied by *anju*, pub snacks in the style of Spanish tapas. Less formal Korean pubs go by the name *makkollijip*.

Can you name the meat Koreans and Korean Americans eat to bolster their strength?

No, it's not beef. Most Koreans and Korean Americans swear by black goat when they need an energy boost, and they often prepare goat as a restorative for patients recovering from a serious illness. To satisfy Korean Americans' hunger for goat, a goat specialty restaurant opened in Koreatown in Los Angeles, where patrons can order anything from barbecued goat to spicy goat stew.

What is traditional Korean medicine?

In A.D. 561, traditional Chinese medicine was introduced to Korea, where it blended with Korean folk medicine to create *hanyak*, traditional Korean medicine. During the Koryo dynasty, Korean medical manuals proliferated, and traditional Korean medicine reached new heights with the publication in 1610 of a twenty-five-volume pharmacopoeia called *Tong-I Pogam*, which means "treasures of Eastern medicine." Korean and Korean American herbal doctors still consult this treatise today.

Hanyak incorporates procedures such as acupressure, acupuncture, moxibustion, pulse analysis, and deep breathing. It also relies on medicinal herbs and substances, and Korean herbal shops stock everything from chrysanthemum petals, snake wine, and dried tortoise to deer antlers, dried reptiles, and insects.

Prevention is at the heart of traditional Korean medicine. In ancient Korea, families hired doctors to monitor each member's health for signs of weakness. If illness befell a patient, the doctor was accused of poor preventive care and was expected to provide a cure at his own expense!

Like Chinese medicine, traditional Korean medicine is based on the assumption that good health depends on harmony between the dual cosmic forces of yin and yang. Herbal potions and acupuncture are both used to reestablish a proper balance of the two.

What is acupuncture and what is acupressure?

Korean Americans often treat ailments with acupuncture, a therapeutic practice that originated in China and involves introducing fine needles at certain points in the skin along what are known as "vital lines of force." These "vital lines of force" may actually be away from the areas of pain or disease in the body. Acupuncture is used to heal all manner of ailments, from cancer to mental disorders, as well as to anesthetize a patient during surgery.

Acupressure targets the same "vital lines of force" as acupuncture, but with massage. Practitioners of acupressure press the hand—primarily the thumb—along the "vital lines of force."

What is ginseng?

The Korean miracle drug, ginseng, more than any other herb, is most intimately associated with traditional Korean medicine. This sweet licorice-flavored root, which originally grew in the forests of Korea and Manchuria, is believed to carry yang energy. Ginseng was brought to China during the Koryo dynasty and was used by the Koreans as a tribute to the Chinese emperor.

Korean ginseng takes from four to six years to mature, and its cultivation requires meticulous care. The composition of the soil is of vital importance: most often ginseng is grown in a rich mulch of chestnut and oak leaves. Thatched mats are used to shield the delicate herb from direct sunlight. After it is harvested, ginseng is washed, peeled, steamed, and dried, and then sorted and classified according to quality. Ginseng comes in two varieties, white and red. The red variety is more potent and more expensive.

Koreans and Korean Americans view ginseng as the elixir of life. The herb has been credited with stimulating the nervous system if taken in small amounts, and with increasing mental and physical stamina if taken in larger doses. It is also considered a cure for impotence. Recent scientific studies reveal that active components found in ginseng include glycosides, saccharides, fatty substances, B-vitamins, enzymes, and alkaline substances. The traditional ginseng brew is made from ginseng root, dried jujubes, and pine nuts, which are boiled with a small amount of sugar.

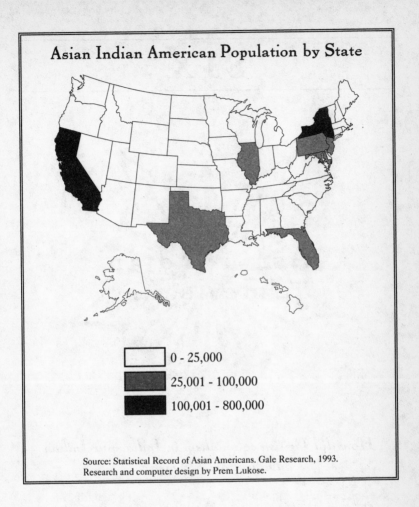

Asian Indian American Population by State

0 - 25,000

25,001 - 100,000

100,001 - 800,000

Source: Statistical Record of Asian Americans. Gale Research, 1993.
Research and computer design by Prem Lukose.

SIX

Asian Indian
Americans

*How did British colonialism in India spur Indian
immigration to America?*

*Who are the Sikhs and why is it easy to tell them apart
from other Asian Indians?*

When did Asian Indians first come to America?

*Why did the California Fruit Growers' Association
seek out the Punjabis as a source of labor?*

Were Indians treated better than other Asian immigrant laborers?

What happened to those Asian Indians already in the United States; or, how did the Indians change color?

Who was Tarak Nath Das?

How else were Asian Indians affected by the Supreme Court's decision to deny them citizenship?

How did World War II alleviate the problems Asian Indians faced in America?

How did Asian Indian immigration change after 1968?

What kinds of problems have Asian Indians faced as they acculturate to America?

Who are the "dotbusters"?

Who are some prominent Asian Indian Americans?

What is a sari?

What is the difference between Hindi and Hindu?

How do Hindus worship in America?

What does the swastika have to do with Hinduism, Jainism, and Buddhism in India?

Who is Deepak Chopra?

*What national holidays do Asian Indians
in America celebrate?*

What foods do Asian Indian Americans prefer?

*What are some essential herbs and spices in Asian
Indian cooking?*

Which hand do Asian Indians traditionally eat with?

What is traditional Asian Indian medicine?

What is yoga?

The majority of Asian Indians in the United States, also referred to as East Indians or Indo-Americans, are South Asian Indians from the Republic of India or their descendants. At the turn of the century, only a few thousand Asian Indians resided in America. Asian Indians from the state of Punjab began immigrating to the United States in substantial numbers after 1905.

After the passage of the Hart-Celler Act in 1965, which did away with racial and national quotas, these Asian Indians were joined by immigrants from areas that now constitute the countries of Pakistan, Bangladesh, and Sri Lanka. In 1990 the total Asian Indian population in the United States hovered at around 815,500.

While Asian Indians who immigrated to the United States from 1904 until the end of World War II were crippled by discrimination and limited access to the mainstream, the highly educated professionals who have come to America since around 1947 have met with extraordinary success. In fact, a higher percentage of Asian Indians occupy professional and managerial positions than any other Asian American group.

How did British colonialism in India spur Indian immigration to America?

When the British instituted a capitalist agricultural economy in India in the early 1800s to replace the traditional Indian land tenure system, they placed the small landowners in dire economic straits. Many landowners had to turn to money-lenders who charged exorbitant interest rates and required borrowers to sell their land in the event of late payments. Economic difficulties, plus a famine that lasted from 1899 to 1902, forced small landowners and peasants from the fertile Doab and Malwa regions of Punjab State to leave their home-land for the British West Indies, Uganda, British Guiana, and Canada. Many Asian Indians eventually made their way from these countries to the United States. A small number of these Punjabis were Hindus and Muslims, but the majority were Sikhs.

Who are the Sikhs and why is it easy to tell them apart from other Asian Indians?

A Sikh is an adherent of Sikhism, a reform religion which broke away from Hinduism in the sixteenth century. Its founder, **Guru Nanak** (1469–1539), sought to reconcile Muslims and Hindus by teaching a monotheistic creed and by stressing meditation and religious exercises as paths to enlightenment. He challenged the Hindu caste system, idolatry, rituals, and the existence of a priesthood.

Sikhism remained a pacifist religion until the tenth and last guru of the Sikh line, **Govind Singh** (1666–1708), hastened the militarization of the Sikhs in order to resist Muslim persecution. He ordered all male Sikhs to adopt the surname Singh, meaning "lion," and all female Sikhs to take the surname Kauer, or "lioness," and introduced practices that persist today, including wearing a turban, carrying a dagger, and never cutting the hair or beard.

When did Asian Indians first come to America?

While a handful of Asian Indians ventured to America in the 1790s as slaves and indentured servants involved in U.S.-India trade, and approximately two thousand Asian Indians called America home by 1900, Asian Indian immigration did not pick up substantially until after 1905.

In 1907, a number of Punjabis who had made their way to Canada headed south along the railroads and found jobs in the lumber mills of Washington State, unleashing the first wave of Asian Indian immigration. The competition for work was fierce, and other laborers were openly hostile to the Indians. In September 1907, angry white workers stormed into the Asian Indian enclave in Bellingham, Washington, and drove seven hundred Punjabis out of town. Two months later, white workers forced Asian Indians out of Everett, Washington. Some Punjabis fled back across the Canadian border or headed south to work on the Western Pacific Railroad in northern California. When the railroad work ran out in 1910, they turned to agriculture.

From 1907 until 1917, when Congress prohibited immigration from India, sixty-four hundred Asian Indians, mostly Sikhs and farmers from Punjab, came to America's West Coast. Fewer than 1 percent of these early Asian Indian immigrants were women.

Why did the California Fruit Growers' Association seek out the Punjabis as a source of labor?

As the twentieth century dawned, California fruit growers capitalized on the Indians' misfortunes. They lured Asian Indian laborers to their farms with promises of competitive wages, and then turned around and paid them twenty-five to fifty cents less per day than was paid to Japanese laborers. The fruit growers also pitted the Indians against the Japanese to discourage labor unrest. The growers had an explicit policy of hiring heterogeneous groups of workers—Japanese, Mexicans, southeastern Europeans—as a way to minimize the possibility of a workers' strike. After a time, some of the Punjabis managed to escape these horrendous conditions by pooling their earnings until they had scraped up enough money to lease or purchase farmland.

Were Indians treated better than other Asian immigrant laborers?

Hardly. Americans essentially lumped Asian Indians into the same category as the Chinese and the Japanese, and treated them just as miserably. America's racist sentiments and animosity toward Asians, including Indians, were explicitly laid out in the remarks of **Samuel Gompers**, the president of the American Federation of Labor. In 1908 Gompers declared that "[s]ixty years' contact with the Chinese, and twenty-five years' experience with the Japanese and two or three years' acquaintance with Hindus should be sufficient to convince any ordinarily intelligent person that they have no standards . . . by which a Caucasian may judge them."

The white labor force in America resented the Asian Indians, as they did all Asians, for driving down wages with their willingness to work for a pittance and supposedly lowering living standards. After the hostile incidents against Asian Indians in Bellingham and Everett, Washington, the Asiatic Exclusion League in San Francisco hopped on the bandwagon and campaigned for an end to Indian immigration, citing "the undesirability of the Hindus, their lack of cleanliness, disregard of sanitary laws, petty pilfering, especially of chickens, and insolence to women."

In 1917, Congress responded to this wave of anti-Asian exclusionism spreading across the land by prohibiting any more Indian laborers from entering the United States. The Immigration Act of 1917 designated India as one of the Asian countries in the "barred zone."

What happened to those Asian Indians already in the United States; or, how did the Indians change color?

The future of Asian Indians already in America was up in the air. The U.S. government categorized Asian Indians as Caucasians because they and Scandinavians are racially and linguistically related. Since the government had managed in 1790 with the passage of federal laws to exclude Chinese, Japanese, and Korean immigrants from citizenship by declaring that naturalized citizenship was reserved for "whites" only, theoretically, Asian Indians in America should have been granted naturalization rights. American exclusionists soon realized that the only way to exclude Asian Indians from naturalization was to somehow "change" their skin color.

Exclusionists went about this by simply narrowing the definition of "Caucasian." The Asiatic Exclusion League, one of a handful of organizations opposing citizenship rights for Asian Indian immigrants, conceded that Asian Indians, or "the Hindus" as they were called, were "members of the same family" as Europeans. However, the organization made the distinction that the ancestors of Europeans "pressed to the west, in the everlasting march of conquest, progress, and civilization . . . [while] . . . the forefathers of the Hindus went east and became enslaved, effeminate, caste-ridden and degraded." Therefore, according to the Asiatic Exclusion League, Asian Indians should be barred from citizenship.

The U.S. government elaborated on this argument and further challenged the legitimacy of categorizing Asian Indians as Caucasians to clear the path for anti-Indian legislation. To this end, United States Attorney General **Charles J. Bonaparte** declared in 1907 that "under no construction of the law can natives of British India be regarded as white persons." Sixteen years later, in 1923, the United States Supreme Court echoed Bonaparte's sentiments in *United States v. Bhagat Singh Thind*, in which it ruled that Asian Indians could not be given naturalized citizenship rights due to differences in skin color. The Supreme Court held that "[i]t may be true that the blond Scandinavian and the brown Hindu have a common ancestor in the dim reaches of antiquity, but the average man knows perfectly well that there are unmistakable and profound differences between them today."

After the Supreme Court's decision, federal authorities nullified citizenship rights that lower courts had previously granted to certain Asian Indians. The revocation of American citizenship left such Asian Indians in a terrible bind—they were citizens of no country.

Who was Tarak Nath Das?

Tarak Nath Das was a political activist and writer who waged a hard battle against anti–Asian Indian legislation in Canada and the United States in the early 1900s. In 1907 he began publishing a monthly journal, *Free Hindustan*, in Vancouver, in which he condemned Canadian and American immigration exclusion laws and challenged Asian Indians to stand up for themselves and fight the laws.

Das himself fought a long battle to obtain U.S. citizenship. While he was naturalized in 1914, the U.S. government kept him under surveillance because of his anti-British stance, and found "sufficient cause" to arrest him for "anti-American plots" during World War I. Tarak Nath Das spent several years in prison, where he was threatened with deportation. With the aid of Friends for the Freedom of India, an organization he himself had founded in 1921, Das was able to show that it was unlawful for the U.S. government to deport him since he was an American citizen. The government then set about looking for a way to denaturalize him. Ultimately Das was set free, but the government continued its efforts to denaturalize him until 1927.

How else were Asian Indians affected by the Supreme Court's decision to deny them citizenship?

The Supreme Court's decision meant that anti-miscegenation laws could be applied to Asian Indians. During the Great Depression, Asian Indians were also ineligible for certain federal relief programs, since they were classified as aliens ineligible for citizenship. And Asian Indians could no longer own land under the California Alien Land Act. As a matter of fact, within weeks of the Supreme Court's decision in *United States v. Bhagat Singh Thind*, California Attorney General **Ulysses Sigel Webb** began nullifying all land purchases made by Asian Indians. Asian Indian farmers were stripped of their land, and had to take jobs as laborers.

Asian Indians found a way around the Alien Land Act restriction by registering their land under the names of their children born in America (who therefore had U.S. citizenship), just as the Japanese in America did. However, unlike the Japanese, many Asian Indian men did not have families and had to devise other strategies to outsmart the Alien Land Act. Many leased land under the names of white farmers, who gave their consent in return for a share of the Indians' crop.

How did World War II alleviate the problems Asian Indians faced in America?

The India Welfare League fought a hard battle to rid America of anti–Asian Indian discrimination. The organization made some headway in 1939 when a bill was introduced in Congress that would extend citizenship to all Asian Indian immigrants who had been in the United States since 1924. The bill never made it out of Congress, where it was vehemently opposed by various groups, including the American Federation of Labor.

In 1940, an Indian by the name of **Khairata Ram Samras** turned to the courts for remedy against discrimination. Samras filed a petition in the federal court challenging the Supreme Court's *Thind* decision, which denied naturalized citizenship to Asian Indian immigrants.

Before the court issued its decision, President Franklin Roosevelt and Prime Minister Winston Churchill signed the Atlantic Charter, upholding the right of peoples to self-determination. The India Welfare League and the India League of America based their claim for independence for India, and naturalization rights for Asian Indians in the United States, on the principles embodied in the Atlantic Charter.

America's struggle in World War II and its obligation to foster democracies abroad forced the U.S. government to extirpate racism from its immigration policies regarding Asian Indians and other groups. More to the point, India was of utmost strategic importance, since Japanese forces could win India's favor and then press westward to meet up with German troops in the Near East. Hence the United States sought to strengthen relations with India to ward off a Japanese-Indian alliance by complying with Asian Indian demands.

In 1946, Congress enacted legislation granting naturalization rights to Asian Indians and providing for a small quota of 100 immigrants per year. Similarly, China was given a quota of 105. The quota for Poland, by contrast, was set at 6,524. Congress passed the Immigration and Nationality Act, also called the McCarran-Walter Act, in 1952, which ended all exclusion of Asians per se. However, it also created a national bias with the formation of a large geographical "Asian-Pacific Triangle," which included most of South and East Asia. By contrast, European immigrants were subject only to the national-origin quotas of the 1924 Immigration Act.

Between 1947 and 1965, the Asian Indians who had become naturalized U.S. citizens numbered 1,772. Historians contend that if immigration laws had gone unchanged in 1946, the Asian Indian community in America would have died out.

How did Asian Indian immigration change after 1968?

America's doors swung wide open to Asian immigration with the passage of the Hart-Celler Act in 1965, which did away with the racial and country-of-origin quotas. Visas were awarded based on familial relationships or scarce occupational skills, and Indians were now able to enter the United States in substantial numbers.

The total population of Asian Indians in the United States stood at fifteen hundred in 1946. After 1968, however, immigrants from South Asia came to American shores in far greater numbers. By 1970, 20,000 had arrived from Pakistan, half of whom were Punjabis. By 1985 the total population of Asian Indians, including those from Pakistan, Sri Lanka, and Bangladesh, in America had risen to 525,000, and by 1990 it had reached 815,447, according to U.S. Census reports.

Unlike the first wave of Asian Indians, who were mainly laborers, the second wave of newcomers has been comprised mainly of highly educated, English-speaking professionals from major urban areas who immigrated with their families. High unemployment in India and the promise of finding satisfying jobs in the States were factors that pushed these professionals to emigrate. Since so many Asian Indians are highly trained, as a group they have enjoyed the highest rate of employment as professionals of all the Asian Americans. In 1980, for instance, 47 percent of adult Asian Indians in America held professional or managerial jobs, while only 30 percent of Chinese, 28 percent of Japanese, and 22 percent of Koreans were professionals or managers.

Since the 1980s a substantial number of Asian Indians have been opening their own small businesses, predominantly hotels, motels, convenience stores, and gas stations. Others took to driving taxis; today over 40 percent of all cab drivers in New York City are Asian Indians.

What kinds of problems have Asian Indians faced as they acculturate to America?

Asian Indian men have had concerns about the effect of Western feminism on Indian women. Most women in India are committed solely to duties related to the household, but once in America they become liberated from traditional constraints and often venture into the workforce. Asian Indian parents also worry that their children will lose respect for their elders, and that their daughters will assert the American prerogative of choosing a career path and a spouse on their own.

As a way of maintaining ties to the Old World and passing on their heritage to their children, Asian Indians have set up special schools that teach regional languages, dance, and music, and have established societies and fraternal groups devoted to social and cultural events.

Asian Indian national and regional organizations have also cropped up. One of the largest is the Association of Indians in America (AIA), which defends Asian Indian interests in American society. For instance, the AIA fought for the classification of Asian Indians as Asian Americans in the 1980 U.S. Census so that they would be eligible for affirmative action programs. In the 1990s the AIA has been joined by the Federation of Indian Associations, which represents the interests of Indian merchants.

Who are the "dotbusters"?

Discrimination against Asian Indians in America has subsided since the turn of the century, but in no way has it disappeared. Racists who sometimes go by the name "dotbusters" have made a despicable habit of attacking Asian Indians. "Dotbuster" makes reference to the *bindi*, the decorative red dot some Asian Indian women wear between their eyebrows to indicate their married status or nowadays even just as a fashion statement. The term was first used by white youths who killed two Asian Indian Americans in New Jersey in 1987. After that, "dotbusters" warned that they would identify and harass more victims by searching phone books for the common Indian name Patel.

Asian Indian Americans have also faced discrimination from the general public. For instance, cases have been documented of how insurance companies cancel policies when they realize the holder is Asian Indian, and of how companies will not sell franchises to Asian Indian Americans out of fear that this will drive away customers.

Who are some prominent Asian Indian Americans?

Dalip Singh Saund, a Sikh originally from Chhajalwadi, India, was the first Asian Indian American—and the first Asian American—to succeed in national politics. In 1919 he settled in California, where in ensuing years he farmed in the Imperial Valley. As he wrote in his autobiography, entitled *Congressman from India*, Dalip Singh Saund had always dreamed of becoming a naturalized citizen: "I saw that the bars of citizenship were shut tight against me. I knew if these bars were lifted I would see much wider gates of opportunity open to me, opportunity as existed for everybody else in the United States of America." Saund wasted no time once he was granted citizenship in 1949, when Asian Indians in the United States became eligible for naturalization. Californians elected him congressman in 1956, and then kept him in the House of Representatives for three terms, until January 3, 1963.

The astrophysicist **Subrahmanyan Chandrasekhar** was honored with the Nobel Prize for Physics in 1983 for his theoretical studies on how stars evolve. He shared the award with William A. Fowler from the California Institute of Technology. Chandrasekhar was born in Lahore, India, on Oct. 19, 1910. He settled in the United States in 1936, when he was appointed to the faculty of the University of Chicago. He became a naturalized U.S. citizen in 1953.

Zubin Mehta, who was born in Bombay, India, on April 29, 1936, became the youngest conductor in America to be appointed to a major orchestra, when in 1962 he joined the Los Angeles Philharmonic Orchestra. Mehta stayed with the Los Angeles Philharmonic until 1978, when he became director of the New York Philharmonic. During his tenure with the New York Philharmonic—which lasted until 1991—Mehta fostered such young talents as Japanese American violinist Midori. In 1969, Mehta was named director of the Israel Philharmonic, and in 1981 became that organization's Director for Life.

Yellapragada Subba Row, a physician and medical researcher, made valuable contributions in the development of cures for numerous diseases, including sprue and macrocytic anemia, and in the development of vital drugs such as teropterin, used to treat cancer, aminoterin, used to treat leukemia, and hetrazan, a drug used in the treatment of filariasis. Born in Madras State, India, in 1896, Subba Row came to the United States in 1924 and was soon accepted into the graduate biochemistry program at Harvard University Medical School. In ensuing years he taught at Harvard and conducted research at Lederle Laboratories Division of the American Cyanamid Company, where most of his work in the development of cures and medicines was conducted. Due to restrictions in U.S. immigration, Yellapragada Subba Row had to wait to become an American citizen until 1946, when the Luce-Celler Bill was passed, which restored naturalization rights to nationals of India.

Entrepreneur, political activist, and philanthropist **Gobindram Jhamandas Watumull** met with enormous success in the retail business in Honolulu. With his brother **Jhamandas Watumull**, G. J. Watumull set to work in 1917 transforming a small retail store in downtown Honolulu into a flourishing enterprise. By 1957 the Watumull brothers' business had blossomed into ten major department stores and numerous other commercial properties. In 1942 G. J. Watumull launched the Watumull Foundation, an organization dedicated to improving conditions in India, fostering U.S.-India relations, and engaging in philanthropic, educational, and cultural projects in Hawaii.

Jane Singh, a descendant of one of the first Sikh families to come to California in the early twentieth century, has broken new ground in ethnic studies as a professor at the University of California at Berkeley. In addition to her invaluable work in the classroom, Singh has contributed to both Asian Indian American and Asian American women's scholarship as an editor of *South Asians in North America: An Annotated and Selected Bibliography* (1988) and *Making Waves: Writing By and About Asian American Women* (1989).

What is a sari?

Among the many traditional garments that Hindu women wear is the *sari*, a robe consisting of six yards of untailored cotton or silk fabric that is simply wrapped around the body and draped over the head or shoulder. When it comes to the sari, one size fits all. The sari is so popular among Indian women that it has been elevated to the national dress.

The color and fabric of a woman's sari reveal much about her age, occupation, religion, ethnicity, and marital status. For instance, Hindu widows wear plain white cotton saris, while newly married women don brightly colored saris. Women from the north and central regions of India tend to wear pastels, while women from the south favor dark fabrics with gold trim.

What is the difference between Hindi and Hindu?

Hindi is the official language of India. It has many dialects and, like Sanskrit, is written in Devanagari script, with its long, horizontal strokes at the top of most characters.

A Hindu is a person who follows Hinduism, one of the oldest living religions in the world. Approximately 83 percent of Indians are Hindus. Hinduism has no one founder, since it developed over a period of four thousand years in syncretism with devotional, philosophical, and cultural movements in India. The religion brought to India by the Aryans in 1500 B.C. had a great impact on Hinduism. Hinduism spawned three other religions: Buddhism and Jainism in the sixth century B.C. and Sikhism in the fifteenth century A.D.

As a result of its long development, Hinduism has numerous sacred writings: the four *Vedas*, the *Upanishads* (dialogues between the teachers and devotees), the *Bhagavad Gita*, the *Puranas*, and two epic poems, the *Mahabharata* and the *Ramayana*. This literature is an essential component of Hindu worship, as are pilgrimages to sacred places, and *puja*, the worship of enshrined deities.

Hindus believe in an omnipotent force, *Parabrahma*, which has three principal deities which assume countless forms: *Brahma*, the Creator; *Vishnu*, the Preserver; and *Shiva*, the Destroyer. In addition, Hinduism has a vast pantheon of "minor" deities that are considered separate manifestations of the one Supreme Being. Each has a myth, a name, a set of gestures, and physical attributes such as animal parts or extra arms. The purpose of the physical representation of the deities is to enable the spiritually unevolved to learn about the divine and find the path to true enlightenment.

Hindus believe that life entails birth, death, reincarnation, and the transmigration of souls. In Hinduism the path of enlightenment leads to the ultimate goal of *moksha*, or *mukti*—liberation from suffering and from the cycles of rebirth. To reach *mukti* the devotee must first of all adhere to the Hindu code of behavior based on *dharma*, performing one's moral duties as called by conscience. *Dharma* is directly linked to *karma*, the law of cause and effect whereby a person reaps the results of good and bad action in this life and the next lives.

Caste is one of the most pervasive aspects of Hinduism. Hindu society is divided into four castes, with the Brahman at the top, then the Kshatriyas (warriors), Vaishyas (merchants), and Shudras (farmers, craftspeople, and laborers). It is widely accepted that fair-skinned Aryans invented and instituted the caste system in order to maintain separation from the darker indigenous people of the region.

ASIAN AMERICAN HEARTTHROBS

1. Tia Carrere

Filipina American singer and actress Tia Carrere first made a splash with her role as Jade on the TV soap opera *General Hospital.* She later starred in the motion pictures *Rising Sun* (1990), *Wayne's World* (1992), *Wayne's World II* (1993), and *True Lies* (1994).

2. Michael Chang

Top-seeded Chinese American tennis player Michael Chang made history in 1989 when he became the youngest male player to capture the French Open.

3. Joan Chen

Chinese American actress Joan Chen has fans in China as well as America. She is best-known for her role in the hit 1990–1992 television series *Twin Peaks.* Chen has also appeared in major motion pictures such as *Dim Sum* (1985), *Tai-Pan* (1986), *The Last Emperor* (1987), *Turtle Beach* (1992), *Heaven and Earth* (1993), and *The Joy Luck Club* (1993) among others.

4. Connie Chung

One of the highest-paid, most influential, and most sought-after woman broadcast journalists in the nation, Chinese American Connie Chung has anchored the news for both NBC and CBS. She has cowritten and hosted numerous documentaries.

5. Dustin Nguyen

Vietnamese American actor Dustin Nguyen survived the fall of Saigon and went on to earn fame for his role as Officer Harry Ioki, an undercover cop in the 1980s TV drama *21 Jump Street*. He made his television debut in 1984 in *Magnum, P.I.*, and later appeared in *General Hospital*. On the big screen Nguyen starred in *Heaven Can Wait* (1993) and *3 Ninjas Kick Back* (1994).

6. Jenny Shimizsu

Japanese American model Jenny Shimizsu has been featured in many American and European magazines and is a fixture on the runways. She is known for her exotic tattoos and her appearances in Madonna's music videos.

7. Tamlyn Tomita

Japanese American actress Tamlyn Tomita has appeared in many box office hits such as *The Karate Kid* (1984), *The Karate Kid Part II* (1986), *Come See the Paradise* (1990), and *The Joy Luck Club* (1993).

8. Russell Wong

Chinese American actor Russell Wong garnered critical applause for his role in the film *New Jack City* (1991). He has acted in numerous other motion pictures, including *China Girl* (1987), *Eat a Bowl of Tea* (1989), and *The Joy Luck Club* (1993).

How do Hindus worship in America?

The first Hindus in America had no temples where they could pray and give offerings before a high-caste Brahmin priest, so they worshiped and read the *Bhagavad Gita* on their own.

They established religious centers, such as the Vedanta Society and the Ramakrishna-Vivekananda Center in New York City, but these were geared toward non-Indians with an interest in Asian Indian religions.

Nowadays Hindus in New York City have the choice of worshiping at small shrines at home or attending one of at least six temples for group services on weekends and holidays. The Hindu Temple of North America in Flushing, New York, is just one possibility. It was constructed by a hundred skilled craftsmen from the southern state of Andhra Pradesh in India. In 1976 the twenty-ton granite structure was transported to Flushing, where twenty-five of the craftsmen carefully reassembled it. Statues of deities from the Hindu pantheon, such as Shiva, Lakshmi (the goddess of wealth), and Ganesha (the elephant-headed god), adorn the elaborate temple.

The elephant god Ganesha stands for both wisdom and gluttony. In September, Hindus from southern India celebrate Ganapathy in commemoration of Ganesha's rise from the underworld. On this holiday Hindu women strew flowers on Ganesha and offer him a feast of avocados, oranges, bananas, and coconuts. Worshipers bow to the altar and toss fistfuls of rice. Occasionally they touch first a flame carried on a silver tray and then their foreheads. A vegetarian banquet follows, and then the Hindus drive to the Flushing Meadow Lake, where they place a replica of Ganesha in the water so that he may return to the land of the dead.

Hindus have erected temples in other regions of America as well. For instance, Hindus near Malibu Beach in southern California attend Sree Venkateswara Hindu Temple, which was constructed by Tamil craftsmen.

What does the swastika have to do with Hinduism, Jainism, and Buddhism in India?

The swastika probably originated with the early Aryans who invaded India in 2000 B.C. It is prevalent in the Hindu, Jain, and Buddhist faiths, and is an auspicious mark of good fortune for Indians.

Who is Deepak Chopra?

Prominent Asian Indian American **Deepak Chopra**, is a physician and the best-selling author of numerous spiritual-motivational books, including *Creating Affluence* (1993) and *The Seven Spiritual Laws of Success* (1994). In his writing and lectures, Deepak Chopra sheds light on a mind-body approach he has devised that combines Eastern wisdom and state-of-the-art Western science, and practical knowledge and spiritual law.

What national holidays do Asian Indians in America celebrate?

Many Asian Indian Americans celebrate Indian Independence Day, which falls on August 21. In New York City the Federation of Indian Associations sponsors a parade with marchers from organizations representing all the many regions of India. Indian dance troops, Indian beauty queens atop floats, and marching bands parade by the throngs that have gathered on the sidewalks. A highlight of the Indian Independence Day parade is the floats that depict how India won its freedom. Asian Indians also celebrate India's sovereignty on Republic Day, which falls on January 26, a holiday commemorating the birth of the Republic of India in 1950.

One of the most holy days for Hindus falls in February or March and is celebrated with the one-day festival *maha-shivaratri* in honor of the god Shiva, which usually takes place on March 1. Hindus, even those who do not worship Shiva, pay a visit to the temple on *maha-shivaratri* to pay homage to the god. On the ninth day of the ascending moon, sometime between mid-March and mid-April, Hindus celebrate the birth of Rama, one of the ten incarnations of Vishnu, with the festival *ramnavami*. During *ramnavami*, Hindus go to the temple with offerings of money, food, and clothing for the Brahmins, monks, and the poor. They also sing songs in honor of Rama, recite the *Ramayana*, the story of Rama's life, and go to the movie theater to see *Ramayana* films.

All Hindus in the United States observe *Divali*, also known as Deepawali, the festival of lights, which falls on the first day of the new moon when the sun reaches Libra, sometime between mid-October and mid-November. As part of the celebrations, Hindus light lamps to guide departed souls in their journey back to earth and as a celebration of the defeat of darkness with light. In New York City and elsewhere around the country, *Divali* celebrations include a procession of floats bedecked with huge shrines decorated with numerous Hindu deities.

One of the most sacred days for Sikhs, who celebrate an equally large number of religious holidays, is *Baisakhi* Day, which falls on April 13. *Baisakhi* Day commemorates the initiation of Sikhs into the Khalsa fraternity, which was founded on April 13, 1699. Sikhs celebrate this day by visiting a Sikh temple, where they attend a religious service that entails readings from the *Guru Granth Sahib*, or holy scriptures. Baisakhi Day is also an important day on the Hindu calendar, for it commemorates the descension of Ganga to earth and signifies the beginning of the New Year.

What foods do Asian Indian Americans prefer?

It all depends on their religious beliefs. Punjabi Sikhs and some Hindus prefer a strict vegetarian diet, while Muslims eat most foods except pork. As Asian Indians acculturate to America, they tend to develop American tastes, although most try to gather for at least one traditional Indian meal a day.

Asian Indian cooking is as varied as the peoples of the Indian subcontinent. In the wheat-growing north, whole-wheat breads such as *chapati* and *paratha* dominate, as does *tandoori*, seared meats made in the Near Eastern clay ovens the northerners adopted. In the subtropical, vegetarian south, rice and *dal*, lentils and beans, reign supreme. Vegetable curries made with "wet" *masalas*, or "spice blends," and *papadam*, crispy wafers made of *urad dal*, are just a handful of the popular southern dishes. The western state of Gujarat is the home of Mahatma Gandhi and Jainism, and Kathiawari and Surati vegetarian cuisine with its ubiquitous vegetable curries, vegetable fritters, and *dhokla*, or chickpea flour cake sprinkled with mustard seeds and cilantro.

What are some essential herbs and spices in Asian Indian cooking?

Turmeric, chile powder, cumin, coriander, ginger, garlic, mustard seeds, cloves, cardamom, cinnamon, peppercorns, parsley, fennel seeds, nigella seeds, white poppy seeds, curry leaves, saffron, and more. Asian Indians make frequent use in the kitchen of hundreds of pungent spice blends, such as the traditional *garam masala*, an aromatic mix of cloves, cinnamon, cardamom, cumin, and peppercorns.

Asian Indians consider more than just flavoring when they add seasonings to dishes, since according to the ancient Indian medical system of Ayurveda, all spices and herbs possess medicinal properties. For example, cloves tone the heart, while tamarind and coriander cure constipation.

Which hand do Asian Indians traditionally eat with?

Asian Indians traditionally eat with their right hand and not with utensils. They reserve the left hand for serving food or picking up glasses of beverage.

Northerners prefer to use just the tips of their fingers, while southerners use their whole hand. These customs prevail in many Asian Indian communities in the United States.

What is traditional Asian Indian medicine?

The traditional system of medicine in India is known as *Ayurveda*, from the word *ayus*, meaning "life," and *veda*, meaning "knowledge." Traditional Indian medicine emphasizes physical, mental, and spiritual balance achieved through regimented daily living and yoga. When an imbalance occurs, doctors who practice Ayurveda rely on yoga, homeopathy, and spices and herbs to restore health. According to Hindu belief, the first herbalist was the god Shiva, who is often depicted with a pot of herbs in one hand and a lotus flower in the other. Asian Indians in America have made invaluable contributions to Western medicine by enlightening hospital staffs about ways to balance their procedures with religious beliefs.

What is yoga?

Yoga, a Sanskrit word meaning "harnessing" or "union," is an ancient discipline designed to integrate the body, the mind, and the spirit so that the individual may experience a union with Brahman, the universal soul. Yoga training consists of eight stages. In the first stage the yoga practitioner must undergo ethical training, and refrain from lying, stealing, and using violent means to achieve an end. The second stage involves mental restraint, that is, the acceptance of life cycles, while the third stage is designed to exercise the body and the mind through *asanas*, or postures, and exercises. The headstand and the cross-legged lotus position are some of the more famous asanas in yoga.

In the fourth stage, the yoga practitioner incorporates breathing exercises, while in the fifth stage the practitioner emancipates her or his mind from the senses. The sixth and seventh stages involve concentration and meditation. Finally, by the eighth stage, the practitioner achieves *samadhi*, a deep state of meditation that entails union with Brahman.

If performed correctly, yoga asanas produce a therapeutic effect on the body by improving blood circulation and eliminating tension. Master yogis have been known to control the rhythm of their heartbeats, to hold their breath for long periods of time, and to withstand extremes of both heat and cold.

Yoga arrived in the United States in the early twentieth century, which saw a phenomenal rise in Asian Indian immigration.

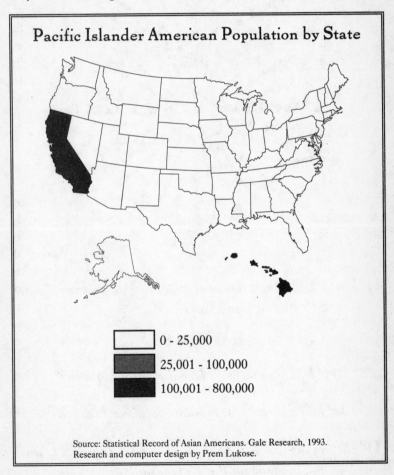

Pacific Islander American Population by State

0 - 25,000

25,001 - 100,000

100,001 - 800,000

Source: Statistical Record of Asian Americans. Gale Research, 1993.
Research and computer design by Prem Lukose.

SEVEN

Pacific Islander Americans

When did Pacific Islanders first migrate and immigrate to America?

HAWAIIANS

Why is the term "Hawaiian" ambiguous?

When did the Polynesians colonize Hawaii?

What impact did Captain Cook's discovery of Hawaii have on the Polynesians?

What was the Great Mahele of 1848?

What did the company Dole Pineapples have to do with Hawaii becoming the fiftieth state of the Union?

When did Hawaii finally become a state?

Why is Hawaii known as a state of tolerance?

Has traditional Hawaiian culture been preserved in Hawaiian schools and how do native Hawaiians fare in public school?

How have native Hawaiians fared economically in their own land?

What is the hula?

Did the Hawaiians invent the sport of surfing?

What language do the indigenous Hawaiians speak?

What is a lei?

What is the Hawaiian custom of hanai?

What religion is prevalent on the Hawaiian Islands?

What is a luau?

SAMOANS

How did American Samoa become a U.S. territory?

When did the Samoans first migrate to the United States?

When did American Samoans begin to migrate in significant numbers to the mainland United States?

What does a Samoan tattoo signify?

What is an aiga?

GUAMANIANS

How did Guam become an American territory?

What triggered Guamanian migration to America?

What's a fandango?

What is breadfruit and how did it save the Guamanians?

TONGAN AMERICANS

Where is Tonga?

If life is so carefree in Tonga, why did Tongans start coming to America?

Where have Tongans settled in the United States?

The Pacific Islands, numbering in the hundreds, lie in the middle of the vast Pacific Ocean, a region known traditionally as Oceania. Oceania was long ago divided into three smaller groups: Micronesia (small islands), Polynesia (many islands), and Melanesia (black islands).

Polynesia, the largest in area, consists of the volcanic and coral islands of the South Pacific, among them the Hawaiian Islands, the Cook Islands, French Polynesia, American Samoa, Western Samoa, and Tonga. Robert Louis Stevenson called the Polynesians "God's best, at least God's sweetest work." Despite their wide geographic distribution, Polynesians are closely related in terms of culture and language. Before they were claimed by the United States, Hawaii and American Samoa were Polynesian nations, and so Hawaiian and American Samoan migrants are considered even though their movement is on U.S. soil, not between sovereign nations.

The major countries in Micronesia, with its more than 2,000 smaller coral atolls and volcanic islands in the mid-Pacific, include the Marshall Islands, the U.S. territory of Guam, and Saipan in the Mariana Islands. Peoples from Guam and Saipan are collectively referred to as Chamorros.

Melanesia is composed of many countries including New Caledonia, Papua New Guinea, Fiji, the Solomon Islands, and New Hebrides, with Fiji wielding the most influence.

Migration and emigration from the Pacific Islands to America is a relatively new phenomenon; before 1950 few Pacific Islanders lived in the U.S. According to the 1990 United States Census 365,024 Pacific Islanders reside in the continental United States, approximately 5 percent of the total Asian American population. This number was up 46 percent from 1980, when only 259,566 Pacific Islanders made their home in the continental U.S.

Of the 365,024 Pacific Islanders counted in the 1990 U.S. Census, 211,014 were Hawaiians (in the continental U.S.), 62,964 Samoans (including both Western Samoan Americans and American Samoans in the continental U.S.), 49,345 Guamanians (in the continental U.S.), 17,606 Tongans, and 7,036 Fijians. For the purpose of this book, we shall discuss the Hawaiians, Samoans, Guamanians, and Tongans (who are the only immigrant group of the four since Tonga is a sovereign nation), for they have contributed the largest number of Pacific Islander migrants and immigrants to the continental U.S. population.

When did Pacific Islanders first migrate and immigrate to America?

The first major wave of Pacific Islander migration and immigration to the continental United States began relatively recently. Between 1950 and 1970, scores of migrants and immigrants from the Pacific Islands abandoned their homes in search of a better way of life. Most did not migrate or immigrate directly to the American mainland but rather stopped along the way in major urban centers such as Guam, Saipan, Yap, Nauru in Micronesia, and American Samoa and Tahiti in Micronesia. The Tongans, however, immigrated to America without taking any detours along the way, mainly because missionaries brought them directly to the United States.

Pacific Islander migration and immigration is partially an unintended manifestation of the wanderlust that is a traditional phase in reaching manhood. Throughout history, young men in the Pacific Islands came of age by making long voyages to distant islands in canoes or other boats. These voyagers, at least in Micronesia, would only return home after several years had passed, and then would marry, settle down, and have children. Migration and immigration to the United States mainland has also been a safety valve for increased pressure on the natural resources in the Pacific Islands. Many also have left to pursue higher education.

Many Pacific Islander groups are better represented in the continental United States than in the Pacific Islands themselves. For instance, by the late 1970s, around 50,000 American Samoans resided in the continental United States, while

Samoans in American Samoa numbered somewhere between
30,000 and 40,000. The same is true of the Chamorros, whose
number in the continental United States ranges between 30,000
and 50,000—about equal to the population of Guam and
Saipan together. The Tongan population in America is roughly
one-tenth of the population in Tonga. The loss of citizenry has
had a critical impact on the dynamics of these tiny countries.

HAWAIIANS

Why is the term "Hawaiian" ambiguous?

In the strictest sense, the term *Hawaiian* refers to the descendants of the original Polynesian inhabitants of the Hawaiian
Islands. However, given Hawaii's history of immigration and
high rate of intermarriage, "Hawaiian" includes peoples of
Portugese, Chinese, Japanese, Filipino, Korean, and Puerto
Rican ancestry and their mixed offspring in Hawaii. Some
who are considered Hawaiian may be genealogically pure,
while others may only be one-sixteenth Polynesian.

Persons of Polynesian or part-Polynesian ancestry represent the third-largest ethnic group in Hawaii after Americans
of European ancestry and Japanese Americans. Many other
Hawaiians of Polynesian ancestry reside on the U.S. mainland, particularly in California, where they are often confused
with the Tongans and American Samoans.

When did the Polynesians colonize Hawaii?

Around 1,500 years ago, Polynesian voyagers, mostly from the
Marquesas Islands, set off in double-hulled sailing canoes in
search of a new home. They crossed 2,000 miles of open sea, navi-
gating by the stars and praying to Laamaomao, god of the winds,
until they reached the Hawaiian Islands. Then, around A.D. 1200,
other Polynesians made their way to Hawaii from Tahiti. It is believed that both groups of voyagers were originally Southeast

Asians who had settled earlier in Tahiti and the Marquesas Islands. According to legend, Polynesian settlers named the islands Hawaii in honor of their chief Hawaii-loa, who led them to the island.

The Polynesians lived in isolation on the Hawaiian Islands for fourteen centuries, before the arrival of the *haoles*, foreigners, late in Europe's Age of Discovery. For two centuries explorers had navigated the Pacific expanse, but it was only in 1778 that the Europeans in the person of British explorer Captain **James Cook** finally stumbled upon Hawaii while they were searching for the legendary Northwest Passage. The moment Captain Cook made landfall on Kauai, Hawaii's destiny was changed forever. Cook named the island chain the Sandwich Islands, after John Montagu, the fourth earl of Sandwich. At the time of his discovery about 300,000 people of Polynesian descent inhabited Hawaii.

What impact did Captain Cook's discovery of Hawaii have on the Polynesians?

After Cook's discovery of Hawaii, all the major seafaring nations—Britain, the United States, and France—sent ships to the islands for exploration and trade. Before long the Europeans had a hand in politics and helped Hawaii's King Kamehameha unite his kingdom under a strong rulership in 1810. They also took over the economy, bringing iron, cattle, horses, melons, and pumpkins to Hawaii—along with dreaded diseases, such as smallpox, to which most Pacific Islanders lacked immunity. By 1858, Hawaii's population had declined from 300,000 to only 60,000 as a result of contact with the West. The decline and the massive immigration of Japanese, Chinese, Puerto Ricans, Filipinos, and other aliens, who were brought in to labor on the sugar and pineapple plantations established in the mid–nineteenth century, made Hawaiians an ethnic minority in their own country. By 1900, Hawaiians of Polynesian ancestry constituted just 24.4 percent of the population.

Yet from 1810, when **Kamehameha I** unified Hawaii under

his rule after a ten-year war, until 1893, Hawaii managed to remain a modern sovereign country. Nonetheless it was a country under siege. By 1820, missionaries from the first New England Congregationalist Church swarmed the islands. In accordance with the liberal Calvinism of the era, they were intent on not only converting the natives to Christianity and replacing Hawaiian customs, such as the *hula,* with Christian practices, but also setting up schools, hospitals, and a democratic government. The Hawaiians did not put up a fight. Kamehameha's son, Liholiho, became **Kamehameha II** upon his father's death in 1819, and abolished the native religion, with its many gods and goddesses and *Kapus,* a system of strict taboos, making it easy for the New England Congregationalist Church to install Christianity.

What was the Great Mahele of 1848?

In 1842 the United States recognized the Kingdom of Hawaii as an independent government, but before long Americans would control the economic life of the island kingdom. Until 1848, the concept of private ownership of land did not exist in Hawaii. Pressure to open up land to aliens resulted in the reallocation of land rights in 1848, what is known as the Great Mahele. Counseled by white advisers, **Kamehameha III** set aside one-third of the land for himself, one-third for the chiefs the king wished to reward, and allocated the remaining one-third as land which could be sold.

Since Hawaiians had no concept of land ownership, many sold the titles to their property for a meager sum without any idea that once sold, the land would no longer be in their possession. The land essentially fell into the hands of business-savvy foreign investors, many from the United States, who converted acre after acre into large sugar and pineapple plantations.

The felony was compounded when plantation owners turned around and used the natives for cheap labor, further demoralizing the people of Polynesian ancestry. By 1890 the native population of Hawaii had dwindled to 40,000 and with their sugar plantations thriving, owners supplemented native labor by recruiting immigrants from Asia to work the fields. So began the long reign of "King Cane" and a wave of Asian immigration that would dramatically alter the makeup of Hawaiian society.

The first laborers were recruited from China in the 1870s. Soon plantation owners began to fear that they would lose control of the Chinese immigrants who flooded into Hawaii, so to create an ethnic counterbalance and disarm the Chinese, they began importing Portuguese laborers in 1878. The plantation owners also recruited the Japanese, although early recruitment attempts in Japan in 1868 were met with fierce resistance from the Japanese government. An emissary of the Hawaiian king even tried to persuade Japan that emigration was in its interest with the story that both the Japanese and the native Hawaiians were descendants of a common ancestor. The Japanese apparently were not impressed. Only in 1886, when Hawaii and Japan signed a convention allowing Japanese workers to go to Hawaii, could plantation owners count on Japanese to work their fields.

The first group of Koreans, hired by the Hawaiian Sugar Planters' Association, arrived in Hawaii in 1903. Between 1907 and 1931, almost 120,000 Filipinos were imported to the Hawaiian Islands as plantation workers. From the 1940s on, sizable numbers of immigrants from several places went to Hawaii, including Puerto Ricans, Spaniards, and Samoans.

"King Cane" would rule Hawaii's economy until after World War II, and thus the wealthy sugar plantation owners exerted extraordinary control in the political arena. As most white plantation owners in Hawaii were from the United States, they wielded enormous influence on the kinds of treaties Hawaii would enter into with the United States. Such treaties tended to favor U.S. interest—for example, the treaty agreed upon by King **Kalakaua**, called the Merry Monarch, which conferred on the United States exclusive rights to a naval base at Pearl Harbor.

What did the company Dole Pineapples have to do with Hawaii becoming the fiftieth state of the Union?

As the decade of the 1890s dawned, Americans in Hawaii became increasingly alarmed that Queen **Liliuokalani**, King Kalakaua's successor, would reestablish an absolute monarchy and change the balance of power in the Kingdom of Hawaii, to the detriment of their interests. They also worried that the duty-free status on the importation of Hawaiian sugar into the United States would be altered. In 1893, American business executives, backed by sailors and marines from a U.S. naval ship, forced Queen Liliuokalani to abdicate her throne and called for the establishment of a provisional government headed by **Sanford B. Dole**, a white plantation owner and pineapple king of Dole Pineapples.

And so the Republic of Hawaii was born in 1894, with Sanford B. Dole as its first and only president. Dole was a major proponent of the campaign to have Hawaii annexed by the United States, since he and other plantation owners would receive a special payment when shipping sugar to the mainland U.S. Dole met with success on August 12, 1893, when the United States under President McKinley formally annexed Hawaii by the Joint Resolution of Annexation, despite opposition from Hawaiians.

On June 14, 1900, Hawaii officially became a U.S. territory through the signing of an Organic Act, and all Hawaiians were granted U.S. citizenship, though as territorial citizens they did not gain the right to vote. Sanford B. Dole was named governor of Hawaii. Statehood would be deferred until 1959 due to America's racist stance toward the large population of people of color in Hawaii and arguments that Hawaii was much too far away to become a state.

When did Hawaii finally become a state?

The Japanese bombing raid on the U.S. Pacific Fleet at Pearl Harbor on December 7, 1941, thrust Hawaii into the center of global affairs. As the Allies sought to contain Imperial Japan, Hawaii became a strategic player in the American defense apparatus, contributing to the success of American operations in World War II. America was united with the cry "Remember Pearl Harbor!" and Hawaii's war efforts did not go unnoticed.

Hawaii's contributions helped to break down the racial prejudice against Hawaiians of color that mainstream Americans harbored, paving the way for Hawaii to be officially admitted as the fiftieth state in the union on March 12, 1959. Interestingly, this was the same year that Boeing introduced its 707 jet airplanes that could fly from California to Honolulu in an amazing five hours, breaking all previous speed records by two hours. Boeing brought Hawaii closer to the continental U.S.

When word that Hawaii was the fiftieth state reached the people, celebrations erupted all over the Hawaiian Islands. The day after Congress passed the statehood bill for Hawaii, making it the only state that was once a royal kingdom, voters elected **Hiram Fong**, a Chinese American and **Oren Ethelbert Long**, a schoolteacher born in Kansas, as Hawaii's U.S. senators. **Daniel Inouye**, a Japanese American, was elected to represent Hawaii in the U.S. House of Representatives. Statehood created endless possibilities for Hawaiians to pursue education and careers on the U.S. mainland, and a good number ventured to the West Coast and beyond to start new lives.

Why is Hawaii known as a state of tolerance?

Hawaii's tolerance of diversity has been applauded for many decades. In fact, civil rights marchers in the South in the 1960s carried signs that read: "Hawaii Knows Integration Works." Hawaiians got to be so tolerant because throughout Hawaii's history, the island's racial groups intermarried and interbred. In fact, by 1960 pure-blooded Hawaiians made up less than two percent of the population. Today four out of ten Hawaiian marriages are interracial, over ten times that on the mainland, and six out of ten Hawaiian babies are of mixed blood.

A further contributor to Hawaii's tolerance of difference was the unique immigration it experienced. Immigrants came to the mainland United States in waves that were spread out over the centuries, allowing each group to settle in and develop a sense of superiority over later arrivals. By contrast, immigrants in Hawaii generally arrived within the same fifty-year period—for the purpose of working on Hawaii's plantations and thus they were on equal terms.

Has traditional Hawaiian culture been preserved in Hawaiian schools and how do native Hawaiians fare in public school?

The school system in Hawaii was originally set up by the white missionaries who arrived in 1820. Although the schools were distinctly American in style, children were originally taught in their native Hawaiian language as a way to preserve indigenous Hawaiian culture. Over time, however, missionary schools made English the official language.

After annexation, mandatory schooling became the norm, and a completely American-oriented school system was put in place. Hawaiian students, who constitute 30 percent of the student body, have fared poorly in these schools; only 5 percent make it to graduation, a startlingly high dropout rate of 83 percent.

How have native Hawaiians fared economically in their own land?

Unfortunately, not too well. The economic status of the native Hawaiians is poor. Not only is the cost of living in Hawaii high in comparison to the rest of the United States, but the income of Hawaiians tends to be low as well. The median income is approximately $6,485 for Hawaiian men and $2,931 for Hawaiian women. The high cost of living in Hawaii has caused a significant number of Hawaiian-born Americans to settle on the U.S. mainland, particularly in California.

What is the hula?

The *hula* is a famous Hawaiian dance with origins in Hawaiian religious ceremonies. In the past hula dancers were hand-picked by the *kahuna*, a priest of the temple, and trained by a *kumu hula*, a dance master. Only after years of training in the religious, mental, and physical aspects of the hula dance were students deemed ready to graduate.

When Protestant missionaries from New England first arrived in Hawaii in 1820, they exerted pressure on Hawaiian chiefs to ban the hula dance, which they considered lascivious. Queen **Kaahumanu**, who became a Christian convert, responded by issuing an edict in 1830 prohibiting the public performance of the hula. For the next twenty years, the hula disappeared from the public scene. Then, in 1851, public performances were allowed once again, but only after payment of licensing fees.

During the reign of Kalākaua (1874–1891), who sought to revive Hawaiians' sense of pride by resuscitating Hawaiian culture and tradition, the hula was celebrated publicly once again, much to the chagrin of the Protestant community. Hawaiian chiefs openly embraced the old custom of celebrating with the hula, and in 1883, when King Kalākaua was coronated, hula dancers were invited to perform in the coronation ceremonies.

Unfortunately, in the twentieth century the hula dance has been neatly packaged for Western consumption in the form of shows like the *Kodak Hula Show* in Waikiki, a kitschy spectacle of sex, corny comedy, show biz, and "cultural instruction," complete with "hula girls" with oversized carnation leis.

Still, not all hula is performed for the tourists in Waikiki. The 1970s ushered in a Hawaiian Renaissance, and with it the establishment of hula *halau*, schools where Hawaiians study ancient and modern styles of hula, and learn about their rich culture.

A hula dancer trained in a halau is taught not just the movements of the hula dance but also Hawaiian culture, myths, and legends. Through the dance, Hawaiian gods are remembered and celebrated in chants and dances. The hula is performed to the accompaniment of traditional Hawaiian instruments, such as the *pahu*, a drum made from sharkskin, the *puniu*, a drum made of coconut shell and traditionally tied to the leg, the *ipu*, a gourd used as percussion, and the *ili ili*, stones used as castanets. Musical instruments borrowed from other cultures also make an appearance in hula. For instance, Hawaiians borrowed the guitar from white missionaries, and then loosened the strings to produce an interesting effect.

Did the Hawaiians invent the sport of surfing?

It has been said that surfing is a combination of two sports brought to Hawaii by its earliest settlers, the Polynesians and the Tahitians. From Polynesia came *paipo*, in which thrillseekers rode waves by lying prone on a rounded board, and from Tahiti came *paka*, in which surfers rode the waves by standing on a canoe. The combination of the two pastimes contributed to the emergence of a new sport, surfing, which the chiefs of Hawaii and the natives of Hawaii embraced as their own.

By the 1800s, however, surfing was condemned by New England missionaries and did not enjoy a resurgence until 1904, when **Duke Kahanamoku**, the famous Hawaiian Olympic swimming champion, promoted the sport and popularized it as a Hawaiian pastime once again.

What language do the indigenous Hawaiians speak?

Hawaiian. The Hawaiian language is a melodic Polynesian language that had no writing system until the eighteenth century, when European settlers began arriving on the islands. Hawaiian should not be confused with the pidgin spoken by some of the locals, which has its roots in the fractured English spoken by early Chinese traders in Hawaii.

The Hawaiian language is dying out, mainly due to the influence of the early missionaries and a policy that makes English the official language of Hawaii. On the island of Niihau, however, the Hawaiian language still survives, although fewer than 2,500 people still speak it.

What is a lei?

A *lei* is a wreath of flowers and leaves that native Hawaiians wear around the neck. The lei came to Hawaii with Polynesian settlers, who used it as an offering to the gods in exchange for a blessing. When used as an offering, the flowers on a lei are carefully chosen to reflect a god's preferences.

There are two types of leis: permanent and temporary. Permanent leis are made of feathers plucked from exotic birds, shells, nuts, paper, and even bones. One of the most ancient leis, the *lei niho palaoa*, was worn by royalty and is composed of one single pendant, a whale's tooth strung on a rope of human hair.

Temporary leis are made from greenery and fragrant flowers. One of the most popular materials used is the fruit of the hala, which produces a scent as rich as the richest French perfume.

What is the Hawaiian custom of hanai?

Hanai is a traditional Hawaiian custom conferring on the grandparents the task of parenting. Boys are taken to their paternal grandfather's house, while girls go to their maternal grandmother's. Although *hanai* is not as prevalent now as it once was, the practice still exists.

What religion is prevalent on the Hawaiian Islands?

The native Hawaiian religion barely survived the onslaught of European missionaries who sought to replace what they viewed as "paganism" with Christianity. Like the Greeks and the Romans, Hawaiians had a god for almost every natural phenomenon—a god of thunder and agriculture, a god of war and male fertility, and a creator and head god. In their pantheon of gods is Kane, the god of creation, who is also worshiped as the god of light and fresh water. Kanaloa is the Hawaiian god of the sea, creator of the freshwater springs in Hawaii. Ku, the god of the rising sun, is also worshiped as the god of male virility, while Lono is the god of agriculture, clouds, winds, and fertility. The most famous goddess is Hina, the goddess of the sunset who, together with Ku, embodies the balance of male and female.

With the arrival of so many immigrant groups, each bringing with it a different religion, there is now a wide array of religions on the island.

What is a luau?

The *luau* is a Hawaiian native feast famous for its pièce de résistance—the roast pig baked in an *imu*, a ground oven. When Polynesians first came to Hawaii, they brought with them their livestock—pigs. Since then pork has become a favorite meat among the Hawaiians, and pig roasted the authentic Hawaiian way is prized among Hawaiians as well as tourists from all over the world.

Slaughtered and skinned, the pig is rubbed inside and out with rock salt and soy sauce, while an *imu*, a trench about eighteen inches deep is filled with hardwood logs and *imu* stones and lit. The pig is left to soak in the soy sauce marinade until the *imu* stones are red hot. Hot rocks are then placed in the body cavity of the pig, which is then wrapped in chicken wire, lowered into the imu, and covered with fresh corn husks, banana leaves, bananas, sweet potatoes, and fish. Last the imu is insulated with burlap bags soaked in water, then smothered with fresh earth to keep the steam from escaping as the pig roasts for approximately four hours. Guests at the luau invariably crowd around the imu as the roasted pig is hoisted onto a wooden platter. They then take their places at long tables and devour the roast pig with other Hawaiian delicacies such as poi.

SOME POPULAR ASIAN AMERICAN DISHES

1. **Kung Pao chicken** (Szechwan chicken with cashew nuts)

The spiciness of Kung Pao chicken comes from hot pepper paste, an integral component in Szechwan cooking. Cashew nuts transform this dish into a pièce de résistance.

2. **Dim sum** (Chinese snacks)

Dim sum, Cantonese for "heart's delight," is a wide assortment of little dishes such as steamed or fried shrimp, pork, beef, or vegetable dumplings, tiny spare ribs in black bean sauce, spring rolls, taro turnovers, crab claws, sticky rice, and steamed lotus buns filled with sweet bean paste, to name but a few. Waiters wheel carts filled with small portions of these delicacies among diners, who choose whichever dishes whet their appetite. Dim sum restaurants abound in Chinatowns across the nation, where Chinese Americans often gather in the early afternoon to enjoy conversation and a few "heart's delights."

3. **Misoshiru** (Japanese miso soup)

Misoshiru is a light broth flavored with white or red soybean paste and garnished with various combinations of ingredients such as tofu and scallions, or daikon and scallions. Miso soup is traditionally served toward the end of the meal.

4. **Nigiri sushi** (Japanese shrimp sushi)

Sushi is a piece of molded vinegared rice (the shapes and sizes

---

are endless) adorned with either raw or cooked fish, seafood, vegetables, or egg. *Nigiri sushi* is an oblong of rice garnished with cooked, butterflied shrimp. Like all sushi and sashimi, it is served with *wasabi* (a paste of green horseradish) and soy sauce.

5. **Sinigang** (Filipino chicken, beef, or fish with vegetables)

Sinigang is a marvelous stew made of meat, onions, tomatoes, and *daikon*, seasoned with fish sauce, hot chile pepper, and lemon.

6. **Kalbi** (Korean barbecued beef short ribs)

Kalbi are beef ribs that are first marinated in a delicious sauce containing ingredients typical in Korean cuisine such as soy sauce, onion, garlic, and ginger. The ribs are then grilled over a barbecue until they turn golden brown.

7. **Tandoori** (Indian oven-barbecued chicken or meat)

Tandoori is meat, or poultry, roasted on a spit in a *tandoor*, a clay oven, into which burning charcoal has been placed. *Tandoori* meats are first marinated in a flavorful sauce made of yogurt, onions, garlic, ginger root, chile peppers, cumin, and a red coloring agent, which imparts to tandoori its trademark orange tinge.

8. **Kimchee** (Korean pickled cabbage)

The Korean national dish, kimchee is a spicy and pungent condiment that accompanies almost every Korean meal. Kimchee is made of fermented vegetables, such as Chinese cabbage and turnips, seasoned with red pepper, salt, and garlic.

9. **Cha Gio** (Vietnamese spring rolls)

Cha Gio, Vietnamese spring rolls, are much lighter than the Chinese version because they are rolled in thin rice wrappers and stuffed with cellophane noodles, pork, shrimp, crab, shredded carrot, and scallions. *Cha Gio* are usually dipped in *nuoc mam,* a fish sauce.

10. **Pad Thai** (Thai noodles)

The queen of all Thai noodle dishes, *Pad Thai* has a wealth of ingredients that give it a vibrant flavor, including rice noodles, lemon juice, fish sauce, chopped peanuts, shrimp, bean-sprouts, garlic, and cilantro. Traditionally the rice noodles are not cut since long noodles are a sign of good luck. And by the way, Thai eat *Pad Thai* with chopsticks, but for most other dishes they use a Chinese-style ceramic spoon.

SAMOANS

How did American Samoa become a U.S. territory?

The mountainous volcanic islands of Samoa, situated in the South Pacific between New Zealand and Hawaii, were isolated from the West until the Dutch "discovered" them in 1722. Life in Samoa changed dramatically in 1816 when Christian missionaries, intent on civilizing the natives, swarmed the islands. The missionaries blazed the trail for eager traders, who recognized in Samoa a rich market to be exploited and developed.

In the nineteenth century, Germany, Great Britain, and the United States staked claims in Samoa. In 1899 Great Britain relinquished its claim, and the islands were partitioned between Germany and the United States. The Germans acquired Western Samoa (1,130 square miles), which they passed on to New Zealand in 1920. New Zealand administered Western Samoa until it became a sovereign nation in 1962.

The United States got American (Eastern) Samoa (76

square miles) in the deal, whose capital is Pago Pago, on the main island of Tutuila. From 1899 to 1951 the U.S. Department of the Navy administered the seven islands of American Samoa as a U.S. territory, and Samoans were accorded the status of U.S. nationals, not citizens. Thus they had limited privileges, such as the right of free entry into the United States. However, they could not vote in U.S. national elections.

American Samoa has never been incorporated as a state, and it is still *unorganized*—that is, it does not enjoy powers of self-government. How American Samoa will hold on to its status as a U.S. territory—or to be more exact, an unincorporated and unorganized territory of the United States—remains to be seen.

When did the Samoans first migrate to the United States?

The first wave of Samoan migrants reached Hawaiian shores in the nineteenth century and consisted of Mormon converts enlisted to build a church in Hawaii. Most of these migrants, whose motivation was religious, not economic, stayed in Laie, a small town about thirty-five miles from Honolulu. It was not until the 1920s that Samoans made their way to the United States.

In 1940 the U.S. Marine Corps made American Samoa into an advance training area and built airstrips, roads, docks, bunkers, and medical clinics. The U.S. Marine Corps provided employment for Samoans and also made the local economy boom. When American troops left after World War II, the Samoan economy slowed down enormously. It took another bad blow in 1951 when the naval station was shut down, unleashing a fierce economic recession and sending a second wave of Samoans to Hawaii. Once there, many Samoan men enlisted in the U.S. Navy, which they viewed as the most appealing avenue to employment. American Samoan officials actually encouraged this migration as a means of alleviating some of the tensions caused by rapid growth in the Samoan population and a sagging economy.

After 1951, American Samoa became an unincorporated territory administered by the U.S. Department of the Interior. Samoans continued to enlist in the Navy, for prestige, adventure, and the higher pay scale it afforded. In 1961 President John F. Kennedy appointed **H. Rex Lee** governor of American Samoa, and Lee undertook a massive campaign to Americanize American Samoa. He poured federal funds into a program of public works, housing, facilities for tourists, and communications. He even brought television to American Samoa.

When did American Samoans begin to migrate in significant numbers to the mainland United States?

In the 1960s, Samoans, who were becoming more American by the minute thanks to H. Rex Lee, became increasingly drawn to the United States, with its endless employment opportunities and quality schools. Once in America, Samoans helped friends and relatives back home to make the journey. Most Samoans have settled in the Los Angeles area, mainly in Carson, California, and in other large coastal cities, such as San Francisco, San Diego, and Seattle. Mormon American Samoans have settled in Salt Lake City. A small number of Western Samoans have actually immigrated to the U.S.

What does a Samoan tattoo signify?

In Samoa, tattooing is regarded as the highest art form and has been in existence for over 2,000 years. Men's tattoos, a sign of manhood, usually run from above the waist down to the knees, while women's start at the knee and go down to the ankle.

For men the entire tattooing process may take months to complete and is extremely painful. Samoans use traditional tattoo instruments, a set of small combs made of turtle shell or pig's teeth, rather than the typical electric pen, to prick the skin with ink. If a man does not go through the entire tattooing process, he is considered a coward and may even bring shame to his family. On the U.S. mainland this custom is waning among American Samoans.

What is an aiga?

The extended family is at the very core of Samoan life. On any given day a Samoan household may contain the nuclear family, the husband and wife's parents and unmarried siblings, as well as friends who have dropped by for a visit and stayed on for a few days or maybe even a year.

An *aiga* is a relative by blood, marriage, or adoption. *Aigas* who are contemporaries are considered brothers and sisters. Samoans can count on their aigas to provide food, shelter, and assistance when necessary, and if they so desire they can even take their aigas' possessions without asking. It is forbidden in Samoan society to marry one's aigas. *Aigas* have played an important role as a support system for Samoan newcomers to the U.S. mailand.

GUAMANIANS

How did Guam become an American territory?

Guam, the gateway to Micronesia, was "discovered" by Ferdinand Magellan, who is believed to have made landfall at Umatac Bay on March 6, 1521. Magellan named Guam and islands to the north Islas de Ladrones, or "Islands of Thieves," because natives stole a skiff from his ship. Spain claimed Guam in 1565 and made it a regular port of call for merchants and sailors plying their trade on the route connecting Mexico and Manila.

In 1688, Padre San Vitores of the Jesuit order of the Catholic Church arrived in Guam, and soon other Spanish missionaries followed to convert the people to Christianity.

The missionaries ripped Chamorro society apart, and in 1672 the natives revolted against Spanish domination. The revolts merely led to a loss of Chamorro lives. Later, Spain administered Guam as part of the Philippines and attempted to integrate both countries into the global economy by encouraging trade with Mexico.

After the Spanish-American War in 1893, Spain ceded Guam to the United States, which turned the island into a naval base and made the natives U.S. nationals. Except for a brief period of Japanese occupation during World War II, the Navy administered the island until 1950. Then on August 1, 1950, Congress passed the Organic Act of Guam, which conferred U.S. citizenship on the inhabitants of the Territory of Guam, established in Guam a civilian administration under the jurisdiction of the U.S. Department of the Interior, and extended control of the local government to the natives.

In 1970, the governorship of Guam became an elected office, rather than one appointed by the president of the United States. Guam has been so Americanized, to the detriment of the indigenous culture, that it has earned the nickname "Guam USA." For the peoples of Micronesia, and tourists from Japan and China, Guam is an "American metropolis in the Pacific," and they flock to the island to sample American-style cosmopolitan living, have a holiday in the sun, and shop duty-free.

What triggered Guamanian migration to America?

Large-scale migration of Guamanians was partially caused by the improvement in relations between the United States and Guam. With the passage of the Organic Act of Guam in 1950, Guamanians had unlimited access to the United States.

Most Guamanians saw this turn of events as a chance to improve their finances. Enlisting in the U.S. armed forces turned out to be the simplest way for Guamanian men to reach the mainland and secure a well-paying job. Figures from the U.S. Immigration and Naturalization Service indicate that 11,930 Guamanians entered the United States, primarily through Hawaii and the West Coast, between 1963 and 1971.

Most of these migrants settled in the very same port cities they first entered, and most found work at naval shipyards. Thus Guamanians are concentrated in large metropolitan areas along the West Coast, mainly San Diego, Los Angeles, and San Francisco.

What's a fandango?

To Spaniards it's a dance, but to Guamanians a *fandango* is a festive wedding reception with music and dancing that is usually held on the Friday night before a Saturday morning ceremony. Tradition dictates that the parents of the betrothed construct an awning of sorts from federico palms to cover tables bedecked with flowers and popular Guamanian dishes of chicken, beef, and pork. The pièce de résistance under the awning is Guamanian wedding cake, a fruitcake with white frosting.

What is breadfruit and how did it save the Guamanians?

Breadfruit is a fruit native to the Pacific that has a bumpy rind and bland flesh that sweetens as it ripens. Breadfruit can be boiled, baked, fried, and grilled, and served as a sweet or savory dish much like plantains. Guamanians use breadfruit to make soups, chowders, chips, and *Gollai Apan Lemmai*, a scrumptious breadfruit and coconut cream dish.

When the Japanese disrupted rice growing in Guam during World War II, Guamanians subsisted on breadfruit.

TONGAN AMERICANS

Where is Tonga?

The Kingdom of Tonga is a Polynesian island chain in the South Pacific, to the east of Fiji, just to the west of the international dateline, and a day ahead of Samoa. According to Tongan legend, the kingdom got its start when the Samoans gave the hero Maui a fishhook, and with it he yanked the Tongan Islands from the sea.

According to archaeologists and historians, the Polynesians from Samoa who roamed Tonga had the islands to themselves until the Dutch showed up in Tongan waters in 1616. Captain Cook explored the islands in 1773, 1774, and 1777, and was so impressed by the natives' hospitality that he named Tonga the Friendly Islands. (Nowadays the Tongan tourist bureau happily capitalizes on Cook's observation.)

From 1799 to 1852 the natives were a little unfriendly to each other and engaged in a fiery civil war. During this time the London Missionary Society sent missionaries to the Tongan Islands, but they were overwhelmed by the fighting. Wesleyan Methodists had better luck in the 1820s and little by little converted the natives.

Just a few decades later, in 1880, the Wesleyan missionary Shirley Baker drafted a constitution for Tonga and placed himself at the helm of the new government. One of the first things Baker did was establish the Free Wesleyan Church, the official church of Tonga. Before long the British, who thought Baker pushy, called for his deportation. In 1901 Great Britain declared the Kingdom of Tonga a protectorate. Tonga, under King Taufa'ahau Tupou IV, the first Tongan to earn a college degree, declared its independence on June 4, 1970.

Today the Kingdom of Tonga boasts one of the lowest mortality rates in the world. Scientists have ventured a guess that the slower pace of life on the islands, the pristine environment and gentle climate, as well as the people's pleasant disposition all contribute to Tongan longevity. Tongans would like to believe that their long life span has something to do with *fakatonga*, doing things "the Tonga way."

If life is so carefree in Tonga, why did Tongans start coming to America?

Thanks to Shirley Baker, Tongans have been churchgoing Wesleyans for over a century. Nonetheless, the Mormon Church managed in the 1960s to rapidly expand its presence in Tonga, precipitating large-scale Tongan emigration to America. Some believe that the Mormons' popularity in Tonga stems from the respect they have shown for ancient traditions, unlike any other missionaries. Three decades later the Church of Jesus Christ of Latter-day Saints, which has churches, schools, and meeting houses everywhere in Tonga, still encourages, and even funds, Tongan emigration to America. Since Tongans do not enjoy the right of unrestricted entry into the United States, they depend on either sponsorship by relatives with United States citizenship or the quota system.

Wesleyan Tongans are generally displeased by the pervasiveness of the Mormon Church in Tonga, but since religious freedom is guaranteed by the constitution, they have little recourse to change the situation. Some question the strength of the Mormon Church in Tonga, claiming that many Tongan Mormons are merely opportunists rather than true adherents who capitalize on the opportunity to send their kids to good schools like Brigham University and then disavow themselves of Mormonism.

Where have Tongans settled in the United States?

The largest Tongan American community, about 4,000 strong, is located in the San Francisco Bay Area. Two to three thousand Tongans also call the Samoan and Chamorro neighbor-hoods of L.A. their home. Approximately 1,000 Tongans live in Salt Lake City, the heart of Mormonism.

SOME SITES WHERE YOU CAN RELIVE ASIAN AMERICAN HISTORY

1. Angel Island San Francisco Bay, California

This 740-acre island dotted with garrisons has served as a mili-tary base, a prisoner-of-war detention center, and an immigra-tion station since 1863. From 1910 to 1940, North Garrison on Angel Island was a holding area for Chinese immigrants anx-iously awaiting permission to enter the United States. They were not allowed to be released until they could somehow convince American authorities that their papers were legiti-mate. As the Chinese immigrants waited, packed in crowded and unsanitary quarters, many vented their frustration by carv-ing poems in the barrack walls. Nowadays North Garrison is a museum that pays tribute to the 175,000 people who were wrongfully imprisoned on Angel Island. Its restored barracks with the poems still visible on the walls were recently opened to visitors, and a photographic display was installed that tells the poignant story of the Chinese immigrants in waiting.

2. Chinatown San Francisco, California

Despite claims to the contrary, San Francisco's Chinatown is home to the largest Chinese community outside of Asia, with the population estimated at around 200,000. The Chinese who settled in San Francisco around 1880 called their enclave Dai Fou or "Big City." For many decades Chinese immigrants flocked to Dai Fou to escape racial hatred and to capture a bit of home amid its Buddhist temples, grocery stores, bakeries, laundries, schools, benevolent associations, and chamber of commerce. In recent decades Filipinos, Thai, Vietnamese, and Koreans have moved in and added their own touches to this overcrowded, bustling, and colorful neighborhood. San Francisco's Chinatown is a popular tourist destination during the Chinese New Year celebration, usually in late January or in February, with its lion dancers, folk dancing, crafts exhibits, martial arts demonstrations, and little red firecrackers. The grand finale of the New Year festivities is a long parade featuring the enormous *gum lung*, the sparkling golden dragon, a beneficent and beloved mythical creature that floats through Chinatown, held aloft by dozens of dragon bearers dressed in black.

3. **Chinatown**, New York City

In 1870 fewer than fifty Chinese had settled on the old Doyer's Farm near the Bowery, the site of New York City's Chinatown. In that decade Asians were such a curiosity in New York City that P. T. Barnum attracted crowds with a display of Chinese in his carnival sideshow. By 1890, Chinatown was bustling with three thousand Chinese, many of whom had crossed the Rockies in search of jobs. Today Manhattan's Chinatown is the first stop for blue-collar Chinese immigrants in New York, who earnestly save their money in hopes of moving one day to middle-class communities in Brooklyn or Queens. Fifty-five percent speak little or no English. The transfer of Hong Kong from Great Britain to the People's Republic of China, scheduled for 1997, has impacted on New York's Chinatown, bringing a steady flow of affluent immigrants from Hong Kong and Taiwan who have made the enclave their center of operations, diversifying the population and sparking heavy investing and a real estate boom. As a result, Chinatown doubled in size between 1980 and 1990. Half the city's Chinese population call Chinatown home. Tourism is big business in Chinatown, where visitors comb the markets for good deals on silks, porcelain, jade and lacquered screens, or exotic ingredients like dried jellyfish or take in kung fu movies. Others flock to Chinatown's restaurants for dim sum in the afternoons or to dine on Peking duck, sizzling rice soup, and other succulent dishes in the evening.

4. **Little Taipei** Monterey Park, California

Monterey Park in Los Angeles is the site of the first suburban and the most affluent Chinatown in America. It bears the nicknames "Little Taipei" and "Chinese Beverly Hills," evidence of the impact of the recent immigration of wealthy and cosmopolitan professionals. For many enterprising Chinese trying to make it in America, Monterey Park epitomizes the fulfillment of the American dream.

5. **Yaohan Waterside Plaza** Edgewater, New Jersey

Also known as "Tokyo on the Hudson," Yaohan Waterside Plaza is the site of the 49,250-square-foot Yaohan Supermarket, the newest, largest, and most complete Japanese market in the United States. Yaohan Waterside Plaza is actually an enclosed mall that entices eager consumers not only with its famous supermarket, but with an array of discount stores, home centers, restaurants, cultural and travel centers, and insurance agencies. Customers come not only from New Jersey but from New York, Connecticut, Pennsylvania, and even Washington, D.C.

6. **Little Tokyo** Los Angeles, California

Little Tokyo in Los Angeles is the center of Japanese American culture in southern California. During the 1920s a Japanese community took shape in the area near First and Central streets, which would later be named Little Tokyo. In the early days it overflowed with pool halls, where Japanese spent their free time. World War II brought the evacuation of Japanese Americans to internment camps, and overnight Little Tokyo turned into a ghost town. African Americans soon moved into the area, but with the end of the war Japanese Americans rushed home. Today, Little Tokyo is a tourist mecca and a thriving neighborhood that boasts the $1 million Japanese American Cultural and Community Center and many restaurants, including Unashin, an establishment dedicated entirely to eel dishes.

7. **Manzanar** Lone Pine, California

Manzanar is one of ten relocation camps where Japanese Americans were interned beginning in 1942. Located on the edge of the desert along the eastern slope of the Sierra Nevada, the camp consisted of a few staff buildings and about 504 barracks surrounded by barbed wire and guard towers. More than 10,000 Japanese people, the majority American citizens, lived within the harsh confines of Manzanar, most for as long as three and a half years. Then in September 1945 the camp closed just as suddenly as it had opened. Today the only physical reminder of Manzanar in Lone Pine is a graveyard with a single monument that commemorates all those who died at the camp. On the last Saturday of April every year Japanese Americans make a pilgrimage to Manzanar, where they participate in a ceremony, Japanese folk dancing, and a tour of the Manzanar exhibit at the nearby Eastern California Museum.

8. **Tule Lake Japanese Relocation Center** Tule Lake, California

In 1942, an area in Tule Lake, California, was transformed practically overnight into an internment camp much like Manzanar, with barracks, watchtowers, and barbed-wire fences. In 1942, 18,000 Japanese Americans were interned at Tule Lake. Today all that remains at the site are a stockade, truck barn, historical marker, and a fence.

9. **Koreatown** Los Angeles, California

Los Angeles boasts the largest Korean American population in the United States and "Little Seoul," situated on Olympic Boulevard between Hoover and Western avenues in central L.A., is the nation's most concentrated Korean American neighborhood. It is a bustling, tightly knit community filled with banks, gigantic Korean supermarkets, Korean churches, and Korean movie theaters, and over 500 Korean restaurants. *Tabangs*, or tearooms, where Koreans Americans come for the gossip rather than the fare, have sprouted around Koreatown, as have *suljips*, or pubs, where Korean Americans drink *makkolli*, or rice wine, the national brew of Korea.

10. **Little Saigon** Westminster, California

One of America's numerous Vietnamese enclaves, Little Saigon in Westminster, California, stretches along Bolsa Avenue. It was officially designated "Little Saigon" in 1988, due to the numerous businesses catering to Vietnamese Americans that had blossomed in the area. Westminster became home to the first American of Vietnamese ancestry to serve in elected office, when Tony Lam was elected a city councilman. Little Saigon in Westminster wields enough influence in California politics to attract candidates to its streets during campaign season. All over Little Saigon restaurants serving *pho* (the national soup dish) have cropped up with names like Pho No. 1, and Pho 86, and the Vietnamese hotly debate who serves the best bowl of *pho*.

Recommended Reading

GENERAL WORKS

ASIAN WOMEN UNITED OF CALIFORNIA, EDS. *Making Waves: An Anthology of Writings By and About Asian American Women.* Boston: Beacon Press, 1989.

BRENNAN, JENNIFER. *The Cuisines of Asia: Nine Great Oriental Cuisines by Technique.* New York: St. Martin's Press, 1984.

BROWN, WESLEY, AND AMY LING, EDS. *Visions of America: Personal Narratives from the Promised Land.* New York: Persea Books, 1993.

CHAN, SUCHENG. *Asian Americans: An Interpretive History.* Boston: Twayne Publishers, 1991.

DANIELS, ROGER. *Asian America: Chinese and Japanese in the*

United States Since 1850. Seattle: University of Washington Press, 1988.

ESPIRITU, YEN LE. *Asian American Panethnicity: Bridging Institutions and Identities.* Philadelphia: Temple University Press, 1992.

FINN, MICHAEL. *Martial Arts: A Complete Illustrated History.* Woodstock, NY: The Overlook Press, 1988.

FONER, PHILIP S., AND DANIEL ROSENBERG, EDS. *Racism, Dissent, and Asian Americans from 1850 to the Present: A Documentary History.* Westport, CT: Greenwood Press, 1993.

GALL, SUSAN B., AND TIMOTHY L. GALL, EDS. *Statistical Record of Asian Americans.* Detroit: Gale Research, 1993.

HAGEDORN, JESSICA, ED. *Charlie Chan Is Dead: An Anthology of Contemporary Asian American Fiction.* New York: Penguin Books, 1993.

HANSEN, BARBARA. *Taste of Southeast Asia: Brunei, Indonesia, Malaysia, the Philippines, Singapore, Thailand, and Vietnam.* Tucson, AZ: HPBooks, 1987.

HASELTIME, PATRICIA. *East and Southeast Asian Material Culture in North America: Collections, Historical Sites, and Festivals.* New York: Greenwood Press, 1989.

HING, BILL ONG. *Making and Remaking Asian America Through Immigration Policy, 1850–1990.* Stanford, CA: Stanford University Press, 1993.

HONG, MARIA, ED. *Growing Up Asian American.* New York: Avon Books, 1993.

HONGO, GARRETT, ED. *The Open Boat: Poems from Asian America.* New York: Doubleday, 1993.

HOOBLER, DOROTHY, AND THOMAS HOOBLER. *The Chinese American Family Album.* New York: Oxford University Press, 1994.

HOYT, EDWIN P. *Asians in the West.* Nashville, TN: Thomas Nelson Inc., Publishers, 1974.

HUNDLEY, NORRIS, JR., ED. *The Asian American: The Historical Experience.* Santa Barbara, CA: Clio Books, 1976.

HUNE, SHIRLEY, HYUNG-CHAN KIM, STEPHEN S. FUGITA, AND

Amy Ling, eds. *Asian Americans: Comparative and Global Perspectives.* Pullman: Washington State University Press, 1991.

Karnow, Stanley, and Nancy Yoshihara. *Asian Americans in Transition.* New York: The Asia Society, 1992.

Kim, Elaine H. *Asian American Literature: An Introduction to the Writings and Their Social Context.* Philadelphia: Temple University Press, 1982.

Kim, Hyung-chan, ed. *Dictionary of Asian American History.* New York: Greenwood Press, 1986.

Kitano, Harry H. L., and Roger Daniels. *Asian Americans: Emerging Minorities.* Englewood Cliffs, NJ: Prentice Hall, 1988.

Knoll, Tricia. *Becoming Americans: Asian Sojourners, Immigrants, and Refugees in the Western United States.* Portland, OR: Coast to Coast Books, 1982.

Lee, Joann Faung Jean. *Asian American Experiences in the United States: Oral Histories of First to Fourth Generation Americans from China, the Philippines, Japan, India, the Pacific Islands, Vietnam and Cambodia.* Jefferson, NC: McFarland, 1991.

Lim, Shirley Geok-lin, and Mayumi Tsutakawa. *The Forbidden Stitch: An Asian-American Women's Anthology.* Corvallis, OR: Calyx Books, 1989.

Lyman, Stanford M. *The Asian in the West.* Reno, NV: Western Studies Center, Desert Research Institute, 1970.

Mangiafico, Luciano. *Contemporary American Immigrants: Patterns of Filipino, Korean, and Chinese Settlement in the United States.* New York: Praeger, 1988.

Melendy, Howard Brett. *Asians in America: Filipinos, Koreans, and East Indians.* New York: Hippocrene Books, 1981.

Min, Pyong Gap, ed. *Asian Americans: Contemporary Trends and Issues.* Thousand Oaks, CA: SAGE Publications, 1995.

Ng, Franklin, ed. *The Asian American Encyclopedia.* 6 vols. New York: Marshall Cavendish, 1995.

ODO, FRANKLIN SHOICHIRO. *In Movement: A Pictorial History of Asian America.* Los Angeles, CA: Visual Communications, Asian American Studies Central, 1977.

OKIHIRO, GARY Y. *Margins and Mainstreams: Asians in American History and Culture.* Seattle: University of Washington Press, 1994.

PERRIN, LINDA. *Coming to America: Immigrants from the Far East.* New York: Delacorte Press, 1980.

REVILLA, LINDA A., GAIL M. NOMURA, SHAWN WONG, AND SHIRLEY HUNE, EDS. *Bearing Dreams, Shaping Visions: Asian Pacific American Perspectives.* Pullman: Washington State University Press, 1993.

TAKAKI, RONALD. *Spacious Dreams: The First Wave of Asian Immigration.* New York: Chelsea House Publishers, 1994.

———. *Strangers from a Different Shore: A History of Asian Americans.* Boston: Little, Brown, 1989.

THERNSTROM, STEPHAN, ANN ORLOV, AND OSCAR HANDLIN, EDS. *Harvard Encyclopedia of American Ethnic Groups.* Cambridge, MA: The Belknap Press of Harvard University Press, 1980.

THOMPSON, RICHARD AUSTIN. *The Yellow Peril, 1890–1924.* New York: Arno Press, 1978.

UNO, ROBERTO, ED. *Unbroken Thread: An Anthology of Plays by Asian American Women.* Amherst: University of Massachusetts Press, 1993.

UNTERBURGER, AMY L., ED. *Who's Who Among Asian Americans, 1994/95.* Detroit: Gale Research Inc., 1994.

WEI, WILLIAM. *The Asian American Movement.* Philadelphia: Temple University Press, 1993.

CHINESE AMERICANS

BALDWIN, ESTHER E. *Must the Chinese Go? An Examination of the Chinese Question.* 1890. Reprint. San Francisco: R and E Research Associates, 1970.

BARTH, GUNTHER. *Bitter Strength: A History of the Chinese in the*

United States, 1850–1870. Cambridge, MA: Harvard University Press, 1964.

CHAN, SUCHENG. *This Bittersweet Soil: The Chinese in California Agriculture, 1860–1910*. Berkeley, CA: University of California Press, 1986.

———, ED. *Entry Denied: Exclusion and the Chinese Community in America, 1882–1943*. Philadelphia: Temple University Press, 1991.

CHANG, PAO-MIN. *Continuity and Change: A Profile of Chinese Americans*. New York: Vantage Press, 1983.

CHEN, HSIANG-SHUI. *Chinatown No More: Taiwan Immigrants in Contemporary New York*. Ithaca, NY: Cornell University Press, 1992.

CHEN, JACK. *The Chinese of America: From the Beginnings to the Present*. San Francisco: Harper & Row, 1980.

COOLIDGE, MARY ROBERTS. *Chinese Immigration*. 1909. Reprint. New York: Arno Press, 1969.

DOBIE, CHARLES CALDWELL. *San Francisco's Chinatown*. New York: D. Appleton-Century Company, 1936.

KINKEAD, GWEN. *Chinatown: A Portrait of a Closed Society*. New York: HarperCollins, 1992.

KUNG, SHIEN WOO. *Chinese in American Life: Some Aspects of Their History, Status, Problems, and Contributions*. 1962. Reprint. Westport, CT: Greenwood Press, 1973.

KWONG, PETER. *The New Chinatown*. New York: Hill and Wang, 1987.

LAI, HIM MARK, GENNY LIM, AND JUDY YOUNG. *Island: Poetry and History of Chinese Immigrants on Angel Island, 1910–1940*. 1980. Reprint. Seattle: University of Washington Press, 1991.

LAI, HIM MARK, JOE HUANG, AND DON WONG. *The Chinese of America, 1785–1980: An Illustrated History and Catalog of the Exhibition*. San Francisco: Chinese Culture Foundation, 1980.

LYMAN, STANFORD M. *Chinese Americans*. New York: Random House, 1974.

MARK, DIANE MEI LIN, AND GINGER CHIH. *A Place Called Chinese America.* 2nd ed. Dubuque, IA: Kendall-Hunt, 1993.

MCCLAIN, CHARLES J. *In Search of Equality: The Chinese Struggle Against Discrimination in Nineteenth-Century America.* Berkeley, CA: University of California Press, 1994.

MCCUNN, RUTHANNE LUM. *Chinese American Portraits: Personal Histories 1828–1988.* San Francisco: Chronicle Books, 1988.

———. *An Illustrated History of the Chinese in America.* San Francisco, CA: Design Enterprises of San Francisco, 1979.

MENG, CHIH. *Chinese American Understanding: A Sixty-Year Search.* New York: China Institute in America, 1981.

NEE, VICTOR G., AND BRETT DE BARY NEE. *Longtime Californ': A Documentary Study of an American Chinatown.* 1973. Reprint. Stanford, CA: Stanford University Press, 1986.

SUNG, BETTY LEE. *Mountain of Gold: The Story of the Chinese in America.* New York: Macmillan Company, 1967.

TAKAKI, RONALD. *Ethnic Islands: The Emergence of Urban Chinese America.* New York: Chelsea House Publishers, 1994.

TSAI, SHIH-SHAN HENRY. *China and the Overseas Chinese in the United States, 1868–1911.* Fayetteville: University of Arkansas Press, 1983.

———. *The Chinese Experience in America.* Bloomington: Indiana University Press, 1986.

WU, CHENG-TSU, ED. *"Chink!": A Documentary History of Anti-Chinese Prejudice in America.* New York: The World Publishing Company, 1972.

WU, WILLIAM F. *The Yellow Peril: Chinese Americans in American Fiction, 1850–1940.* Hamden, CT: Archon Books, 1982.

YUN, LEONG GOR. *Chinatown Inside Out.* New York: Barrows Mussey, 1936.

YUNG, JUDY. *Chinese Women of America: A Pictorial History.* Seattle: University of Washington Press, 1986.

YUNG, WING. *My Life in China and America.* New York: H. Holt, 1909.

JAPANESE AMERICANS

ANDOH, ELIZABETH. *At Home with Japanese Cooking.* New York: Alfred A. Knopf, 1980.

ARMOR, JOHN, AND PETER WRIGHT. *Manzanar.* New York: Times Books, 1988.

BODDY, ELIAS MANCHESTER. *Japanese in America.* 1921. Reprint. San Francisco: R and E Research Associates, 1970.

CHALFEN, RICHARD. *Turning Leaves: The Photograph Collections of Two Japanese American Families.* Albuquerque: University of New Mexico Press, 1991.

CONRAT, MAISIE, AND RICHARD CONRAT. *Executive Order 9066: The Internment of 110,000 Japanese Americans.* 1972. Reprint. Los Angeles: University of California Asian Studies Center, 1992.

DANIELS, ROGER. *Prisoners Without Trial: Japanese Americans in World War II.* New York: Hill and Wang, 1993.

DANIELS, ROGER, SANDRA C. TAYLOR, AND HARRY H.L. KITANO, EDS. *Japanese Americans: From Relocation to Redress.* 1986. Revised edition. Seattle: University of Washington Press, 1991.

FUGITA, STEPHEN S., AND DAVID J. O'BRIEN. *Japanese American Ethnicity: The Persistence of Community.* Seattle: University of Washington Press, 1991.

GLENN, EVELYN NAKANO. *Issei, Nisei, War Bride: Three Generations of Japanese American Women in Domestic Service.* Philadelphia: Temple University Press, 1986.

GRODZINS, MORTON. *Americans Betrayed: Politics and the Japanese Evacuation.* Chicago: University of Chicago Press, 1949.

HATAMIYA, LESLIE T. *Righting a Wrong: Japanese Americans and the Passage of the Civil Liberties Act of 1988.* Stanford, CA: Stanford University Press, 1993.

HERMAN, MASAKO. *The Japanese in America, 1843–1973: A Chronology & Fact Book.* Dobbs Ferry, NY: Oceana Publications, 1974.

Recommended Reading

HOSOKAWA, BILL. *JACL in Quest of Justice.* New York: William Morrow, 1982.

———. *Nisei: The Quiet Americans.* New York: William Morrow, 1969.

HOSOKAWA, BILL, AND ROBERT A. WILSON. *East to America: A History of the Japanese in the United States.* New York: William Morrow, 1980.

HOUSTON, JEANNE WAKATSUKI, AND JAMES D. HOUSTON. *Farewell to Manzanar.* Boston: Houghton Mifflin, 1973.

ICHIOKA, YUJI. *The Issei: The World of the First Generation Japanese Immigrants, 1885–1924.* New York: The Free Press, 1988.

JAMES, THOMAS. *Exile Within: The Schooling of Japanese Americans, 1942–1945.* Cambridge, MA: Harvard University Press, 1987.

KESSLER, LAUREN. *Stubborn Twig: Three Generations in the Life of a Japanese American Family.* New York: Penguin, 1993.

KIKUMURA, AKEMI. *Promises Kept: The Life of an Issei Man.* Novato, CA: Chandler and Sharp Publishers, 1991.

———. *Through Harsh Winters: The Life of a Japanese Immigrant Woman.* Novato, CA: Chandler and Sharp Publishers, 1981.

KITANO, HARRY H. L. *Generations and Identity: The Japanese American.* Needham Heights, MA: Ginn Press, 1993.

———. *Japanese Americans: The Evolution of a Subculture.* 2nd ed. Englewood Cliffs, NJ: Prentice-Hall, 1976.

MCWILLIAMS, CAREY. *Prejudice, Japanese-Americans: Symbol of Racial Intolerance.* Boston: Little, Brown, 1944.

MINATOYA, LYDIA YURIKO. *Talking to High Monks in the Snow: An Asian American Odyssey.* New York: HarperCollins, 1992.

MURA, DAVID. *Turning Japanese: Memoirs of a Sansei.* New York: Atlantic Monthly Press, 1991.

NAKANO, MEI T. *Japanese American Women: Three Generations, 1890–1990.* Berkeley, CA: Mina Press Publishing, 1990.

NIIYA, BRIAN, ED. *Japanese American History: An A-to-Z Reference from 1868 to the Present.* New York: Facts on File, 1993.

O'BRIEN, DAVID J., AND STEPHEN S. FUGITA. *The Japanese American Experience.* Bloomington: Indiana University Press, 1991.

PETERSEN, WILLIAM. *Japanese Americans: Oppression and Success.* New York: Random House, 1971.

SHIMONISHI-LAMB, MILI. *And Then a Rainbow.* Santa Barbara, CA: Fithian Press, 1990.

SMITH, BRADFORD. *Americans from Japan.* Philadelphia: J. B. Lippincott Company, 1948.

TAKAKI, RONALD. *Issei and Nisei: The Settling of Japanese America.* New York: Chelsea House Publishers, 1994.

TAKEZAWA, YASUKO I. *Breaking the Silence: Redress and Japanese American Ethnicity.* Ithaca, NY: Cornell University Press, 1995.

TATEISHI, JOHN, ED. *And Justice for All: An Oral History of the Japanese American Detention Camps.* New York: Random House, 1984.

UCHIDA, YOSHIKO. *Desert Exile: The Uprooting of a Japanese American Family.* Seattle: University of Washington Press, 1982.

WILSON, ROBERT A., AND BILL HOSOKAWA. *East to America: A History of the Japanese in the United States.* New York: William Morrow, 1980.

YANAGISAKO, SYLVIA JUNKO. *Transforming the Past: Tradition and Kinship among Japanese Americans.* Stanford, CA: Stanford University Press, 1985.

FILIPINO AMERICANS

BANDON, ALEXANDRA. *Filipino Americans.* New York: Macmillan, 1993.

BLOUNT, JAMES H. *The American Occupation of the Philippines, 1898–1912.* 1912. Reprint. New York: Oriole Editions, 1973.

BUAKEN, MANUEL. *I Have Lived with the American People.* Caldwell, ID: The Caxton Printers, Ltd., 1948.

BULOSAN, CARLOS. *America Is in the Heart: A Personal History.*

1946. Reprint. Seattle: University of Washington Press, 1973.

CORDOVA, FRED. *Filipinos, Forgotten Asian Americans: A Pictorial Essay, 1763–circa 1963.* Dubuque, IA: Kendall-Hunt, 1983.

CROUCHETT, LORRAINE JACOBS. *Filipinos in California: From the Days of the Galleons to the Present.* El Cerrito, CA: Downey Place Publishing House, 1982.

DEWITT, HOWARD A. *Anti-Filipino Movements in California: A History, Bibliography and Study Guide.* San Francisco: R and E Research Associates, 1976.

FILIPINO ORAL HISTORY PROJECT. *Voices: A Filipino American Oral History.* Stockton, CA: Filipino Oral History Project, 1984.

KARNOW, STANLEY. *In Our Image: America's Empire in the Philippines.* New York: Random House, 1989.

KIM, HYUNG-CHAN, AND CYNTHIA C. MEJIA. *The Filipinos in America, 1898–1974: A Chronology & Fact Book.* Dobbs Ferry, NY: Oceana Publications, 1976.

LEROY, JAMES A. *The Americans in the Philippines: A History of the Conquest and First Years of Occupation with an Introductory Account of the Spanish Rule.* 2 vols. 1914. Reprint. New York: AMS Press, 1970.

NORIEGA, VIOLETA A. *Philippine Recipes Made Easy.* Kirkland, WA: Paperworks, 1993.

PIDO, ANTONIO J. A. *The Filipinos in America: Macro/Micro Dimensions of Immigration and Integration.* New York: Center for Migration Studies, 1986.

QUINSAAT, JESSE, ED. *Letters in Exile: An Introductory Reader on the History of Filipinos in America.* Los Angeles: UCLA Asian American Studies Center, 1976.

VALLANGCA, CARIDAD CONCEPCION. *The Second Wave: Pinay and Pinoy (1945–1960).* San Francisco: Strawberry Hill Press, 1987.

VALLANGCA, ROBERTO V. *Pinoy: The First Wave, 1898–1941.* San Francisco: Strawberry Hill Press, 1977.

SOUTHEAST ASIAN AMERICANS

HAINES, DAVID W., ED. *Refugees as Immigrants: Cambodians, Laotians, and Vietnamese in America.* Totowa, NJ: Rowman & Littlefield Publishers, 1989.

HIGGINS, JAMES, AND JOAN ROSS. *Southeast Asians: A New Beginning in Lowell.* Lowell, MA: Mill Town Graphics, 1986.

SARDESAI, D.R. *Southeast Asia.* 3rd ed. Boulder, CO: Westview Press, 1994.

SCOTT, JOANNA C. *Indochina's Refugees: Oral Histories from Laos, Cambodia and Vietnam.* Jefferson, NC: McFarland & Company, 1989.

STRAND, PAUL J., AND WOODROW JONES, JR. *Indochinese Refugees in America: Problems of Adaptation and Assimilation.* Durham, NC: Duke University Press, 1985.

TENHULA, JOHN. *Voices from Southeast Asia: The Refugee Experience in the United States.* New York: Holmes & Meier, 1991.

Vietnamese Americans

BACHE, ELLYN. *Culture Clash.* Yarmouth, ME: Intercultural Press, 1989.

FREEMAN, JAMES M. *Hearts of Sorrow: Vietnamese-American Lives.* Stanford, CA: Stanford University Press, 1989.

KARNOW, STANLEY. *Vietnam: A History.* New York: The Viking Press, 1983.

KIBRIA, NAZLI. *Family Tightrope: The Changing Lives of Vietnamese Americans.* Princeton, NJ: Princeton University Press, 1993.

MONTERO, DARREL. *Vietnamese Americans: Patterns of Resettlement and Socioeconomic Adaptation in the United States.* Boulder, CO: Westview Press, 1979.

NEWELL, JEAN F. *Vietnamese Americans: A Needs Assessment.* Ann Arbor, MI: University Microfilms International, 1993.

ROUTHIER, NICOLE. *The Foods of Vietnam.* New York: Stewart, Tabori & Chang, 1989.

RUTLEDGE, PAUL JAMES. *The Vietnamese Experience in America.* Bloomington: Indiana University Press, 1992.

Laotian Americans

CHAN, SUCHENG, ED. *Hmong Means Free: Life in Laos and America.* Philadelphia: Temple University Press, 1994.

DONNELLY, NANCY D. *Changing Lives of Refugee Hmong Women.* Seattle: University of Washington Press, 1994.

HAMILTON-MERRITT, JANE. *Tragic Mountains: The Hmong, the Americans, and the Secret Wars for Laos, 1942–1992.* Bloomington: Indiana University Press, 1993.

HENDRICKS, GLENN, BRUCE DOWNING, AND AMOS DEINARD, EDS. *The Hmong in Transition.* Staten Island, NY: Center for Migration Studies, 1986.

MOTTIN, JEAN. *History of the Hmong.* Bangkok: Odeon Store, 1980.

PROUDFOOT, ROBERT. *Even the Birds Don't Sound the Same Here: The Laotian Refugees' Search for Heart in American Culture.* New York: Peter Lang, 1990.

STUART-FOX, MARTIN. *Laos: Politics, Economics and Society.* Boulder, CO: Lynne Rienner Publishers, 1986.

Cambodian Americans

CHANDLER, DAVID P. *A History of Cambodia.* Boulder, CO: Westview Press, 1983.

———. *The Tragedy of Cambodian History: Politics, War, and Revolution Since 1945.* New Haven, CT: Yale University Press, 1991.

CRIDDLE, JOAN D., AND TEEDA BUTT MAM. *To Destroy You Is No Loss: The Odyssey of a Cambodian Family.* New York: The Atlantic Monthly Press, 1987.

EBIHARA, MAY M., CAROL A. MORTLAND, AND JUDY LEDGERWOOD. *Cambodian Culture Since 1975: Homeland and Exile.* Ithaca, NY: Cornell University Press, 1994.

FIFFER, SHARON SLOAN. *Imagining America: Paul Thai's Journey from the Killing Fields of Cambodia to Freedom in the U.S.A.* New York: Paragon House, 1991.

MARTIN, MARIE ALEXANDRINE. *Cambodia: A Shattered Society.* Berkeley: University of California Press, 1994.

NGOR, HAING, WITH ROGER WARNER. *A Cambodian Odyssey.* New York: Macmillan, 1987.

SHANBERG, SYDNEY H. *The Death and Life of Dith Pran.* New York: Viking Penguin, 1985.

SHAWCROSS, WILLIAM. *The Quality of Mercy: Cambodia, Holocaust and Modern Conscience.* New York: Simon & Schuster, 1984.

TOOZE, RUTH. *Cambodia: Land of Contrasts.* New York: The Viking Press, 1962.

WELARATNA, USHA. *Beyond the Killing Fields: Voices of Nine Cambodian Survivors in America.* Stanford, CA: Stanford University Press, 1993.

KOREAN AMERICANS

BARRINGER, HERBERT R., AND SUNG-NAM CHO. *Koreans in the United States: A Fact Book.* Honolulu: Center for Korean Studies, University of Hawaii, 1989.

CHOY, BONG-YOUN. *Koreans in America.* Chicago: Nelson-Hall Publishers, 1979.

HASTINGS, MAX. *The Korean War.* New York: Simon & Schuster, 1987.

HURH, WON MOO, AND KWANG CHUNG KIM. *Korean Immigrants in America: A Structural Analysis of Ethnic Confinement and Adhesive Adaptation.* Rutherford, NJ: Fairleigh Dickinson University Press, 1984.

KIM, HYUNG-CHAN, ED. *The Korean Diaspora: Historical and Sociological Studies of Korean Immigration and Assimilation in North America.* Santa Barbara, CA: ABC-Clio, 1977.

KIM, HYUNG-CHAN, AND WAYNE PATTERSON. *The Koreans in*

America, 1882–1974. Dobbs Ferry, NY: Oceana Publications, 1974.

KIM, ILLSOO. *New Urban Immigrants: The Korean Community in New York.* Princeton, NJ: Princeton University Press, 1981.

LEE, MARY PAIK. *Quiet Odyssey: A Pioneer Korean Woman in America.* Seattle: University of Washington Press, 1990.

LIGHT, IVAN, AND EDNA BONACICH. *Immigrant Entrepreneurs: Koreans in Los Angeles, 1965–1982.* Berkeley, CA: University of California Press, 1988.

MARKS, COPELAND, WITH MANJO KIM. *The Korean Kitchen: Classic Recipes from the Land of the Morning Calm.* San Francisco: Chronicle Books, 1993.

TAKAKI, RONALD T. *From the Land of the Morning Calm: The Koreans in America.* New York: Chelsea House, 1994.

ASIAN INDIAN AMERICANS

ALEXANDER, MEENA. *Fault Lines: A Memoir.* New York: Feminist Press at the City University of New York, 1993.

CHANDRASEKHAR, S., ED. *From India to America: A Brief History of Immigration; Problems of Discrimination; Admission and Assimilation.* La Jolla, CA: Population Review Publications, 1982.

DASGUPTA, SATHI SENGUPTA. *On the Trail of an Uncertain Dream: Indian Immigrant Experience in America.* New York: AMS Press, 1989.

FENTON, JOHN Y. *Transplanting Religious Traditions: Asian Indians in America.* New York: Praeger, 1988.

FISHER, MAXINE P. *The Indians of New York City: A Study of Immigrants from India.* New Delhi: Heritage Publishers, 1980.

GIBSON, MARGARET A. *Accommodation Without Assimilation: Sikh Immigrants in an American High School.* Ithaca, NY: Cornell University Press, 1988.

HELWEG, ARTHUR W., AND USHA M. HELWEG. *An Immigrant*

Success Story: East Indians in America. Philadelphia: University of Pennsylvania Press, 1990.

JAFFREY, MADHUR. *A Taste of India.* London: Pavilion, 1985.

JENSEN, JOAN M. *Passage from India: Asian Indian Immigrants in North America.* New Haven, CT: Yale University Press, 1988.

SARAN, PARMATMA. *The Asian Indian Experience in the United States.* Cambridge, MA: Schenkman Publishing Company, 1985.

SARAN, PARMATMA, AND EDWIN EAMES, EDS. *The New Ethnics: Asian Indians in the United States.* New York: Praeger, 1980.

SAUND, DALIP SINGH. *Congressman from India.* New York: E. P. Dutton and Company, 1960.

WILLIAMS, RAYMOND BRADY. *Religions of Immigrants from India and Pakistan: New Threads in the American Tapestry.* New York: Cambridge University Press, 1988.

WOMEN OF SOUTH ASIAN DESCENT COLLECTIVE, EDS. *Our Feet Walk the Sky: Women of the South Asian Diaspora.* San Francisco: Aunt Lute Books, 1993.

XENOS, PETER, HERBERT BARRINGER, AND MICHAEL J. LEVIN. *Asian Indians in the United States: A 1980 Census Profile.* Honolulu: East-West Center, 1989.

PACIFIC ISLANDER AMERICANS

GIBSON, ARRELL MORGAN, WITH JOHN S. WHITEHEAD. *Yankees in Paradise: The Pacific Basin Frontier.* Albuquerque: University of New Mexico Press, 1993.

HOWE, K.R., ROBERT C. KISTE, AND BRIJ V. LAL, EDS. *Tides of History: The Pacific Islands in the Twentieth Century.* Honolulu: University of Hawaii Press, 1994.

Hawaiians

ANDERSON, ROBERT N., WITH RICHARD COLLER AND REBECCA F. PESTANO. *Filipinos in Rural Hawaii.* Honolulu: University of Hawaii Press, 1984.

BURROWS, EDWIN G. *Hawaiian Americans: An Account of the Mingling of Japanese, Chinese, Polynesian, and American Cultures.* 1947. Reprint. Hamden, CT: Archon Books, 1970.

DAWS, GAVAN. *Shoal of Time: A History of the Hawaiian Islands.* New York: Macmillan, 1968.

GLICK, CLARENCE E. *Sojourners and Settlers: Chinese Migrants in Hawaii.* Honolulu: University of Hawaii Press, 1980.

GRAY, FRANCINE DU PLESSIX. *Hawaii: The Sugar-Coated Fortress.* New York: Random House, 1972.

HAZAMA, DOROTHY OCHIAI, AND JANE OKAMOTO KOMEIJI. *Okage Sama De: The Japanese in Hawai'i.* Honolulu: Bess Press, 1986.

KIMURA, YUKIKO. *Issei: Japanese Immigrants in Hawaii.* Honolulu: University of Hawaii Press, 1988.

OKIHIRO, GARY Y. *Cane Fires: The Anti-Japanese Movement in Hawaii, 1865–1945.* Philadelphia: Temple University Press, 1991.

SAIKI, PATSY SUMIE. *Early Japanese Immigrants in Hawaii.* Honolulu: Japanese Cultural Center of Hawaii, 1993.

TAMURA, EILEEN H. *Americanization, Acculturation, and Ethnic Identity: The Nisei Generation in Hawaii.* Urbana: University of Illinois Press, 1994.

WAKUKAWA, ERNEST K. *A History of the Japanese People in Hawaii.* Honolulu: The Toyo Shoin, 1938.

Samoans

GRAY, J. A. C. *Amerika Samoa: A History of American Samoa and Its United States Naval Administration.* Annapolis, MD: United States Naval Institute, 1960.

SUTTER, FREDERIC KOEHLER. *Amerika Samoa: An Anthropological Photo Essay.* Honolulu: University of Hawaii Press, 1984.

SWANEY, DEANNA. *Samoa: Western & American Samoa.* 2nd ed. Hawthorn, Australia: Lonely Planet Publications, 1994.

Guamanians

THOMPSON, LAURA. *Guam and Its People.* New York: Greenwood Press, Publishers, 1947.

Tongan Americans

RUTHERFORD, NOEL, ED. *Friendly Islands: A History of Tonga.* Melbourne, Australia: Oxford University Press, 1977.

SWANEY, DEANNA. *Tonga.* 2nd ed. Hawthorn, Australia: Lonely Planet Publications, 1994.

Index

356

Ma, Yo-Yo, 55
McCarran Internal Security Act of 1950, 47
McCarran-Walter Act of 1952, 8, 48–49, 50,
   130, 134, 194, 293
McCarthy, Joseph, 48
McCarthy, Nobu, 142
McCoy, John J., 137
McCreary, James Bennett, 36–37
McDougal, John, 11
McKinley, William, 317
McLemore, Henry, 103
Magellan, Ferdinand, 158, 329
Magnuson, Warren, 43
Maha-shivaratri, 303
Mahayana Buddhism, 63, 217
Makkolli, 280
Mako, 143
Malapit, Eduardo E., 178
Manavi, 218
Manifest Destiny, xv, 14
Manilamen, 158
Manzanar Relocation Camp, 107, 337
Mao Tse-tung, 193
Marcantonio, Vito, 43
Marquesas Islands, 313
Marshall, James W., xiv–xv, 8, 10
Martial arts:
   Chinese, 71–72
   Japanese, 150–52
Masaoka, Mike Masaru, 101
Matsui, Robert Takeo, 134
Matsunaga, Masayuki "Spark," 132–33
Mehta, Zubin, 297
Melanesia, 311
Metcalf, Victor H., 96
Mexicans, 170
Micronesia, 311, 329
Mid-Autumn Festival (Moon Festival), 66
Midori, 140, 220, 297
Mien, 226, 228, 229
Military Intelligence Service, 121
Min, Chouhei, 273–74
Min, Queen, 253
Minatoya, Lydia Yuri, 131
Mineta, Norman Yoshio, 134
Mink, Patsy Takemoto, 133, 220–21
Misa de Gallo, 182–83
Misoshiru, 324
Mitchell, Broadus, 43
"Model minority," myth of, xvii–xviii
Montagu, John, 314
Moon, Sun Myung, 267
Morita, Noriyuki "Pat," 142
Mormons, 327, 328, 333, 334
Moxibustion, 70

Mukti, 299
Munemori, Sadao S., 121
Murphy, Frank, 109
Murray, Hugh G., 35
Muschamp, Herbert, 147–48
Muslims, 159, 161, 287
Mutual Aid Associations (MAAs), 197
Myer, Dillion S., 114–15

Nanak, Guru, 287
Nash, J. Carrol, 59
Nationality Act of 1870, 17
National Japanese American Student Relo-
   cation Council (NJASRC), 123, 124
National Origins Quota System, 49, 50
Natividad, Irene, 221
Naturalization Law of 1790, 15, 83, 100
New England Congregationalist Church,
   315, 320, 321, 322–23
New World, discovery of, 9–10
New York Times, The, 241
Ngor, Haing, 238–39, 242–44
Ngo Van Chieu, 222
Nguyen, Dustin, 301
Nguyen, Mike, 272
Nigiri sushi, 324–25
Nisei, 83, 90, 94, 95, 101, 103, 104, 114, 125, 144
   drafting of, 122–23
   education of, 118, 123–24
   Endo case and, 126–27
   in the 442nd Regimental Combat Team,
      120–21
   in the military, 118–20
   in the Military Intelligence Service, 121
   post-war, 129–30
   Supreme Court decisions concerning,
      126–27
   women, 124, 125
Nisei Week, 148
Nitz, Michael, 53–54
Nixon, Richard M., 205, 206, 207, 218, 270
Noguchi, Isamu, 140–41, 147–48
No-No Boys, 117
Nuoc mam, 225–26

Oceania, 311
Office of Refugee Resettlement, 196
Office of Strategic Services (OSS), 200
Office of the United Nations High Commis-
   sioners for Refugees (UNHCR), 196
Oh, Angela, 221, 276
Okei, 84
Okinawa, 150–51
Oland, Warner, 58, 59
1.5 generation, 198–99

Onizuka, Ellison Shoji, 139
Organic Act of Guam of 1950, 330
Orientals, xv–xvii
Oyakawa, Yoshinobu, 143
Ozawa, Seiji, 139

Pacific Islander Americans, 308–38
  described, 311–12
  first migration of, 312–13
  population by state, 307
  see also Guamanians; Hawaiians; Samoans;
    Tongan Americans
Pad Thai, 326
Paek, Jim, 271, 272
Page Law of 1875, 29–30, 45
Paik, Nam June, 274
"Paper sons," 37, 48
  clinging to fake names, 38–39
  government response to, 38
Paris Peace Agreement of 1973, 205–207
  as "leopard spot" arrangement, 206
  reaction to violations of, 207
  South Vietnamese signing of, 206–207
Park, Chan-ho, 271, 273
Patti, Archimedes L. A., 200–201
Pearl Harbor, 41–42, 102–103, 105, 144,
    259, 317–18
  "economic," 137–38
Pei, I. M., 56
Pensionado Act of 1903, 163
People v. Hall, 35
Personal Justice Denied (CWRIC), 137
Phi, 231–32
Phillip II, King, 157, 158
Philippine-American War, 160–61
Philippine Independence Act of 1934, 171–72
Philippines, 157
  independence of, 173–74
  legacy of the U.S. on, 161
  see also Filipino Americans
Pho restaurants, 225–26
"Picture brides," 86–87, 89, 99, 168, 256
Pinoys, 165–66
Pol Pot, 233
  "killing fields" of, 234–35, 241–44
  single parent households due to, 237
Polynesia, 311
  see also Hawaiians
Prostitutes, 29–30, 32
Protestantism, 158, 217, 222
  Hawaiians and, 314–15, 320, 321, 322–23
  Koreans and, 254–55, 256, 264, 267
Punjabis, 286, 287
  California fruit growers and, 288–89
Purcell, James, 126

Quan Yin meditation, 222–23
Queue Ordinance of 1873, 26

Rafu Shimpo, 138
Ramnavami, 303–304
Ranariddh, Norodom, 245
Reagan, Ronald, 137
Reciprocity Treaty of 1876, 85
Refugee Act of 1980, 195
Refugee Relief Act of 1953, 193, 194
Refugees:
  dispersal of, 189
  first-asylum countries for, 195–96
  immigrants and, 192–93
  1.5 generation, 198–99
  organizations that resettle, 196–97
  second-asylum countries for, 196
  traditional U.S. treatment of, 193–95
  see also specific ethnic groups
Relief Appropriation Act of 1937, 172
Repatriation Act of 1935, 172
Rhee, Syngman, 259
rich businessmen, 240–41
Rohmer, Sax, 57–58
Roman Catholicism, 158, 159, 182–83, 199,
    217, 222, 329
Roosevelt, Franklin D., 42, 44–45, 104, 114,
    119, 125–26, 135, 201, 293
Roosevelt, Theodore, 88, 95
  discrimination against Japanese and, 96–98
  Gentlemen's Agreement of 1908 and, 98–100

Sake, 149, 280
Salabat, 184–85
Samoans, 312, 326–29
  aiga and, 329
  migration of, 327–28
  as Mormons, 327, 328
  tattoos of, 328–29
  U.S. territorial status and, 326–27
Samras, Khairata Ram, 293
Sanders, Wilbur Fisk, 40
San Francisco Chronicle, 95
San Francisco earthquake of 1906, 37, 92
Sansei, 83, 144
  achieving the American dream, 131–32
San yi man, 50–52
Sari, 298
Saund, Dalip Singh, 296
Schanberg, Sydney, 241
Schnell, John Henry, 84
Scott Act of 1888, 33–34
Second-asylum countries, 196
Sensu, 146–47
Shaolin monastery, 150

Shek, Emily Lee, 46
Shibuya, Seijiro, 138
Shimizsu, Jenny, 301
Shintoism, 144
Siddhartha Gautama, 63
Sidhu, Jay S., 240
Sihanouk, Norodon, 232, 233
Sikhs, 287–88, 304
Singh, Govind, 287–88
Singh, Jane, 298
Sinigang, 325
Sino-Korean People's League, 261
Smith, P. F., 12
Sojourners:
    Chinese, 14, 28, 51
    Japanese, 85, 89, 91
Southeast Asian Americans, 186–246
    difference between a refugee and an immigrant, 192–93
    dispersal of, 198
    diversity of, 192
    first-asylum countries and, 195–96
    1.5 generation, 198–99
    organizations to resettle, 196–97
    population by state, 185
    second-asylum countries, 196
    treatment of refugees by the U.S., 193–94
    see also Cambodian Americans; Laotian
        Americans; Vietnamese Americans
Spain:
    Guam and, 330
    the Philippines and, 157–60
Spanish American War, 158, 160, 330
Sproul, Robert, 123
Statement of United States Citizen of Japanese Ancestry, 119
Stevens, Durham, 258–59
Stevenson, Robert Lewis, 311
Stimson, Henry L., 119, 137
Subba Row, Yellapragada, 297
Sudden unexplained death syndrome (SUDS), 231
Sukiyaki, 149
Sumner, Charles, 15
Surfing, 321
Swastika, 302–303

Tae-Hanin Kungminhoe (THK), 258
Tahiti, 313
T'ai chi ch'uan, 71
Taiwan, 52–53
Tajima, Renee, 60
Takei, George Hosako, 142–43
Talking to High Monks in the Sow (Minatoya), 131

Tan, Amy, 55, 215, 221
Tandon, Sirjang Lal, 240
Tandoori, 325
Tanomoshi, 264
Taoism, 61–62, 63, 69, 217
Tatami, 146
Tattoos, 328–29
Taufa'ahau Tupou IV, King 332
Taylor, Zachary, 11
Tea drinking, 145
Terasaki, Paul, 139
Tet celebration, 223–24
Tet Offensive, 204
Thakkar, Chuck, 241
Theravada Buddhism, 63, 217, 222, 231–32
Thind, Bhagat Singh, 291, 292, 293
"Thomasites," 161
"Throwing out the anchor," 214
Tiger Brigade, 261
Time magazine, 42, 108
Toguri, Iva Ikuko, 127–29
Tokyo Rose, 127–29
Tolan, John H., 104
Toler, Sidney, 59
Tomita, Tamlyn, 301
Tong, Kaity, 56
Tongan Americans, 312–13, 332–34
    history of, 332–33
    migration of, 333
    settlement of, 333–34
Tongs, 19–20, 29
Tonkin, 199, 232
Triad Society, 19
Truman, Harry S, 49, 120–21, 122, 200
Trumball, Lyman, 15
Tsai, Gerald, Jr., 57, 240
Tsung-Dao Lee, 54
Tule Lake Japanese Relocation Center, 117, 337
Twain, Mark, 160
Tydings, Millard, 171–72
Tydings-McDuffie Act of 1934, 171–72, 174

Umeki, Mihoshi, 141
Unification Church, 267
University of California at Irvine (UCI), 177
Uyeda, Clifford I., 129
Uyeshiba, Morihei, 152

Van Reed, Eugene M., 83–84
Viet kieu, 215
Vietnam:
    division of, into north and south, 202
    French rule over, 199–202
    history of, to the 20th century, 199